Knights of the Black Cross

Knights of the Black Cross

Hitler's Panzerwaffe and its Leaders

by
BRYAN PERRETT

ST. MARTIN'S PRESS
New York

Library of Congress Cataloging-in-Publication Data

Perrett, Bryan.
    Knights of the Black Cross.

    1. World War, 1939–1945—Tank warfare.   2. Germany.
Heer—Armored troops—History.   I. Title.
D793.P46   1987   940.54'13'43   87-16334
ISBN 0-312-01055-9

First published in Great Britain by Robert Hale Limited.

First U.S. Edition

10 9 8 7 6 5 4 3 2 1

Contents

List of Illustrations

Picture Credits

The following photographs have been reproduced by kind permission of: Bundesarchiv: 2, 4, 5, 6, 7, 8, 9, 12, 13, 14, 15, 16, 17, 18, 19, 22, 23, 24, 25, 27, 28, 30, 31, 32, 37, 38, 39; RAC Tank Museum: 1, 26, 33, 34, 35, 36, 40; Ullstein: 3; US National Archives: 10, 11, 20; Colonel Peter Whiteley: 21.

List of Maps

Foreword

by General a.D. Dr F.M. von Senger und Etterlin
*Formerly Commander-in-Chief Allied Forces
Central Europe*

In 1985, while Bryan Perrett was writing this book, the German Army commemorated the 50th Anniversary of the forming of the first three Panzer Divisions which were themselves to become the core of the entire Panzerwaffe. During those early years of re-armament, the German General Staff was confronted with three different schools of thought concerning the employment and organization of modern motorized and armoured formations.

The first, predominant in the United Kingdom, was the 'all-tank' school which envisioned tanks of various types operating in isolation and acting, so to speak, as their own infantry, cavalry and artillery, although it was conceded that a certain proportion of lorried infantry should be included in the division-sized formation. This school led to the formation of the first more-or-less tank-heavy armoured divisions in the United Kingdom and in Germany.

A second school, particularly influential in France, propagated the mechanization of the cavalry for its traditional roles of long-range reconnaissance, pursuit and economy-of-force operations. This theory led to the creation in France of the Divisions Légères Mechaniques (DLM) and in Germany of the four Leichte Divisionen.

A third theory sought to utilize the internal combustion engine as a means of improving the mobility of the three older arms of service, and in many countries this led to the formation of motorized infantry divisions.

Simultaneously, there was a debate as to whether the new arm would be better employed in large formations at the operational level or tactically in support of the traditional arms.

The German Oberkommando des Heeres (OKH), the General Staff of the Army, decided not to decide; because of lack of practical experience, they allowed all three (or four) schools to materialize. However, one thing was already clear even in those

11

early years: this modern element would constitute a 'second-tier'
army, an army within the old army, capable of operating in new
dimensions of time and space and independent of the main mass
which proceeded at the pace of the foot soldier. In the years to
come, this new element would not, for practical reasons, exceed
one fifth of the entire army, although from the outset it was to be
concentrated in large corps-sized formations for deployment in
independent, decisive operations. One must be quite clear about
the magnitude of this organizational structure to understand its
impact in the ensuing years, described in such a vivid and
balanced way in this book. In order to gain experience in the
command and control of such large formations, an Army Group
Headquarters was established which had three, and after the
occupation of Austria four, motorized Armee-Korps (mot AK)
under control. Before the war all the divisions which had been
created in accordance with the three previously mentioned
schools of thought were grouped under these headquarters, and
the peacetime order of battle looked like this:

Heeresgruppenkommando 4 (Leipzig)		Gen.d.Art. v.Reichenau
XIV Armee-Korps	(Magdeburg)	Gen.d.Inf. v. Wietersheim
2 Inf.Div. (mot.)	(Stettin)	Gen.Lt. Bader
13 Inf.Div. (mot.)	(Magdeburg)	Gen.Lt. Otto
20 Inf.Div. (mot.)	(Hamburg)	Gen.Lt. Wiktorin
29 Inf.Div. (mot.)	(Erfurt)	Gen.Mjr. Lemelsen
XV Armee-Korps	(Jena)	Gen.d.Inf. Hoth
1 Leichte Division	(Wuppertal)	Gen.Mjr. v.Loeper
2 Leichte Division	(Gera)	Gen.Lt. Stumme
3 Leichte Division	(Cottbus)	Gen.Mjr. Kuntzen
XVI Armee-Korps	(Berlin)	Gen.Mjr. Guderian, later Gen.Lt. Höpner Chef des Stabes Obst. Paulus
1 Panzer-Division	(Weimar)	Gen.Lt. Schmidt
3 Panzer-Division	(Berlin)	Gen.Lt. Frhr. Geyr v. Schweppenburg
4 Panzer-Division	(Würzburg)	Gen.Mjr. Reinhardt
5 Panzer-Division	(Oppeln)	Gen.Lt. v. Vietinghoff-Scheel

The new Heeresgruppenkommando 5 (Vienna) had under command:

XIX Armee-Korps	(Vienna)	
2 Panzer-Division	(Vienna)	Gen.Lt Veiel
4 Leichte Division	(St Pölten)	Gen.Lt Hubicki

The experience gained during the first year of the war led to the amalgamation of the first two schools of thought on mechanized warfare. For the campaign against the Soviet Union, the Panzerwaffe reached the peak of its organizational structure with the formation of four Panzer Armies (initially designated Panzergruppen), in which seventeen of the existing twenty-one Panzer Divisions were grouped together with a dozen motorized infantry divisions to form ten motorized (later Panzer-) corps (mot AK). Thus, the order of battle on the first day of the offensive in the east looked like this:

Panzer Group 1 (v. Kleist)
    25 Infantry Division (mot)
    III mot. AK (v. Mackensen) with 13 and 14 Panzer Divisions
       and SS Divisions *Leibstandarte* and *Wiking*
    XIV mot. AK (v. Wietersheim) with 9 and 16 Panzer Divisions
       and 16 Infantry Division
    XLVIII mot. AK (Kempf) with 11 Panzer Division and
       mounted infantry formation

Panzer Group 2 (Guderian)
    XXIV mot. AK (Geyr v. Schweppenburg) with 3 and 4 Panzer
       Divisions, 10 Infantry Division (mot) and 1 Cavalry
       Division (mounted)
    XLVI mot. AK (v. Vietinghoff-Scheel) with 10 Panzer Division,
       SS Division *Das Reich* and Infantry Regiment (mot)
       Grossdeutschland
    XLVII mot. AK (Lemelsen) with 17 and 18 Panzer Divisions
       and 29 Infantry Division (mot)

Panzer Group 3 (Hoth)
    XLIX mot. AK (Schmidt) with 7 and 20 Panzer Divisions and
       10 and 14 Infantry Divisions (mot)
    LVII mot. AK (Kuntzen) with 12 and 19 Panzer Divisions and
       18 Infantry Division (mot)

Panzer Group 4 (Höpner)
    SS Division *Totenkopf*
    XLI mot. AK (Reinhardt) with 1 and 6 Panzer Divisions and 36
       Infantry Division (mot)
    LVI mot. AK (v. Manstein) with 8 Panzer Division and 3
       Infantry Division (mot)

The OKH Reserve consisted of XL mot. AK consisting of 2 and 5

Panzer Divisions and 60 Infantry Division (mot.).

Although frequently subject to change, this grouping of armoured and motorized formations constituted the basic organization of the second-tier army and immediately placed it on a higher operational plane than lay within the capacity of the marching and horse-drawn mass.

To sum up, it was the mental mobility of the higher German military leaders which enabled them to grasp quickly the capabilities of the new arm, coupled with their flexibility in grouping and forging the tool into large operational formations. It was the high standard of the command and control system which enabled them to handle this tool up to the level of Field Army. It was the principle of control by directives (*Auftragstaktik*), giving commanders of all levels 'long-distance tickets', which, together with the thorough and uniform standard of General Staff training, exploited creativity and responsible independence to the utmost. All these factors played a much greater role in securing success in the early years of Blitzkrieg than numbers or the quality of tanks.

I am very grateful to Bryan Perrett for his endeavour to draw a balanced picture. The war in the East – almost forgotten today in the West – was fought by millions of German soldiers against the ever-growing Soviet Army not only by units of the Panzerwaffe but also and with equal bravery by those many infantry units which possessed only the same mobility as Napoleon's army.

Can we draw any lessons from this history? Certainly, but only if we are absolutely clear about conditions that existed then but which exist no longer. It is possible to identify many such conditions, facts and factors, but this must be left to the reader who is familiar with the situation as it exists today.

One fact must, however, be stressed since it is of paramount importance. Today there is no such thing as a two-tier army; today every army worthy of the name is mechanized. Higher military commanders therefore do not dispose of an army within their army which they could use for operations with a degree of mobility manifoldly superior to the mass of their own or their opponents' armies. History does not repeat itself but it seems that the story of the Panzerwaffe can teach us one lesson, and that is that, where one element within an army possesses a degree of mobility much superior to the rest, it should not be dispersed by being scattered around at the lower tactical level but concentrated into independent formations at the exclusive disposal of the highest possible command level. It is my conviction that today air-mobility offers this capability, and this is, therefore, a matter for serious consideration by the most senior commanders. This book might pave the way if we learn from the historic lesson it conveys.

Introduction: An Affair of the Intellect

There is a story to the effect that in the prevailing enthusiasm for the things of the First Empire which followed Louis Napoleon's *coup d'état* in 1848, a politician sought to persuade a former sergeant of the Grenadiers of the Old Guard to share a platform with him. The *vieux moustache* eyed him balefully while he outlined his proposition, then spat in disgust. Knowing that the Emperor himself had always referred to the most devoted of his soldiers as *grognards* (old moaners), the politician unwisely persisted.

'M'sieu', he said, 'You have a duty to the younger generation! You have a duty to tell them of the glories of Wagram, of Jena, of Austerlitz!'

'Glory! You wouldn't know it if you put your foot in it!' snarled the old grenadier.

The interview was not going the way the politician intended.

'My friend,' he said sternly. 'You are too modest. After all, you can read of your own achievements and those of your comrades in the history books!'

For a moment the old man stared at him. It was difficult to tell what he was thinking, but suddenly the corners of his moustache began to twitch, then his shoulders began to heave uncontrollably and finally tears streamed down his lined cheeks. Nonplussed, the politician imagined that the fellow was quite overcome by the compliment he had been paid, and patted him sympathetically on the shoulder.

'There, there, *mon brave*!'

Then, to his horror, he realized that the old man was not weeping but laughing.

'*Allez-vous en*!' shouted the grey-haired ex-sergeant, brushing him aside with a wiry and totally unsuspected strength. 'I don't have to read history, you fat wind-bag — I spent twenty years making it!'

The last of the Grenadiers of the Old Guard were laid to rest well over a century ago but, more than any other troops of Napoleon Bonaparte's vast army, they epitomize the spirit of that era. Similarly, in considering the German Army's startling series of victories won between 1939 and 1942, and its protracted struggle against mounting odds during the years 1943 to 1945, it is of Hitler's Panzerwaffe that one tends to think first. Indeed, the men of the Old Guard and the crews of the Panzerwaffe had much in common, for both fought armies drawn from all the nations of Europe in settings which varied between the burning sands of North Africa and the wind-blasted snow-plains of the Russian heartland.

Today it is possible to regard the Old Guard with complete and objective detachment, but the same is not yet true of Hitler's Panzerwaffe, for although two generations have passed since a German tank fired its weapons in anger, the attitudes, the myths and the propaganda provoked by two world wars tend to linger on, distorting one truth and concealing another until the real facts are obscured by over-simplification and legend. Nonetheless, the years have also healed old wounds, and ancient enemies have become allies in a common cause, enabling us to re-examine the subject with a new and less emotional perspective. This is particularly important for the West, as the only NATO army which has inherited practical experience of the Soviet approach to war is that of West Germany. In this context it is necessary to re-state the fundamental objective of grand strategy, which is the defeat of the main mass of the enemy's army, for it was on the Russian Front that the main mass of the German Army was deployed and ultimately defeated; despite the countless books on the subject, the war in North Africa absorbed a mere 2.5 per cent of the total German war effort. That percentage rose sharply when the Western Allies returned to the mainland of Europe, but the war's centre of gravity remained in the East. The term Panzerwaffe, the literal meaning of which is 'armoured weapon', is generic and somewhat imprecise, since it refers to those branches of service which were equipped with armoured fighting vehicles of various sorts, some of which had yet to be fully established when war broke out. The term includes the Army's own tank and armoured-car troops, the armoured artillery (Panzerartillerie) and tank-destroyer (Panzerjäger) troops, and the motor rifle regiments later known as Panzergrenadiers, all of whom had their Waffen SS counterparts. Somewhat apart and able to pursue a jaunty independence to the end was the elite Assault Artillery (Sturmartillerie), equipped with assault guns. The Panzerwaffe was Hitler's only in that it was raised following his repudiation of the restrictive clauses of the Treaty of Versailles in 1935 and thereafter absorbed more of the Führer's interest and attention than any other section of the German armed forces, initially with beneficial results, latterly with catastrophic consequences.

The Panzerwaffe has always been regarded as the superbly equipped and finely honed cutting edge of the German Army, yet today perspective enables us to see that it suffered from very serious deficiencies in a number of areas. In fact, its commanders did not believe that it would be ready for war until 1943, and had it not acquired the Czech tank fleet *in toto*, together with Czech manufacturing capacity, it would have been unable to fight at all in 1939. The reality was that during the early years of the war the Panzerwaffe excelled *only* in organization, technique, command, control and communications, gun control equipment and a commendable prescience which left sufficient spare capacity in the PzKw III and IV designs for these tanks to be up-gunned when the time came. By comparison, contemporary British, French, Russian and, to a lesser degree, American practice was ineffective, although this situation would be reversed as the war progressed.

It was the sheer scale of the Panzerwaffe's victories, particularly in the West in 1940, that led to the creation of the legend. During this period the Panzerwaffe always fought at a numerical disadvantage, although such an admission would have been tantamount to suicide for the contemporary politicians of the defeated nations; rather than admit that the German Army had an instinct for mechanized warfare, it was more expedient to suggest that it was the Germans who had possessed the superior numbers, and since this had been the case in the decisive areas, this piece of selective reportage was willingly accepted. After the war, of course, the truth emerged but by then tempers had cooled a little and Germany had herself been defeated. The British, for example, were now willing to accept the nature of the German victory in 1940, but with the comforting rider that it was they who had shown the way and that the enemy had not been slow to take it. Such a view was even emphasized in his book *Panzer Leader* by none other than General Heinz Guderian, the distinguished German officer who had played such a significant role in establishing the Panzerwaffe and who was appointed Inspector General of Armoured Troops in March 1943 before becoming Army Chief of General Staff in July the following year.

'It was principally the books and articles of the Englishmen, Fuller, Liddell Hart and Martel, that excited my interest and gave me food for thought. I learned from them the concentration of armour, as employed in the Battle of Cambrai. Further, it was

Liddell Hart who emphasized the use of armoured forces for long-range strokes, operations against the opposing army's communications, and also proposed a type of armoured division combining panzer and panzer-infantry units. *Deeply impressed by these ideas I tried to develop them in a sense practicable for our own army.'*

The last sentence is extremely important, for each army has a different set of problems to consider, and no army is an exact mirror-image of another. If we examine group photographs of British and German officers' messes taken prior to the First World War, the faces tell us that much the same sort of people are serving as regimental officers in both armies. Most of the British officers have been educated in spartan public schools, most of the Germans in tightly disciplined cadet academies. Both groups contain officers with generations of military service to the state behind them. Both regarded sport, particularly hunting and shooting, as important, and since their regiments were recruited on a local basis they were expected to play a full part in the social life of their garrison towns, dividing their time scrupulously between the councillors, their wives and their daughters. Subalterns who paused to chat to each other at the Mayor's Ball were quickly confronted by their enraged Commanding Officer and invariably asked if they thought they were there to enjoy themselves!

By and large, officers visiting each other's messes would feel quite at home, with one or two minor differences. Off duty, the German officer remained in uniform, complete with sword; his British counterpart changed into civilian clothes as a matter of course. A visiting German officer would be told that discussion of ladies in a British mess was frowned upon as it caused ill-feeling; this he would have regarded as being incredibly dull, since female conquests were an essential element in the conversation of his own mess and, depending upon what was said, one could find oneself drawn into an illegal duel which would confer much prestige on the participants. A curious reversal of these *mores* was provided by the tango, then considered a highly inflammatory experience. In contrast to the War Office, which wisely offered no guidance to British officers on the subject, the Kaiser protected the moral welfare of his own officers by issuing an order to the effect they would instantly *leave the building* whenever it was played!

A second glance at the photographs would reveal deeper differences in the approach to war of the two groups of officers. The British were clearly the more experienced at the regimental level, and many of them wore campaign ribbons. They regarded soldiering at home as a bore and looked forward to their tours of duty in the distant outposts of the Empire, where they would be unlucky if they did not see active service at least once during their careers. Most were content to spend their years with their regiment, and little thought was given to operations above corps level.

In contrast, hardly any of the Germans had seen active service since the Franco-Prussian War of 1870. If an officer was posted to any of Germany's colonies, he would regard the event as a disaster and wonder what he had done to incur the wrath of those in high places that they should remove him from the mainstream of military life. The ambition of every German officer who wished to reach the heights of his chosen profession was to be selected for and to pass through the Kriegsakademie (War Academy), where the course was so intense and demanding that, it was whispered, its graduates never smiled again; certainly their humour was the drier for the experience. Only graduates of the Kriegsakademie were eligible for a coveted place on the General Staff, the driving force and the brain of the army, famed for its thinking on war at the higher level.

This approach to the subject was inherited by the German Empire from the kingdom of Prussia. An inscription below the statues of Prussian soldiers at the little Temple of Victory, built in the 1820s in Berlin's Unter den Linden, confirms that the thought is not a new one. It reads, 'German war, is an affair of the intellect; the intellect is stronger than any other force.'

The geographical position of Prussia, and later of Imperial Germany, was that of a state surrounded by potential enemies. War on at least two fronts always seemed probable, so that much thought had to be given to the speedy annihilation of at least one of the enemy armies. As John Laffin comments in his study of the German soldier, *Jackboot*, 'Annihilation was possible, as the examples of Epaminondas and Hannibal, Frederick the Great, Napoleon and Moltke proved, only when the attacker initiated a mobile battle with the object of falling upon the enemy's flank or of encircling and destroying piecemeal.'

To this end, therefore, the General Staff evolved a system of strategy consisting of three features: a bold advance, an enveloping attack, and full initiative in the commanders of minor units. The object was to recreate on a huge scale the Battle of Cannae, in which the wings of a Roman army were defeated and driven in upon the centre until the whole became a jumbled, disorganized mob which was slaughtered where it stood. The genius of the General Staff was that it was able to create the conditions for such events even before war had broken out. Thus in 1866 two Prussian armies had converged with precise timing to destroy an Austrian army on the battlefield of Königgrätz. Four years later the most important of the French armies was pinned against the Belgian frontier at Sedan and forced to surrender. Both of these major victories were won only weeks after hostilities had commenced.

It was clearly appreciated from the outset that, while offensive operations were under way against one enemy, it might be necessary to remain on the strategic defensive against another. The nature of that defence was not expected to remain passive. Full advantage was to be taken of mobility and the possession of interior lines to achieve a local superiority which could result in a sharp and unexpected defeat for the enemy.

Guderian and the panzer leaders of the Second World War were products of the old Imperial Army, in which most of them served as company or battalion commanders before and during World War I. Strictly speaking, the term Imperial Army is imprecise, but it has been used as a matter of convenience. The German states which constituted the Empire all maintained their own independent armies, as do the member states of NATO today. However, in time of war the Kaiser was designated Commander-in-Chief, and the Royal Prussian General Staff possessed the prerogative of planning for war. Some states also had bilateral conventions with Prussia under which the peacetime activities of their troops were subordinated to the Prussian authorities.

Guderian was an infantryman, as were Field Marshals Erwin Rommel and Walter Model; so too were Generals Hermann Balck, Heinrich Eberbach, Fritz-Hubert Gräser, Josef Harpe, Gotthard Heinrici, Hermann Hoth, Hans Hube, Walther Nehring, Georg Reinhardt, Rudolf Schmidt, Georg Stumme and Wilhelm Ritter von Thoma. Field Marshal Erich von Manstein, the most brilliant of them all, had served in the Foot Guards, and so had General Hans-Jurgen von Arnim. Field Marshal Ewald von Kleist was a hussar, and so were Generals Eberhard von Mackensen, Hasso von Manteuffel and Gustav Ritter von Vaerst. Generals Ludwig Crüwell, Leo Freiherr Geyr von Schweppenburg and Erich Höpner were all dragoons.

Many of these names will be unfamiliar to the average reader in the West, since their reputations were made on the Russian Front. It is significant that the one name which is instantly familiar, that of Erwin Rommel, usually appears in about tenth place in any

German order of merit. The fact that the list contains so many infantrymen merely confirms that when the Panzerwaffe was formed in 1935 the concepts of strategic mobility absorbed by the former officers of the Imperial Army in their youth provided the best possible seedbed in which the new ideas governing mechanized warfare could flourish and grow, despite the efforts of the conservative element which was present in every army. In 1939 the German Army was lucky in two respects. It alone had experienced a mass attack by tanks and knew exactly what to expect; the rest of the world's armies could only await the event, pondering the tank's alleged invulnerability as they did so. Secondly, Germany's panzer leaders were about to reach the pinnacle of their profession at a time when the influence of the tank pioneers of other nations was in steady decline. In Great Britain, most of these men had retired or were performing tasks which had little or nothing to do with armour, while years of deliberate political neglect had reduced the Royal Armoured Corps to virtual impotence. In France, the emphasis was on the strategic defensive and the writings of such men as the then Lieutenant-Colonel Charles de Gaulle were ignored. In the Soviet Union the Red Army's radical thinkers had all been butchered by Stalin in the Great Purge, and the designated role of armour changed with every shift of the political wind.

The startling successes obtained between 1939 and 1941, therefore, were gained against armies which were seriously flawed. From 1942 onwards that position was reversed, when Hitler assumed the role of Commander-in-Chief, imposing one disastrous decision after another on his troops. In this light one can see that the real merits of the Panzerwaffe lay not in its easy victories but in coping for so long with problems that were insoluble and odds which could never be equalled, the combination of which ultimately destroyed it.

Knights of the Black Cross

1. 'That's What I Want – That's What I'm Going to Have!'

When war broke out in 1914, Germany pinned all her hopes in the West on the Schlieffen Plan, another version of the Cannae theme in which the German line would pivot on the Franco-German frontier while its extended right wing marched through Belgium in a gigantic wheel which would ultimately crush the French left back against its centre and right in a huge vice. Six weeks had been allowed for this operation, and success depended entirely upon speed. On the outer edge of the wheel the troops, belonging to General Alexander von Kluck's First Army, would have to travel further and faster than anyone else. Noted for his ruthlessness, von Kluck had been selected specially for his ability to drive them on, but even he knew that he was asking a lot of men who marched with ninety-pound (forty kg) loads and whose supply lines grew longer and less reliable each day.

The Schlieffen Plan failed narrowly for a variety of reasons, few of which are relevant to this story. Its objective *was* attainable, but only just, and the margin between success and failure was too thin to allow for errors of judgement. It was very dangerous to stake so much on the abilities of marching men, and the limited provision of motor vehicles for the cavalry divisions' Jäger battalions suggests that subconsciously the General Staff was probably aware of the fact. Had most of the First Army been motorized, there can be little doubt that the plan would have succeeded, but even if the General Staff had been less conservative in its outlook, there were at the time not enough motor vehicles in existence within the Empire, let alone men capable of driving them. The plan was a generation ahead of its time, and its potential would provide Western commanders with a fatal distraction throughout the opening months of the next major conflict.

In the East, Germany had remained on the strategic defensive, leaving one army, the Eighth, to defend East Prussia. This fought several inconclusive engagements against the Russian First Army near the eastern frontier of the province, but when the Russian

Second Army began to close in on his right flank from the south, the German commander, von Prittwitz, became seriously alarmed and advocated a withdrawal behind the Vistula. The Chief of General Staff, General Count von Moltke, promptly dismissed him for his lack of resolve, his place being taken by the elderly General Paul von Hindenburg, recalled from his retirement for the purpose. As Chief of Staff Hindenburg was given General Erich Ludendorff, who had recently distinguished himself during the capture of Liège.

At this level in the German service the office of chief of staff was often synonymous with that of *de facto* commander, the reason being that designated army commanders might be members of Germany's royal families or general officers of great seniority who were respected figureheads but who needed the guidance of a professional at the peak of his abilities. Sometimes, when presented with a difficult problem, the army commander and his chief of staff would retire to separate rooms to prepare their own solutions, which were then compared. Frequently they were identical, but if they were not, the best features of each were chosen. In this case, even before he had joined Hindenburg for the journey to East Prussia, Ludendorff worked out a rapid re-deployment of the Eighth Army's corps which made maximum use of the frontier railway network, and then telegraphed orders directly to the corps commanders on 22 August, his action being subsequently approved by Hindenburg. This action had already been predicted in detail by Lieutenant-Colonel Max Hoffmann, the army's Staff Officer (Operations), so that when Hindenburg and Ludendorff arrived next day the necessary movements had already been initiated, the result being that, while a covering force had been left to delay the advance of the Russian First Army, the bulk of the Eighth Army was now concentrated against the Russian Second Army.

The episode demonstrates in the most graphic manner possible the uniform thought-pattern of the General Staff when confronted with an unexpected situation; it also emphasizes the German preference for spoken as opposed to written orders in circumstances where decisions have to be made quickly. The immediate result was that the Second Army marched into a trap and by 31 August had been encircled and crushed at Tannenberg. Hindenburg and Ludendorff now turned their attention to the Russian First Army and a fortnight later managed to destroy a major part of it with another double-envelopment in the area of the Masurian Lakes. Together, these two disasters cost Russia 250,000 of her best troops and 650 guns.

To the student of mechanized warfare, the campaign of Tannenberg and the Masurian Lakes demonstrates the use of mobility to deal simultaneously with the threat posed by two opponents, initially by holding the attention of the first, then moving rapidly to strike an unexpected and decisive blow at the second, and finally returning to attack the first with concentrated resources. This technique was used repeatedly and with telling effect by panzer and panzer-grenadier formations during the defensive phase of the fighting on the Russian Front during World War II, although of course these possessed their own organic mobility and did not have to rely exclusively on a convenient railway system, as did the Eighth Army.

After these opening moves both the Eastern and Western fronts lapsed into bloody stalemate. At first, the German Army gave little thought to the use of armoured vehicles as a means of breaking the deadlock, although in 1915 it did form a number of armoured car units. Its initial reaction to the first British tank attacks was that such vehicles had a purely local application and that the time and effort involved in their construction were barely justified. In the autumn of 1916 it changed its mind and set up a committee to look into the matter. This was known as the Allgemeine Kriegsdepartment 7 Abteilung Verkehrswesen (General War Department 7, Traffic Section), generally shortened to A7V, by which abbreviation Germany's first tank was to become known.

This tank was constructed according to parameters set by the committee and in essence consisted of an armoured box mounted on an underslung chassis. The vehicle was armed with a captured 57mm Russian gun and six machine-guns. It was protected by 30mm frontal armour and was manned by a crew of no fewer than eighteen, who travelled in extreme discomfort. The prototype was demonstrated to the General Staff at Mainz on 14 May 1917. In September it was decided to form two five-tank operational units designated Sturmpanzer Abteilungen 1 and 2. Unfortunately the slow rate of delivery from the factories seriously restricted the growth of the German tank arm, so that, while seven tank units had been formed by December, only three of these possessed A7Vs; the remainder were equipped with captured British Mark IVs, in some cases re-armed with 57mm guns. An eighth unit was formed during 1918 with captured Whippets. A basic infrastructure was set up in October 1917 with the formation of a Kraftfahrversuchskompanie (delivery squadron), and a tank depot was established behind the lines at Charleroi in Belgium. Ambitious plans were laid in 1918 for a major expansion of the arm, including a new heavy tank, the A7VU, and mass production of a copy of the Whippet, the LK II, but the war had ended before this belated enthusiasm bore fruit.

The task of the tanks was to eliminate pre-designated strongpoints and areas of likely resistance, and thereafter it seems that individual tank commanders could either engage opportunity targets or retire to the rally-point at their discretion. After the initial attack, the tanks were not expected to keep up with the infantry. According to the brief tactical notes that were issued, 'The infantry and tanks will advance independently of one another. No special instructions regarding co-operation with tanks will be issued. When advancing with tanks infantry will not come within 160 yards of the tanks on account of the shells which will be fired at them.'

Twenty tanks went into action on the St-Quentin sector on 21 March 1918, the first day of Ludendorff's great Michael offensive, achieving complete success. In subsequent actions the fortunes of the arm were mixed. British and German tanks clashed briefly at Villers-Bretonneux on 24 April, with loss to both sides, and fought a major action south of Cambrai on 8 October when the Sturmpanzer Abteilungen were concentrated for what transpired to be an abortive counter-attack. The last German tank attack of the war was delivered three days later at St-Aubert by four A7Vs, all of which were hit by artillery fire, and the following month an armistice was concluded. Thus the short but honourable history of the Imperial German Army Tank Force came to an end, apparently without an heir to inherit its traditions. It was too small and its officers were too junior for its former members to have much influence in the radically re-structured post-war German Army, although one of its sergeant-majors, a Bavarian named Josef Dietrich who had joined the 1st Lancers as a trooper in 1911, would rise to the heights of his profession and, a generation later, command an entire Panzer Army.

In another area of mechanized warfare, however, the Germany Army had achieved a spectacular success in what can justly be regarded the grandfather of all panzergrenadier and mechanized infantry operations. In 1916 Romania had entered the war on the side of the Entente Powers. German troops had quickly secured the important Vulkan Pass on the country's northern border but were unable to press their advantage because the poor roads in the area were incapable of carrying supplies in the quantity required for a major advance. This difficulty could be resolved if the main railway line which ran from Romania's western frontier could be secured. The problem was that the railway passed through the famous Danube gorge known as the Iron Gate, a naturally strong position lying some fifty miles (80 kms) south-west of the Vulkan Pass. This was held by a Romanian division which was offering the most determined resistance, while close behind was the town of Turnu Severin, which was surrounded by a ring of forts. It was decided to capture Turnu Severin with an *ad hoc* motorized battlegroup despatched from the Vulkan Pass. This would break into the town from the east, i.e. the least-expected direction, the consequence being that the Romanians would have to abandon their positions covering the Iron Gate.

The battlegroup was commanded by a Captain Picht and consisted of an infantry battalion, three machine-gun platoons, two mobile anti-aircraft guns, a signals section and a troop of dragoons, a total of 500 men, all of whom, with the exception of the dragoons, rode in lorries. Setting off at dawn on 20 November, Picht seized the town with a daring *coup de main* that evening and held it against all comers for the next thirty-six hours. Resistance at the Iron Gate quickly collapsed and the road into the Romanian heartland was open. Quite apart from the outstanding achievement of Picht and his men, what makes this operation so very interesting is the fact that the benefits of the indirect approach and the consequent strategic paralysis inflicted on the enemy were already fully understood by the Imperial German Army some years before Fuller and Liddell Hart began to write on these subjects. This, coupled with the instinctive use of mobility as a weapon of offence and defence, was its principal legacy to the as yet unborn Panzerwaffe.

As the year 1918 ended, the old Army completed its orderly withdrawal across the Rhine and then, like that of the Tsar the previous year, it disbanded itself. Most of the rank and file simply went home, so that the majority of units were reduced by events to a mere cadre of officers and NCOs, but in some cases regiments followed the Bolshevik precedent and established Soldiers' Councils which even dismissed those officers that remained.

The Kaiser had abdicated on 28 November, and the government was now in the hands of republican politicians who had neither police nor troops to enforce their will. Armed gangs of Spartacists (the German equivalent of the Bolsheviks), naval mutineers from Kiel and assorted revolutionary movements all roamed the countryside and the cities seeking to impose their own will and to destroy what remained of established authority. These were hard times indeed for those loyal officers who remained at their posts, for in barracks they were no longer saluted and were obeyed only if the Soldiers' Councils approved their orders, while outside they risked being spat upon, having their epaulettes torn off or being assaulted or even murdered.

There was a reaction to this which the government mobilized in the hope that its own authority could be established. This was the Freikorps movement in which former officers raised units of their own to fight the revolutionaries. These units were incorporated in the central command structure early in 1919, but the fact that their loyalties very clearly lay to their own unit commanders rather than to the elected government has tended to give them a somewhat sinister reputation. To many, including the government, they were heroes doing their duty, but to others they were sadistic thugs. The latter opinion is somewhat severe, and it must be remembered that it is in the nature of civil wars to induce a bitterness and savagery on both sides which is rarely present in a conflict between nations. After the revolutionaries had been defeated in Germany, the Freikorps were employed in the formerly Russian Baltic provinces where the native German minority was fighting to keep the Bolsheviks at bay. During the fighting it seems to have been Freikorps crews which manned such tanks and armoured cars as Germany still possessed.

On 28 June 1919 the Allies concluded a peace treaty with Germany at Versailles. Many Germans, already embittered by the unsatisfactory outcome of the war, unable to believe that their army had been defeated in the field and deeply concerned by the chaos into which the country had fallen, were stunned by the terms of the treaty, which deliberately left them *Heerlos, Wehrlos und Ehrlos* – disarmed, defenceless and dishonoured. Among other humiliations unwisely imposed by the Allies, Germany was forbidden military aircraft, heavy artillery and fighting vehicles of every sort, with the exception of a few unarmed armoured personnel carriers for internal security purposes. Further, the Great General Staff was dissolved, the number of cadet academies was drastically reduced and the size of the Army was restricted to 100,000 men.

At this period Germany had about 400,000 men under arms, the majority belonging to Freikorps units. Many left the service quite voluntarily when the civil war was over, but about 15,000 officers and a proportionately higher number of senior NCOs who believed that their futures were secure were discharged. The anger of such men is understandable, for they were the ones who had actually fought the revolutionaries on behalf of the same government which was now abandoning them; to compound their sense of betrayal, it was soon obvious that the better jobs in the new regular army, the Reichsheer, were going to men who had remained in barracks the while with the rump of the old army. Thoroughly disillusioned, they became natural recruits for the infant Nazi Party, bringing organization and discipline to its gangs of uniformed street thugs, the Sturm Abteilungen (SA), so that the latter easily defeated their less regimented enemies of the Iron Front, which included both Socialist and Communist private armies in its ranks. From such a sowing of dragon's teeth there was to emerge a terrible harvest, although the direction history was to take was little apparent to the ex-service SA members of the 1920s, some of whom were later to emerge as competent panzer leaders in the Waffen SS. Nonetheless, the SA's victory was a major factor in Hitler's rise to power, and once an evil of this magnitude had been unchained, the tragedy could but pursue its course.

The Reichsheer was the bedrock on which the German Army of 1933-45 was built. It was the creation of its first Commander-in-Chief, General Hans von Seeckt, who came from Schleswig-Holstein on the Danish border.

Seeckt had first come to the attention of his superiors when, as a lieutenant of the Kaiser Alexander Garde-Grenadier Regiment Nr 1, he had commanded a company at the lying-in-state of Kaiser Wilhelm I at Berlin Cathedral in 1888. The late Emperor had been both liked and respected by his people, and a crowd wishing to pay its respects grew to such proportions that several barriers collapsed because of the crush. Seeckt, feeling that the dignity of the occasion was seriously threatened, ordered his men to fix bayonets and cleared the area by force, earning the highest praise for this somewhat extreme reaction. In 1914 he was a lieutenant-colonel and chief of staff of a corps in von Kluck's First Army, where he was able to witness the reasons for the failure of the Schlieffen Plan at first hand. He always expressed sincere admiration for the quality of the British Expeditionary Force with which First Army had clashed violently at Mons and again at Le Câteau, remaining a convinced advocate of the small professional army in preference to the *levée en masse*. In 1915 he served as chief of staff to Field Marshal von Mackensen during the major defeat inflicted on the Russians at Gorlice, and he continued to serve on the Eastern Front for the remainder of the war.

Von Seeckt was unpopular with the Hindenburg-Ludendorff circle, but this in itself made him the more acceptable to the Allies when he attended the peace conference as military adviser to the German delegation. German politicians, too, found him an easier

man to deal with than they had been used to in either Hindenburg
or Ludendorff, although his own professional colleagues were not
endeared to him by his haughty manner and caustic wit. He used
silence as a weapon, betraying few of his thoughts and earning
himself the nickname 'the Sphinx'. His period of office lasted
from 1920 until 1926 and was terminated when, without
consulting the Minister of Defence or the republican government,
he permitted the Kaiser's grandson, Prince Wilhelm of Prussia, to
attend the army manoeuvres wearing the uniform of the First
Footguards. The public outcry was such that, with little personal
regret, President Hindenburg demanded his resignation. This was
an uncharacteristic lapse on the part of a man whose first edict to
his officers was that the Army must remain above politics, and it
can be explained only on the grounds that he allowed his affection
for the monarchy to cloud his judgement.

The army created by von Seeckt numbered 4,000 officers and
96,000 other ranks, consisting of eighty-one cavalry and
twenty-one infantry regiments organized into three cavalry and
seven infantry divisions. By forbidding conscription and fixing
the term of enlistment at twelve years, the Allies sought to
prevent Germany's amassing a large trained reserve, but this was
a fruitless exercise as there was already an excess of trained
manpower which would last for several years. It was a policy
which suited von Seeckt very well, since what he aimed to
produce was an army of leaders and instructors trained beyond
the level of their present rank so that, when expansion came, it
would proceed smoothly and efficiently. It also enabled the Army
to apply selective recruiting, taking only the best of those who
offered themselves for service. The value of tradition was
particularly emphasized, each squadron or company of the
Reichsheer assuming the traditions, honours and customs of a
regiment of the Imperial Army.

There was intentionally a great deal about the Reichsheer that
the Allied Control Commission for the Disarmament of Germany
(1920-7) either did not know or suspected but could never
prove. For instance, despite the official disappearance of the
Kriegsakademie, highly trained staff officers were still being
produced by clandestine methods; Lufthansa, the state airline
formed in 1926, was organized so as to provide the perfect
infrastructure for the Luftwaffe when it appeared; a respectable
financial and industrial statistics company named Stega, with its
head office in Berlin and branch offices throughout the country,
had actually been set up by the Ordnance Directorate with the
task of collating information on armaments-manufacturing

capacity, this being put to good use when the Army expanded so dramatically in 1933.

Most interesting of all was the activity which went on behind the apparently dull façade of the Transport Troops Inspectorate. This department was responsible for two different types of organization, the Fahrtruppe (horse-drawn transport troops), who wore light-blue branch-of-service piping on their uniforms, and the Kraftfahrtruppe (mechanical transport troops), who wore pink piping, both of whom concealed their real purpose beneath their routine daily activity. It is sometimes forgotten that most of the German Army's transport *and* field artillery relied exclusively on the horse before and throughout World War II and therefore required men who were familiar with horse-management. The reality was that the Fahrtruppe provided a cover for more trained gunners than were strictly permitted but who could perform the transport role and were officially transferred to the artillery during the Army's period of expansion. The seven battalions of the Kraftfahrtruppe, however, were technical troops, and when Germany formed her first tank units since World War I, it was they who provided the necessary cadres. Subsequently the now depleted ranks of the transport troops were filled with men recruited direct from civilian life.

After the signing of the Versailles Treaty, Germany scrapped or sold her few tanks and armoured cars, the last of the A7Vs being purchased by the newly created state of Poland, which used them against Tukhachevsky's Bolsheviks during the Battle of Warsaw, before being scrapped themselves in 1921. Despite this the Reichsheer did not altogether lack practical experience during the next decade, gaining useful technical data from work carried out discreetly in Sweden. In addition, a secret agreement was reached with the USSR under which an AFV testing station was established at Kazan on the River Kama, deep inside Russia, to the mutual benefit of both parties as the Russians were completely inexperienced in this field and the Germans needed an area in which to test their ideas far from the prying eyes of the Allied Control Commission. The presence of the Commission did nothing to inhibit the design and construction of turreted heavy and medium tank prototypes within Germany under their espective cover names of *Gross Traktor* and *Leichter Traktor* (large and light tractors), the former armed with a 75mm gun and weighing 23 tons and the latter, of 12 tons, mounting a 37mm gun. Six heavies and three mediums were despatched to Kazan in 1928.

It was, however, in the area of theoretical employment of tanks that the most significant developments took place. The reports of German military attachés and observers posted to trouble-spots around the world where armour was in use were read with intense interest. The majority of stimulating ideas stemmed from the United Kingdom, where Fuller, Liddell Hart, Martel and Stern were predicting the course armoured warfare would take and where the Royal Tank Corps, as it then was, demonstrated the validity of their theories in exercises which saw the movement of entire formations controlled by means of a radio network. Interesting as these developments were, there were many senior officers in every army, including the Reichsheer, who have been accused of a collective conservatism because of their lukewarm reaction, but whose reservations stemmed from very reasonable doubts that, with the rudimentary equipment available at the time, it would be extremely difficult to fulfil the promises made by the prophets of the armoured idea. Once the various technical problems had been solved, most doubts vanished. What struck a particular, if occasionally unconscious, chord in the mind of German officers who had been schooled in the traditions of von Moltke the Elder and von Schlieffen was the similarity in the basic thought-process expressed by Fuller in his famous Plan 1919, which consisted of three phases:

I. A deep penetration by what he termed a Disorganizing Force, aimed at the elimination of the enemy's higher headquarters, accompanied by close air support and air interdiction behind the enemy's lines;

II. A breaking or holding operation intended to engage the main mass of the enemy army;

III. A pursuit maintained for up to 150 miles (240 kms).

Plan 1919 provided the framework upon which the Blitzkrieg technique is based, and historical experience confirms that the best results are obtained if Phase II, the breaking or holding phase, actually precedes or runs concurrently with Phase I. Attempts to apply the technique using Phase I, the deep penetration phase, without the support of Phase II, have rarely yielded satisfactory results and have sometimes ended in complete failure. Most military writers and historians are guilty of placing too much emphasis altogether on the undoubtedly dramatic aspects of Phase I, and too little on the rather less obvious but equally vital aspects of Phase II. In certain circumstances there has been no need to implement Phase III, the pursuit phase, as the enemy army has already been destroyed.

In the light of experience, therefore, it is possible to define the Blitzkrieg technique itself in the following terms:

Ground troops with air support employing their mobility to secure an *attainable* objective, the loss of which will paralyse the enemy's command system, destroy his morale and lead to the disintegration of his army. The actual method consists of concentration in overwhelming strength at the point of impact during the break-in phase, deep penetration beyond the zone in which the enemy is capable of response, and attainment of the objective by means of an indirect approach; *the whole accompanied by a breaking or holding operation intended to involve the main mass of the enemy's force.*

The traditional German approach to war, based on creating the conditions which would result in the encirclement and destruction of the enemy, has already been discussed briefly. This was known as the *Vernichtungsgedanke* (annihilation concept), and the new ideas differed from it only slightly, in that the emphasis had shifted from the enemy's flank to a strategic objective in his rear, while the disintegration of his army following the paralysis of its command structure had been substituted for its physical destruction.

Another factor which was to be of immense benefit to the German Army in its conduct of mechanized operations was its appreciation that war is fought simultaneously on several levels. At this period most Western armies thought only in terms of strategy, i.e. the planning of campaigns, and of tactics, the manner in which they are fought. The Germans interposed a third level, then known as the operative but now more commonly as the operational level, involving operations of approximately corps or army size. For example, the war in North Africa was fought throughout by the Axis powers at the operational level since the forces involved never approached the size of an army group. It was, in fact, in the handling of armour at the operational level that German commanders demonstrated a clear superiority during the early years of World War II.

It was also inevitable, in an army which historically had employed mobility as a weapon that flexibility should be the keynote of operational procedure. The formation of *ad hoc* battlegroups for specific tasks, such as that commanded by Picht to open the Iron Gate in 1916, was a natural part of German military life. So too were 'saddle orders', a reliance on spoken rather than written orders in the field to a degree not practised in other armies to anything like the same extent.

Most of the Reichsheer's formative thoughts on the use of armour had their origins inside the Transport Troops Inspectorate. Here in 1922 the then Inspector, General Erich von

Tschischwitz, was engaged in studying the application of mechanical transport to the problems posed by Germany's long frontiers and the lack of troops to defend them. Much of the detailed work was carried out by a former light infantryman and communications specialist, Captain Heinz Guderian, who found Tschischwitz a hard taskmaster but, contrary to his own expectations, soon began to take an interest in mechanized warfare. One of his colleagues, a Lieutenant Volckheim, was compiling a survey on the use of armour during the war and provided him with sufficient material to stimulate his interest in this aspect of the subject. He also read avidly whatever books and articles about armour could be obtained from Britain and was soon contributing articles of his own to the *Militär-Wochenblatt* which were generally well received. 'Since nobody else busied himself with this material,' he commented, 'I was soon by way of being an expert!'

Guderian got on less well with Tschischwitz's successor, Major-General von Natzmer. On his suggesting publicly in 1924 that the mechanical transport troops could perform a combat role, Natzmer reacted angrily: 'To the devil with combat – they're supposed to hump flour!' Perhaps Guderian's suggestion was a little too close for comfort to the Reichsheer's concealed intentions, for Natzmer was not quite the dyed-in-the-wool reactionary the remark suggests; in fact, his comment was actually made on the conclusion of a series of theoretical exercises which examined the use of tanks with cavalry in the reconnaissance role, and it was, of course, during his period in office that the secret armour school was set up at Kazan.

In October 1926 von Natzmer was succeeded by Major-General A. von Vollard-Bockelberg, an officer whose contribution to the story of Germany's armoured troops has seldom been acknowledged. It was he who was responsible for the regular training of the Kraftfahrtruppe officers in the theory of armoured warfare, based on the British Army pamphlet *Provisional Instructions for Armoured Vehicles 1927*, and under his direction exercises were commenced with mock-up cardboard tanks mounted on automobile chassis. In 1929 he moved to the Ordnance Department, where he stayed until the end of 1933, during which period he accelerated the process of motorization within the Army, formed the first motor-cycle and mechanized reconnaissance units and set in train the design phase of what were to become Germany's first mass-produced tanks, the Panzerkampfwagen (PzKw) I and II.

Meanwhile, in 1928 Guderian had been promoted major and

embarked on a series of tactical lectures to Transport Corps personnel. He now believed that the tank's full potential could be realized only by the formation of armoured divisions which also contained a balanced complement of supporting arms, but the following year these views attracted unfavourable comment from Major-General Otto von Stülpnagel, who had replaced von Vollard-Bockelberg as Inspector. Stülpnagel thought that armoured divisions belonged to a world of fantasy and promptly forbade the discussion of tactical problems in which *theoretical* tanks were organized in formations greater than regimental strength! A clever man but clearly of limited vision, he expressed the view that, 'Neither of us will see German tanks in operation in our lifetime.'

Guderian went away to command a motorized transport battalion, and when he returned to the Inspectorate as a lieutenant-colonel in October 1931, it was as Chief of Staff to its new commander, Major-General Oswald Lutz, an old friend under whom he had served in a Bavarian motorized transport battalion for three months in 1922. Lutz shared Guderian's views, and much of their time was spent trying to convince colleagues in other branches of the service that the proposed armoured formations could really deliver what their advocates promised. In this they achieved considerable success by staging large-scale exercises which attracted the approval of President Hindenburg. They also took over the role of reconnaissance from the cavalry, introduced new armoured-car designs, continued clandestine tank development and began the motorization of the infantry divisions' anti-tank units. Although there was a degree of opposition to the growth of mechanization from a few conservatively minded officers in the cavalry, artillery and infantry, it was by no means the uphill struggle Guderian hints at occasionally in his memoirs. A number of very senior officers also favoured the idea, including the War Minister, General von Blomberg, the Chief of the Reichswehr Ministerial Office, Colonel-General Walter von Reichenau, with whom Guderian got on extremely well, and the Army's Commander-in-Chief from 1 February 1934, Colonel-General Freiherr von Fritsch. On the other hand, Guderian was on the worst possible terms with the Chief of General Staff, General Ludwig Beck, whom he scathingly described as 'a paralysing influence wherever he appeared'. It is, perhaps, as well to remember that Guderian's widely read memoirs often provide a very personal view, reflecting his impatience with those who failed to agree with him at once. The truth was that Beck was far from hostile to new ideas, and it was during his term of office that the Panzerwaffe was established. For his part, Beck regarded Guderian as an *arriviste*, and a pushy one at that. In the final analysis, this clash of personalities mattered not at all, for the panzer arm's most enthusiastic proponent was none other than Adolf Hitler, Germany's new Chancellor, who had exclaimed, on witnessing one of Guderian's demonstrations involving a motor-cycle platoon, two armoured car platoons, a platoon of experimental PzKw Is and an anti-tank platoon: 'That's what I need! That's what I'm going to have!' With such allies it was inevitable that the panzer arm would expand rapidly when the moment came.

The moment arrived as a result of the sinister political climate which had existed since the Nazis were voted into power, quite legally, in January 1933. Throughout the rest of that year the SA ruthlessly suppressed all other political parties. Now 400,000 strong, this organization considered itself the rival of the Reichsheer, towards which it maintained a hostile and highly provocative attitude. More to the point, Hitler was well aware that the SA could unseat him if it chose to, so on the night of 30 June 1934, subsequently known as 'the Night of the Long Knives', its leadership throughout Germany was murdered by members of his own bodyguard, the Schutzstaffeln (SS), and of the security service, the Sicherheitsdienst (SD); in addition to the leaders of the SA, Hitler's deathlist included anyone against whom he had a grudge, including two generals. In the Reichstag he was to insist that these killings had been necessary to protect the integrity of the German Army and preserve it as the non-political instrument of the nation.

President Hindenburg was now failing visibly, and perhaps he did not fully understand just what had taken place, for he sent Hitler a congratulatory telegram. On 2 August the old Field Marshal died and Hitler combined the offices of President and Chancellor in one title, that of Führer. The armed services were immediately ordered to swear the soldier's oath of unconditional loyalty and obedience not to their country or its constitution but to Adolf Hitler, 'the Führer of the German Reich and Commander-in-Chief of the Wehrmacht'. This was a very different matter from swearing loyalty to a monarch, which the majority of senior officers had once done, and many accepted it with serious reservations since its effect was to make the Army and Navy the private property of a politician. Having once taken the oath, most officers considered themselves honour-bound by it, and in the long term this was to have terrible consequences for Germany.

At this period Hitler's popularity was at its height. His strange, magnetic personality contained facets which appealed to most men, particularly his avowed intention of restoring Germany's honour and her fortune. Having bound the services to himself and had his position ratified by plebiscite, he now embarked upon the policy of expansion and confrontation which was to lead directly to the Second World War. On 16 March 1935 he repudiated the restrictive clauses of the Treaty of Versailles and made it clear that Germany would re-arm as she thought fit. Conscription was introduced, with the object of the Army's being able to fight a full-scale *defensive* war by 1939 and an *offensive* war by 1943. The 100,000-strong Reichsheer lost its title and was submerged under the flood of conscripts as its units split and split again, amoeba-like, to form fresh regiments, which in turn would themselves produce their own offsprings. This so diluted the quality of units that it was several years before the lost ground was regained. In form the new Army resembled neither the Reichsheer nor the Kaiser's Army, for it was an army which was intended for short wars rather than the sort of protracted struggle which had taken place between 1914 and 1918; it was, in fact, an army which re-armed in breadth but not in depth, most of the modern equipment being issued to the armoured and motorized formations which would form its cutting edge, while the rest continued to rely on the horse as a prime mover. As far as the Panzerwaffe is concerned, its birth is described by Colonel Albert Seaton in his excellent study *The German Army 1933-45*:

> Some idea of the confusion that must have existed at that time can be gained by tracing the forming of the first six panzer regiments that made up the three panzer divisions. Panzer Regiments 1 and 2 were formed on Kraftfahrkampftruppe cadres, their numbers being made up to establishment by the addition of officer and other rank drafts from the cavalry. Panzer Regiment 3 had its first battalion based on officers and men transferred from Cavalry Regiment 12; its second battalion was formed from drafts from six other cavalry regiments. Within a year, however, Panzer Regiment 1 broke up to form Panzer Regiment 5 and, together with the main body of Cavalry Regiment 4, formed Panzer Regiment 6. Panzer Regiment 2 was renamed as the new Panzer Regiment 1, but it threw off a framework so that Panzer Regiment 2 should continue in existence, most of the officers and other ranks for the new Panzer Regiment 2 coming from Cavalry Regiment 7. Then Panzer Regiments 1, 2 and 3 gave up drafts to form a new Panzer Regiment 4. This process continued during 1936 and 1937, Panzer Regiment 7 being formed from further drafts from Panzer Regiments 1, 2 and 4, and Panzer Regiment 8 from 3, 5 and 6. And so it went on, with little apparent stability anywhere.

The first three panzer divisions were set up on 15 October

1935, the 1st at Weimar under Major-General Freiherr von Weichs, the 2nd at Würzburg under Colonel Heinz Guderian, the 3rd at Berlin under Major-General Fessmann. The 4th and 5th Panzer Divisions were formed in 1938, and the 10th in April the following year. At this period the divisional establishment consisted of a panzer brigade, a motorized infantry brigade, a motorized artillery regiment, reconnaissance, anti-tank, signals and engineer battalions (joined later by an anti-aircraft battalion), plus service units. The panzer brigade consisted of two regiments each of two battalions, each battalion containing one heavy and three light companies, giving a total theoretical tank strength of 562 vehicles, which never came close to being fulfilled. The motorized infantry brigade contained one two-battalion lorried infantry regiment and a motor-cycle battalion. The organization of the reconnaissance battalion was that of a miniature battlegroup, including two armoured reconnaissance squadrons each with one heavy and two light armoured car troops; a motor-cycle machine-gun squadron; and a heavy squadron with towed light field gun and anti-tank gun troops and an assault pioneer troop. This reflected the deep reconnaissance concept essential to the techniques already discussed, assisted by the necessary firepower to get the cars through the enemy's forward defended localities.

The Panzerwaffe's understandable wish to control its own destiny had not gone unchallenged by the still influential infantry and cavalry lobbies. The infantry naturally wanted tank support for their own operations and, as this could not reasonably be denied, two independent panzer brigades, the 4th and 6th, and one independent panzer regiment were formed for this purpose. The cavalry, most of which had now been mechanized but was still employed on its traditional tasks, also demanded tanks for its four Light Divisions, which were formed in 1938. These divisions included one panzer battalion, four motor-rifle battalions known as Kavellerie Schützen to commemorate their traditions, and reconnaissance, artillery and engineer elements. The problem was that infantry and cavalry requirements absorbed an unwelcome proportion of the country's already unsatisfactory tank-production figures which would otherwise have benefited the panzer divisions.

As defined by the Ordnance Department, the Panzerwaffe's tank requirements were based on four vehicles, the PzKw I, II, III and IV.

The PzKw I, armed with twin machine-guns, was an intentionally simple little machine designed for basic crew-training. The PzKw II was a slightly larger and more sophisticated light tank armed with a 20mm cannon and a co-axial machine-gun and was intended originally for the reconnaissance role, although much more was to be demanded of it than this.

The PzKw III was conceived as the main battle tank which would equip three of the panzer battalion's four companies. Senior tank officers had recommended that it be armed with a 50mm gun, a sensible provision at a time when the British were beginning to fit a 40mm 2-pdr gun into their new Cruiser tank series and the Russians were already employing a 45mm gun in their BTs and T-26s. However, the Ordnance Department demurred, pointing out with the backing of the Artillery Inspectorate that the infantry was already in possession of the 37mm anti-tank gun, which was in quantity production, and the obvious convenience of standardization. An intelligent compromise was reached by which the tank officers accepted the 37mm, while the turret ring was constructed wide enough to accommodate the 50mm gun if necessary.

The PzKw IV was intended as the equipment of the panzer battalion's fourth or heavy company, and its main armament consisted of a 75mm L/24 howitzer, the idea being that the direct fire of this weapon with high explosive ammunition would eliminate the enemy's anti-tank guns from a range at which the latter could not make effective reply. The secondary armament of both the PzKw III and IV consisted of co-axial and hull machine-guns.

On the basis outlined above, it is unlikely that Hitler would have gone to war in 1939 had he not acquired the Czech tank fleet and manufacturing capacity in that year, for although the PzKw III and IV were essentially sound designs, their development phase was plagued by suspension problems and they were leaving the factories only in small numbers. However, from the Czechs the Panzerwaffe inherited just sufficient PzKw 35(t)s and PzKw 38(t)s, both of which were armed with a 37mm gun and could be substituted for the PzKw III, to give it an offensive capacity.

At this period little interest was expressed in the heavy or breakthrough tank which was so popular with the French and Soviet armies, but in 1934 two prototype versions were produced under the transparent cover title of Neubaufahrzeug (new construction vehicles), generally shortened to NbFz. These were heavily influenced by the multi-turreted design of the British 'Independent' and, although it was decided not to proceed with quantity production of the NbFz, the prototypes were retained on the active list. In addition, from 1937 onwards, design work proceeded at a fairly leisurely pace on the project which, in due course, was to evolve into the legendary Tiger.

Following his appointment as commander of the 2nd Panzer Division, Guderian's star continued to rise swiftly. On 1 August 1936 he was promoted major-general; on 4 February 1938 he was promoted lieutenant-general and appointed commander of the XVI Corps at Berlin; on 20 November that same year Hitler promoted him *General der Panzertruppen* and appointed him Chief of Mobile Troops. As a former signals specialist, he was well aware of the connection between operational flexibility and good communications, and it was at his insistence that every tank was fitted for radio and that armoured command vehicles containing the appropriate number of sets were developed for the various command levels within the Panzerwaffe. Serious training from the level of company upwards was commenced to give commanders and staffs the feel of handling formations on the move.

Much emphasis was placed on the facts that the panzer division was a balanced weapon designed for offensive use and that much of its success would depend on its ability to generate violence during the break-through phase. With its tank brigade spearheading the assault, and with close co-operation from the Luftwaffe, it would attack a sector of the enemy front not more than 5,000 yards (4,500 metres) wide. During the approach march the tanks might be concentrated in a *Keil* (wedge) but for the assault itself would deploy into either two consecutive waves known as *Treffen* (clubs) or two parallel groups known as *Flugel* (wings), for both of which the quadruple organization of tank units had been designed; each club or wing would be responsible for the elimination of a specific aspect of the defence. The sheer speed and weight of the attack would generally take it right through the defended zone, and then the panzer brigade would *accelerate* towards its strategic objective, avoiding areas of resistance wherever possible. Through the gap created by the tanks would pour the rest of the division: the armoured reconnaissance battalion, which would go into the lead and operate several miles ahead of the advance; the motor rifle battalions, which would deal with isolated areas of opposition along the divisional centre-line and hold selected areas of captured ground; the motorized artillery batteries, ready to support tanks or riflemen as the situation required; the anti-tank gunners, capable of deploying their weapons rapidly into screens with which to beat off an armoured counter-attack; and finally the divisional service units with their facilities for vehicle recovery, replenishment, supply and maintenance. Given sufficient time, most of this force was to have ridden on tracked or half-tracked chassis, but this was not to be, and by 1939 the only developments in this direction were the use of the already obsolete PzKw I as a mounting for a Czech 47mm anti-tank gun and the German 150mm Heavy Infantry Gun 33. Work was also in hand on the SdKfz 251 armoured personnel- and weapons-carrier series, but the first examples were not issued until 1940 and deliveries never amounted to more than a fraction of the total demand; the vast majority of motor riflemen had to put up with lorries or, at best, unarmoured versions of the half-track chassis.*

Guderian's intention regarding the Light Divisions was that their strength should be augmented until they attained full armoured status, but this ambition had been only partially realized by the time the Polish crisis deepened. The additional tanks came from the independent panzer brigades, which also provided the nucleus of the 10th Panzer Division, their commitment to infantry support being transferred to the embryo Sturmartillerie (Assault Artillery), soon to become an elite branch of service within its own right.

The Sturmartillerie had its origins in a memorandum submitted in 1935 to General Beck, the Chief of General Staff, by the then Colonel Erich von Manstein, in charge of the Operations Branch. Manstein's memo indicated that technical studies had shown the need for an armoured self-propelled gun to work under infantry control and give direct gunfire support as required; he also suggested that each infantry division should contain an organic assault gun battalion consisting of three batteries each of six guns. Beck thought the idea a good one and passed it on to von Fritsch, the Commander-in-Chief, who agreed, and the project was approved.

The artillery was given the task of designing the weapon system under the supervision of the General Staff's Technical Section 8, commanded by Colonel Walter Model. To save time it was decided to employ the chassis of the PzKw III as a carriage. On this was placed a low, fixed superstructure with overhead cover and heavy frontal armour, mounting a limited-traverse 75mm L/24 howitzer. The completed prototype was ready for trials on Kummersdorf Ranges early in 1937 and proved entirely satisfactory. Thereafter it was hoped that by the autumn of 1939 each active infantry division would have its assault gun battalion, as would each reserve division sometime in 1940, although the

* SdKfz = Sonderkraftfahrzeug (special-purpose vehicle). All German fighting vehicles had an SdKfz number.

number of guns had been reduced to four. In the event, such optimism was quite unfounded.

First it had to be decided who was going to man the new assault guns and a conference was held during which the Inspector Generals of Infantry, Artillery and Panzertruppen, accompanied by their personal staffs, met to discuss the subject. The infantrymen began by explaining that their branch of service did not possess the necessary technical or logistic infrastructure required to maintain the guns in the field, and rather than have these insuperable difficulties thrust upon them, they were prepared to let the whole idea drop. This was a professional evaluation and was accepted. The panzer contingent then suggested that the project be scrapped on the grounds that it was interfering with tank production. The reply to this was that, if the assault guns were not produced, it would be the tanks which would have to perform their work. The tank men would accept neither this nor that there had been an improvement in PzKw III chassis deliveries.

Tempers were already frayed when someone maliciously commented that the assault gun's roomier superstructure enabled a larger weapon to be mounted than that carried by the tanks, and that this would confer on the Sturmartillerie the capacity to destroy enemy armour at a greater range than their beloved panzers. At this point one tank officer completely lost control and, banging the table furiously, yelled that the conference 'had just passed sentence of death on the panzer arm!' In an attempt to induce a calmer atmosphere, the Inspector-General of Artillery intervened and in so doing brought the meeting to its memorable climax, apparently without understanding that the weapon system under discussion was a twenty-two ton (23,500 kg) tracked armoured vehicle. Modern technology was all very well, he said, but before any major decisions were taken, perhaps trials should be held to decide whether the new support gun would not be better horse-drawn, in the manner of the Great War! While jaws gaped in astonishment, his embarrassed personal staff gathered round to explain von Manstein's ideas on tactical employment and also the nature of the weapon itself. Once *au fait* with the position, the Inspector-General began to warm to the concept, which he agreed was best handled by artillerymen, much to the relief of everyone present. The Artillery School at Jütebog was detailed to establish basic training facilities and a tactical instruction wing.

In the autumn of 1937 an Experimental Battery was set up by the 7th Motorized Artillery Demonstration Regiment, and this carried out a variety of exercises throughout the following winter. After the results of these had been evaluated, the Experimental Battery spent the next year carrying out combined trials with the Infantry Demonstration Regiment at Doberitz, during which tactical principles were established for the benefit of both arms. During gunnery trials the assault gun crews did rather better than their tank counterparts, who used the same howitzer fitted to the PzKw IV, being quicker onto the target and using less ammunition to destroy it. Unfortunately, the protracted nature of the troop and gunnery trials, which in themselves had proved entirely satisfactory, combined with other factors to delay the series production of assault guns, so that the first battery was not available for active service until 1940.

The Panzerwaffe had its first experience of active service during the Spanish Civil War, to which Hitler and Mussolini sent troops and equipment to support Franco's Nationalists, while Soviet Russia did likewise for the Communists. The German contingent was known as the Condor Legion, and the first of its 180 PzKw Is began arriving in January 1937, commanded by Colonel Wilhelm Ritter von Thoma. Training of Spanish crews was commenced at once, and eventually von Thoma had four tank battalions under his command, each three companies strong with fifteen tanks in each company; he was also responsible for thirty anti-tank batteries, equipped with six 37mm guns apiece. Franco wanted the tanks parcelled out among his infantry units, and von Thoma had to resist this, proving that the best results were obtained when they fought together. There were a number of successes but no striking victories, for neither side appreciated the critical importance of pushing motorized infantry through the gap created by the tanks, so that much of the ground won had to be abandoned because there were no troops available to consolidate it. Nonetheless, much practical experience was gained in co-operation with ground-attack aircraft and in developing the sword-and-shield technique which was to be of such value in North Africa and Russia. This involved the aggressive use of anti-tank gun screens onto which the panzers would draw the enemy armour by feigning retreat; once the latter had been written down, the German tanks would counter-attack and complete the rout. Spain also revealed the glaring inadequacy of the PzKw I as a combat vehicle to such an extent that von Thoma offered a reward of 500 pesetas for every Russian T-26 captured, this tank being armed with a 45mm high-velocity gun and a co-axial machine-gun. To this challenge Franco's Moors responded with alacrity. Like the French Army's *Goumiers*, to whom they were related, they liked darkness and were unpleasantly handy with their knives, so that in due course no fewer than four of von Thoma's companies were fully equipped with Russian tanks.

The Spanish experience provided the Panzerwaffe with a taste of action and its first decorations, but at the higher levels more was learned during the dry run into Austria in March 1938. Guderian was horrified when this exposed a breakdown ratio of thirty per cent in his 2nd Panzer Division, although it must be stressed that the division had covered 420 miles in two days. Once installed as Chief of Mobile Troops, he implacably set about eradicating failures in the tank recovery and repair system. The subsequent occupation of the Sudetenland in October that year and of Czechoslovakia in March 1939 revealed a greatly improved situation, and in this context it is worth remembering that the little PzKw I and II were light enough to be ferried long distances on unadapted lorries into their operational zones, thereby saving priceless track mileage.

The year 1938 saw Hitler tighten his grip on the Army yet further, and in the shabbiest way possible. In January General von Blomberg, the widower Minister of War, married for the second time. Immediately after the ceremony, rumours began to circulate that the new Frau von Blomberg had a dubious past, a matter regarded so seriously in Prussian military circles that the Minister was compelled to resign, his function being assumed by Hitler himself. Shortly after, the Commander-in-Chief, General von Fritsch, was accused of homosexual practices and resigned in his turn. His replacement was General Walther von Brauchitsch, a capable and intelligent artillery officer whose task, by tradition, demanded that he must never shrink from speaking honestly and, if necessary, with brutal frankness to the Head of State if, in his opinion, the situation warranted it. Unfortunately, he was not the man to carry such responsibility for he was completely dominated by Hitler, whose uncontrolled rages could shatter his nerves for hours at a time. Next to go was Beck, the Chief of General Staff, whose fussy, fastidious ways annoyed Hitler as much as they did Guderian and whose open criticism of the Nazi hierarchy made his removal inevitable. He was replaced by his deputy, General Franz Halder, a Bavarian and a Catholic who despised Hitler and was actually involved in a plot to assassinate him. Similarly, those other senior officers who were unable to come to terms with the spirit of the times were removed from office and given appointments far removed from the centre of power.

Halder, like von Brauchitsch, was an artilleryman. So, too, were von Fritsch, Beck, Fromm, the Chief of Army Equipment and commander of the Replacement Army, and Keitel, Jodl and Warlimont of the Armed Forces Supreme Command (OKW). This domination of the upper command levels stemmed as much from the fact that the artillery sustained proportionately fewer casualties than either the infantry or the cavalry during World War I as it did from the intellectual standards demanded by the arm. Many were simply not prepared to accept Guderian's ideas at his own valuation without the necessary proof, and for this he referred to them in scathing terms as 'the Gentlemen of the Horse Artillery', conditioned to a certain style of warfare by five centuries of drawing their guns 'with the muzzle pointing backwards'. Naturally this antipathy was, in many cases, quite mutual. Guderian was not, as he was constantly reminded, a Kriegsakademie man; he was a technician with inadequate understanding of the higher strategic thought process. His impatience, his intolerance and his brusque manner did nothing to assist his case. The Army High Command had two nicknames for him, both of which said a great deal about his personality: the first was *Schnelle Heinz*, Heinz-in-a-hurry; the second was *Brausewetter*, emphasizing his unsettled, volatile temper.

The truth was that, although by the summer of 1939 the standing of the Panzerwaffe in the eyes of the general public was high, because of its impeccable performance on parade and during exercises, to the rest of the Army and indeed to itself it remained an unknown quantity. It was well below its war establishment strength and was heavily outnumbered by both the French and Russian tank fleets. Most of its tanks were stop-gap designs, and the signs were that even the PzKw III and IV were already obsolete even as their quantity production began; a visiting delegation from Russia refused to believe that the PzKw IV was the most powerful design being built, the state of the art in their own allegedly backward country having reached this point some years previously. Nor, because of the unfounded belief that the next major war would be a short one, had any provision been made for the design of a second generation of main battle tanks. Further, the theories upon which the Panzerwaffe was organized and which formed the basis of its training had yet to be proved.

At this juncture the last thing the Panzerwaffe wanted was a war, yet suddenly Hitler's instinct for brinkmanship proved fallible and Germany found herself in the very situation which her statesmen and soldiers had always striven to avoid – that of facing foes simultaneously on two fronts. The United Kingdom and France had stood shamefully by while Austria and

Czechoslovakia were removed from the map of Europe, but the uncompromising nature of the Polish question left them with no alternative other than to resort to arms. For Guderian and the other panzer leaders it remained to be seen whether their creation could deliver a quick victory; at the regimental level the outlook was less than optimistic, for on mobilization there were barely sufficient tanks to equip three companies in each battalion, while the fourth company had to be left behind in its depot.

2. The Annihilation Concept at Work

The only possible grand strategy for Germany was to remain on the defensive behind the newly constructed Siegfried defences in the west while simultaneously concentrating most of her effort on the destruction of Poland's armies. Few had any serious doubts that this could be accomplished, the only question being whether the task could be completed before the French Army mobilized a sufficient proportion of its strength to commence offensive operations against the thinly stretched garrison of the West Wall.

From the outset, the conditions existed for a campaign in the precise mould of *Vernichtungsgedanke*. From East Prussia in the north to the Slovak border in the south the Polish armies, strung out along the 1,750-mile (2,800 km) common frontier in a gigantic horseshoe, were already deployed in a manner which could not have served the Germans better, since a breakthrough on the flanks would inevitably lead to the isolation and encirclement of all those troops west of the River Vistula. Further, the political conditions for the defeat of Poland had been created by Hitler's signature of a non-aggression pact with Stalin as recently as 23 August, a pact with secret clauses which divided the carcass of the victim between Nazi Germany and Soviet Russia.

The nature of the Polish Army, too, made a German victory inevitable. Emotionally wedded to the great achievements of the War of 1920, when well-led cavalry had seen off Tukhachevsky's ill-organized Bolshevik hordes, the Poles had made but slow progress towards mechanization. On 1 September 1939, the day of the German invasion, they could field just over 700 tanks, although of these some 450 were TK/TKS-type tankettes and little better than tracked machine-gun carriers, fifty-five were World War I Renault FTs and fifty were more recent Renault R.35s which offered a slight improvement; the remainder were variations on the Vickers six-ton (6,500 km) theme, the most numerous type being the 7-TP, which was armed with a 37mm gun. Most of the Polish armour was allocated in company or battalion strength to higher formations, but one all-arms mechanized formation, the 10th Cavalry Brigade, had been set up

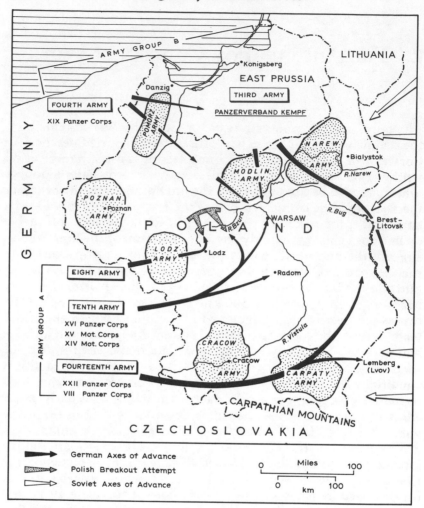

Poland 1939, showing the disposition of German armoured formations

in 1937 with offensive operations in mind. The principal strength of the army lay in its thirty infantry divisions, adequately equipped with field and anti-tank artillery and numerous anti-tank rifles, and in its eleven mounted cavalry brigades. This loyalty to the horse was not entirely sentimental, for it alone conferred complete mobility in a landscape of forest, streams flowing through low-lying marshland and the sandy roads known locally as *trakts*. Much the same conditions prevailed in large areas of eastern Germany; hence the continued use of horse-drawn transport and artillery in the German Army. What neither side could be quite certain of in 1939 was the extent to which such terrain would inhibit the movement of *large* mechanized formations, and both were, to a certain extent, gambling.

The German plan of attack had been drawn up in June by von Brauchitsch and, predictably, consisted of a double envelopment, the inner jaws closing on Warsaw and the outer jaws on Brest-Litovsk. The southern arm of the pincers was formed by Field Marshal Gerd von Rundstedt's Army Group A and consisted of three armies, the Eighth, Tenth and Fourteenth; the northern arm was formed by Field Marshal Fedor von Bock's Army Group B and consisted of only two armies, the Third in East Prussia and the Fourth in Pomerania. The total German strength available amounted to forty infantry, six panzer, four light and four mechanized infantry divisions, and one mounted cavalry brigade. Most of the armoured formations were concentrated in the south with Army Group A. Under the Tenth Army, responsible for the drive on Warsaw, was the XVI Panzer Corps (1st and 4th Panzer Divisions) and XV Motorized Corps (2nd and 3rd Light Divisions); in addition, the 1st Light Division was detailed to form the spearhead of the XIV Motorized Corps. On the Fourteenth Army's sector was the XXII Panzer Corps (2nd Panzer and 4th Light Divisions), plus the 5th Panzer Division attached to the VIII Corps. To the north Guderian's XIX Panzer Corps (3rd Panzer Division reinforced by the Panzer Demonstration Battalion, plus the 2nd and 20th Motorized Divisions) formed part of General von Kluge's Fourth Army, with the newly raised 10th Panzer Division initially allocated to army reserve. In East Prussia the Third Army's armoured element consisted of an *ad hoc* grouping named *Panzerverband Kempf* after its commander, including Panzer Regiment 7, I/Panzer Regiment 10 and several Waffen SS units including the motorized infantry regiment *Deutschland*, an artillery regiment and a reconnaissance battalion.

The tank strength of the various panzer and light divisions

varied considerably and of course never approached the figure of 562 specified as the establishment. As the senior formation, the 1st Panzer Division received a larger allocation of the few medium tanks available, each of its battalions containing 14 PzKw IVs, 28 PzKw IIIs, 18 PzKw IIs and 17 PzKw I; these, together with headquarters and command tanks, gave a divisional strength of 324. The battalion establishment of the remaining five panzer divisions was six PzKw IVs, five PzKw IIIs, 33 PzKw IIs and 34 PzKw Is; when the command tanks were added, this produced a tank strength of 328 per division. The 1st Light Division, whose strength had now been increased to three tank battalions, could muster a total of 221 tanks, including a handful of PzKw IIIs and IVs, but was actually one of the strongest armoured formations in the field since the balance of its tank strength included 112 PzKw 35 (t)s. Conversely, the 2nd and 4th Light Divisions each had fewer than a hundred tanks, and of these the PzKw II predominated. The 3rd Light Division, however, was reinforced with a battalion of fifty-nine PzKw 38 (t)s, giving it a strength of approximately 150 tanks. It was, therefore, upon the light tanks that the burden of the Polish campaign fell, but in this context it should be remembered that in 1939 very few soldiers had experience of being attacked by armour and that to the average infantryman a tank was a tank, terribly dangerous and apparently invulnerable, whatever shortcomings it may have possessed.

The campaign followed the course intended for it by the German Supreme Command. The Luftwaffe failed to achieve strategic surprise but experienced little difficulty in winning command of the air from the hopelessly outnumbered Polish Air Force. It then carried out interdiction missions before turning to direct tactical support, the psychological effects of sustained dive-bombing doing much to break the enemy's spirit. For two days the Poles resisted fiercely before commencing their retreat into the trap which was already beginning to close around them. Once the German armoured formations had broken through the cordon of armies guarding the frontier, they accelerated the pace of their advance in accordance with their training, disrupting the Polish command and logistic network as they went, their movement being too rapid for the latter's own High Command to co-ordinate an adequate response. Simultaneously, reinforcements were often unable to reach the front because the roads were jammed with refugees trying to escape from the war zone, neither the Luftwaffe nor the tank crews being slow to exploit terror as an additional weapon whose use might induce a speedier end to the fighting; from this time onwards panzer units engaged in offensive operations would open up with their weapons when driving through villages and woods, whether or not they were fired at themselves, not only as a precautionary measure but also to discourage thoughts of resistance and to encourage surrender.

On 5 September the Germans crossed the Vistula, and the pincers began to close on those Polish armies west of the river. On 8 and 9 September the 4th Panzer Division launched a premature attack through the outskirts of Warsaw but was repulsed with the loss of some sixty tanks by dug-in anti-tank and field artillery and a weak battalion of 7-TPs, thereby learning the sharp lesson that unsupported armour soon finds itself in difficulty if it attempts to fight in built-up areas. 9 September also witnessed an attempt by the Pomorze and Poznan Armies to break out of the trap in which they now found themselves by mounting a strong counter-attack along the line of the River Bzura. Making full use of the flexibility inherent in the German system, General von Reichenau, the Tenth Army's commander, re-directed the XVI Panzer Corps west from Warsaw, simultaneously ordering the 1st Light Division north from the reduction of a pocket which was forming around Radom and which eventually yielded 60,000 prisoners. Together the 1st Panzer and 1st Light Divisions were the most powerful in the German order of battle, and they succeeded in halting the Polish drive, though at some cost. Infantry divisions from the Fourth Army began to close in on the enemy's rear, and when the 2nd and 3rd Light Divisions arrived from Radom, the fate of the two armies was sealed and a further 170,000 men marched into captivity.

Elsewhere, only a remarkable delaying action by the 10th Cavalry Brigade prevented the Fourteenth Army's XXII Panzer Corps' completing a similar encirclement near Cracow, but by now the die was cast. Guderian's XIX Panzer Corps, having crossed the Polish Corridor into East Prussia, had been reinforced with the 10th Panzer Division and was now driving south along the Bug with a view to effecting a junction with Fourteenth Army units moving north from their bridgeheads over the San. Polish troops continued to stream eastwards through the inexorably closing jaws of this outer pincer, but on 16 September the Soviet Army crossed the frontier to establish its claim on the spoils, announcing blandly that it had intervened in the Poles' best interests and to put a stop to the fighting. Warsaw held out until 27 September, and isolated Polish groups did not lay down their arms until 6 October.

The Polish Campaign of September 1939 has been called by some a pure application of *Vernichtungsgedanke* and by others the first Blitzkrieg with modern weapons, but, as events fell, the border between the two is so blurred that either definition will suffice. The 1½ million-strong Polish Army had been destroyed, effectively within the first ten days' fighting, at a cost to Germany of 8,000 men killed and 32,000 wounded. It was also admitted that 218 panzers had been lost, approximately ten per cent of the total engaged, the breakdown being as follows: PzKw Is – 89; PzKw IIs – 78; PzKw IIIs – 26; PzKw IVs – 19; PzKw 35(t)s – 6. In the light of subsequent strength returns, and the tendency of Dr Goebbels' propaganda apparatus to gild the lily, these figures were regarded with some suspicion, and a scrupulously fair post-war examination of contemporary German documents by Polish historians confirms than this scepticism is justified. What actually appears is a reduction in the Panzerwaffe's operational tank strength by 674 vehicles, partly the result of enemy action and partly because of mechanical failure and other causes. If it is accepted that one third were immediately written off, one arrives close to the published German figure. A further third should simply be regarded as being beyond local repair, and these would have been re-built in Germany. The remainder, whether battle casualties or breakdowns, fall into the category of being beyond economic repair, and in this respect it is worth remembering that the PzKw Is and IIs were comparatively frail machines and that the more elderly of them had already reached the limit of their service life. The full extent of the German tank loss, therefore, almost certainly exceeded 400 vehicles, twenty per cent of the total, and this, balanced against deliveries of new and repaired vehicles, is reflected in the line-up for the offensive in the West the following year. Temporary loss of tanks due to mechanical failure was later revealed as being twenty-five per cent at any one time.

Whatever the full extent of the Panzerwaffe's loss, it emerged from the Polish Campaign as the arm of decision, its reputation established, its confidence enhanced and its operational techniques tried and tested. Some years later General von Thoma, who commanded the 2nd Panzer Division's panzer brigade during the campaign, gave the late Captain Sir Basil Liddell Hart a number of reasons for the success of the German armoured forces in this and other offensive campaigns which took place during the early years of World War II. These included the need for divisional and corps commanders to be present at the forward edge of the battle; air superiority and close co-operation with the air arm; concentration of strength at the point selected for the breakthrough; exploitation by road *during the hours of darkness*;

an organic fuel supply adequate for 90-125 miles (150-200 km), which could be supplemented by paradrop if the need arose; three days rations carried aboard the tanks, three more with the regimental supply echelon and three more with the divisional column. Von Thoma considered a daily advance of thirty miles (48 km) to be about average, and Guderian was to exceed this on numerous occasions. During the early stages of the Polish Campaign, however, panzer divisions were covering only an average of eleven miles (eighteen km) a day due to an understandable reluctance to embark on quite unprecedented and probably dangerous drives deep into the enemy's hinterland. Guderian and other senior commanders had to point out, with considerable force at times, that continuous movement provides its own defence and that a deep penetration was actually safer than a shallow one. With specific regard to the campaign in Poland, the terrain had not proved the obstacle the enemy hoped it might. Tanks had bogged down in some numbers, it was true, but a day's operational experience is worth a month's training, and most crews cut themselves a small fascine of pine logs to keep their vehicles out of trouble, stowing this across the engine deck. A further sharp lesson was that the white cross which distinguished German vehicles proved too prominent for safety, so that after the first few days it was either smeared with mud or painted over in yellow; after the tanks had returned to their depots, this device was replaced by the black-outlined-white national cross, which was retained for the duration of the war.

Hitler, overjoyed by his victory, was anxious to initiate a similar offensive in the West as soon as the troops could be re-deployed. Without exception, his generals were totally opposed to the idea, believing that this would probably end in stalemate and a prolonged war for which the Army was simply not equipped. In addition, they were far from satisfied with the performance of certain categories of the reserve infantry divisions in which lack of enthusiasm had actually bordered on indiscipline at times. It was now the duty of von Brauchitsch (described by von Manstein in his memoirs as having 'all the hallmarks of the aristocrat, dignified in bearing, correct, courteous and charming, slightly inhibited and certainly rather sensitive') to make known the Army's collective view to Hitler. The unfortunate meeting took place on 5 November. Hitler bluntly rejected Brauchitsch's opinion that the Army was not yet ready to take on the French and flew into an insane rage at the suggestion that the force he had created compared unfavourably in any way with the old Imperial Army, shrieking personal insults at the unhappy

Commander-in-Chief, who emerged from the encounter 'chalk white and with twisted countenance', arriving back at his own headquarters still shaking and quite incoherent. From this moment it was clear that the Führer had no use for the Army's most senior officers, save as instruments of his own will. As if to ram the point home, on 23 November every general officer down to the level of corps commander, together with their Luftwaffe and Naval counterparts, was subjected to a three-hour harangue in which Hitler screamed that, 'He would ruthlessly destroy anyone who opposed *him* and *his* plans for the offensive.'

Naturally there were many who deeply resented having their patriotism and integrity insulted in this way. Guderian, who now ranked high in Hitler's estimation, was granted an audience some days later and protested in the frankest manner possible. Hitler's mood had changed somewhat and he listened seriously to what the panzer general said, then explained to him why he felt such distrust of his generals, and particularly of von Brauchitsch. In practical terms, however, the conversation yielded precisely nothing, and it remains a mystery why Hitler chose to discuss the Army's Commander-in-Chief and his possible successor with a comparatively junior officer, for on the evening of 23 November Brauchitsch had actually tendered his resignation, only to have it rejected.

It was lucky for Germany, and most unfortunate for the West, that two factors inhibited the launching of any sort of offensive during the winter of 1939/40. The first was that after Poland half the tanks were off the road with mechanical problems, and unit tank strength remained inadequate for several months. The second, and probably more important of the two, was that continuous bad weather seriously affected the ability of the Luftwaffe to provide critical ground support.

The nature of the German plan, code-named Yellow, had been decided as early as 19 October, and in essence it involved three army groups – Army Group B under von Bock deployed along the border with Holland and Belgium, Army Group A under von Rundstedt facing Luxembourg, and Army Group C under von Leeb opposite the Maginot Line – in what amounted to nothing more ambitious than a mechanized reconstruction of the opening phases of the old Schlieffen Plan. At best this would secure most of Belgium including the coastline and might just bring the German Army to the positions from which it had withdrawn in 1918, since it was exactly what the Allies expected and was, in fact, the one situation to which they were capable of reacting constructively. This was certainly not *Vernichtungsgedanke*, nor

was it Blitzkrieg, nor did it contain any hint of the German genius
for creating victory during the planning stage. Rather it suggested
a head-on encounter with indecisive results, whose long-term
effects would favour the Allies. Small wonder that, despite
Hitler's attempts to generate enthusiasm for the idea, it evoked so
little.

During this period the headquarters of von Rundstedt's Army
Group A was located in Koblenz. Rundstedt was now in his
middle-sixties but his abilities remained at their peak and he was
universally respected and liked, being regarded as representative
of the best qualities of the German officer corps. He had a secret
vice, that of reading detective novels, which he kept in an open
drawer in his desk; if anyone entered the office, the drawer would
be hastily shut, despite the fact that he was an army group
commander. In Poland his Chief of Staff had been von Manstein,
who remained with him during this fresh assignment and would
often join him for his morning stroll along the Rheinpromenade.
'Even in that freezing winter, when the Rhine was already
covered with ice, Rundstedt still wore only a thin raincoat. When
I protested that he would catch his death of cold, he merely
retorted that he had never possessed a greatcoat in his life and was
certainly not going to buy one at his age! And neither did he, for
even after all these years the old gentleman still bore the imprint
of his spartan training in the Cadet Corps.'

Manstein was to emerge from the war with the reputation of
possessing the finest operational mind in the German Army, and
possibly in any army of the era. It was clear to him, and to many
other senior officers, that Plan Yellow as written contained an
inherent flaw that would inhibit its success from the outset. Like
the Schlieffen Plan, it required a strong right wing, and for that
reason all the armour was concentrated under von Bock in Army
Group B. This meant that it would effectively be denied its
greatest asset, its mobility, because it was being forced to operate
in a landscape of rivers, streams and canals. On the other hand,
thought Manstein, Plan Yellow could be used as a matador's cloak
to lure the British and French armies north into the Low
Countries. This was nothing less than Fuller's holding Phase II of
Plan 1919, and as soon as the Allies were firmly inside the trap,
Manstein's intention was that Army Group A would execute a
rapid panzer-led deep penetration through the Ardennes and
across the good tank country of northern France to the Somme
estuary. The enemy armies inside the pocket thus formed would
then be destroyed in the traditional battle of annihilation. The
only doubt was whether the rolling, heavily forested hills of the

Ardennes were really as tank-proof as the French believed. Guderian was asked for his opinion and he said they were not. Having satisfied himself that what he proposed was practical, Manstein obtained von Rundstedt's approval and sat down to draft his variation on Plan Yellow, which he called Sichelschnitt (Sickle Cut) to describe the sweep of the panzer divisions through the enemy's rear areas to the coast. Then, with his chief's backing, he submitted his idea to OKH on 31 October.

It was ignored. Manstein submitted it again three times in November, twice in December and once in January without extracting a direct response, although on the last occasion Rundstedt enclosed a note of his own requesting that the memorandum be shown to the Führer. But Brauchitsch was having serious trouble with Hitler during this period and neither he nor Halder, his Chief of Staff, felt justified in raising a fresh issue in which they lacked confidence. Halder in particular seems to have been opposed to the idea; a precise man who took pleasure in mathematics, he probably felt that the stakes were too high and the uncertainties of this new form of warfare too great to warrant Sichelschnitt's acceptance. Manstein's importuning was clearly regarded with such disfavour that finally OKH took the decision to remove him from the mainstream of activity. On 27 January he was promoted and sent to command a corps based on Stettin, far removed from the concerns of the West.

Nonetheless, Manstein had friends at Army Group A who did not consider themselves obliged to work through the recognized channels. These included Colonel Blumentritt and Lieutenant-Colonel von Tresckow, the latter a personal friend of Hitler's adjutant, Colonel Schmundt. When Schmundt paid a routine visit to Koblenz, he was advised of Manstein's idea and, knowing that Hitler had himself once expressed some interest in the Somme estuary as a strategic objective, advised the Führer of the situation on his return to Berlin. The sheer originality of the idea appealed to Hitler, and Manstein was ordered to present himself on 17 February. Ostensibly the occasion was a lunch for newly appointed corps commanders but afterwards Hitler invited him into his study and encouraged him to talk at length about the Sichelschnitt concept. Manstein then returned to his corps, having found him 'surprisingly quick to grasp the points which our Army Group had been advocating for many months past, and he entirely agreed with what I had to say'.

Next morning Brauchitsch and Halder were instructed to prepare fresh directives based on Sichelschnitt, which Hitler claimed as his own idea, and since OKH had been reduced to virtual impotence, there the discussion ended. To be fair to OKH, it had recently become more sympathetic to the Manstein variation, having subjected it to the test of war games. Furthermore, on 10 January Plan Yellow itself had been thoroughly compromised when a German military aircraft strayed over Belgium and was forced down by bad weather. The briefcase of one of the passengers contained details of the projected offensive, which the Belgians promptly passed to the Dutch, French and British governments. Whether or not the Allies regarded the papers as a plant, it was now definitely in Germany's interest that they should be viewed as genuine, since they provided the first flourish of the matador's cloak.

While planning went ahead for the re-structured offensive in the West, events in Scandinavia also claimed the Wehrmacht's attention. One of the subjects which had been discussed at the lunch attended by Manstein was the seizure of the German vessel *Altmark* by the British destroyer HMS *Cossack* inside neutral Norwegian waters. The affair underlined the vulnerability of Germany's iron ore supplies, which travelled by rail from Swedish Lapland to Narvik in northern Norway and thence south by sea down the Leads. Hitler decided to safeguard the route by occupying Norway, and Denmark too for good measure. The method chosen for this operation, code-named Weserubung, involved first the dropping of paratroops to secure important airfields, followed by air-landing formations and amphibious landings at strategic points along the coast. The Panzerwaffe was required to contribute one tank battalion, and this was drawn from Panzer Regiment 35 of 4th Panzer Division. Known as Panzerabteilung 40, the unit possessed between forty and fifty tanks, the majority being PzKw I, II and 38(t). None of the priceless PzKw IVs could be spared for the operation but instead the battalion was issued with the old NbFz prototypes, which also possessed a 75mm howitzer as their main armament. After the campaign was over, Goebbels was able to turn this deficiency into a propaganda success by describing these vehicles as PzKw Vs, upstaging the real PzKw V, better known as the Panther, by several years and causing some groundless concern in Allied intelligence circles.

Weserubung began on 9 April and achieved complete success in spite of British and French landings to assist the Norwegians. The cost to Germany was the crippling of her surface fleet but in all other respects Hitler attained his objectives. Panzerabteilung 40 was employed in support of infantry operations against the British in the wide valley of Gubrandsdalen, leading north from

Lillehammer, and against the even more poorly equipped Norwegians in the parallel Osterdalen to the east. The Allies had no armour of their own, and the Luftwaffe possessed complete air superiority, so that together the German artillery and dive-bombers were able to pulverize opposition. Repeatedly, infantry were able to take the high ground and outflank the Allies in the valley below, causing the latter to withdraw. If they made a stand, the tanks provided direct gunfire support as they led the attack. On occasion they were able to smash their way through makeshift roadblocks but latterly lost two light tanks to the 25mm anti-tank guns of the 15 British Brigade, newly arrived from France. An NbFz also had to be blown apart with demolition charges when it bogged down in the middle of a critically important ford. By 3 May, however, the Allies had completed their withdrawal from central Norway, and the battalion's mission had ended.

This fresh success simply added to the sense of inferiority which had afflicted the Allies since the war began. The morale of the French Army in particular had declined dramatically in the months since mobilization. Led by its sixty-eight-year-old Commander-in-Chief, General Maurice Gamelin, it was, thanks to the casualties of World War I and a falling national birthrate, an elderly army which had developed a fortress mentality behind the barrier of the Maginot Line and was firmly committed to a doctrine of strategic defence. It had, in fact, made no attempt to invade Germany while the Wehrmacht was fully committed in Poland, although it could have reached the left back of the Rhine without undue difficulty, and by May 1940 whatever fighting spirit might have existed in September 1939 had evaporated as a result of political disillusionment, poor conditions, low pay, lack of leave, sheer boredom and an unsatisfactory relationship between officers and men. In some respects, notably those of anti-aircraft defence and communications, the Army showed signs of serious neglect, but it was able to field a tank fleet of some 3,000 machines which actually outnumbered the Panzerwaffe by a wide margin, even if the light PzKw Is and IIs, of no value at all in the tank battle, were included in the latter's total. This quantitative imbalance was compounded at the qualitative level, for the 37mm gun carried by the PzKw III, PzKw 35(t) and PzKw 38(t) could hardly be compared with the 47mm of the Char B and the Somua as an armour-defeating weapon. Again, 30mm plate was the best protection available to German tanks but the Char B possessed 60mm armour and the Somua 55mm. To some extent this impressive technical combination was discounted by the limited operational radius of the tanks and the French preference for one-man turrets, which required the vehicle commander to act as his own loader and gunner with the result that he performed neither of these functions well under pressure.

The French possessed two entirely different types of armoured formation. The first were the three *Divisions Légère Méchaniques* (DLMs), whose function was to provide a screen for the main body of the army, carry out reconnaissance *en masse* and be available to exploit a victory; in short, to execute a mechanized version of the cavalry's traditional role. The second were the *Divisions Cuirassées* (DCRs) which had been hastily formed following the dramatic success of the Panzerwaffe in Poland. Each DCR consisted of two demi-brigades, each equipped with one battalion of thirty-four Char Bs and one battalion of forty-five Hotchkiss H.35s, thereby giving a divisional tank strength of 158; plus a motor rifle battalion and two motorized twelve-gun artillery battalions. By the end of April three DCRs had been formed, although they lacked the important experience of working together, and a fourth was being raised. Unfortunately, the concept of the DCR was that of a break-through force, and therefore neither it nor the DLM was capable of the same flexibility as the German panzer divisions. An even greater deficiency was the lack of specially trained corps or higher formation headquarters to handle a possible concentration of armoured divisions, a fatal flaw which underlined the persistent French view that they were tactical entities and must therefore be regarded as subordinate to the demands of an infantry-dominated battle. Altogether, the French had 500 tanks serving with the DCRs and 800 with the DLMs and mounted cavalry divisions, the remainder of their tank fleet being dispersed in infantry support battalions.

During the inter-war years the British armed services had been subjected to such a criminal degree of political neglect that even now, seven months after Field Marshal Lord Gort's British Expeditionary Force had arrived in France, it numbered only ten infantry divisions, although these were of good quality. Serving with the BEF were 210 machine-gun-armed light tanks of two light armoured reconnaissance brigades and the divisional cavalry regiments, and the incomplete 1st Army Tank Brigade with one hundred heavily armoured (80mm) Infantry tanks, of which the majority were the little Mark Is, joined recently by a handful of 2-pdr (40mm) Mark IIs, better known as the legendary Matilda. In theory the 1st Armoured Division, still in Britain with its 174 light and 156 2-pdr Cruiser tanks, could also be shipped across the Channel at short notice.

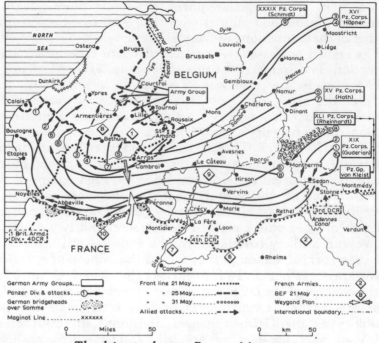

The drive to the sea, France, May 1940

Gamelin's plan in the event of a German attack on the Netherlands and Belgium was for his best troops to race north and join the eleven Dutch and twenty-three Belgian infantry divisions in halting the invaders' advance along the line of the River Dyle; indeed, he actually looked forward to this accretion of strength, which he felt would give him a decisive edge in the land battle. The rest of his front was to be held by second- and third-line reserve divisions, including the very sector opposite the 'tank-proof' Ardennes on which the break-through phase of von Manstein's Sichelschnitt was to take place. Thus, in this the Panzerwaffe's most complete and spectacular victory, success was not only attained in the planning stage and long before the first shot had been fired, so following the inherited tradition of the Great General Staff, but virtually guaranteed by the enemy's own strategy.

None of this was readily apparent to the German tank crews at the time and, frankly, they were not looking forward to beginning a fresh campaign under the triple disadvantages of being outnumbered, out-gunned and under-armoured. They would have been astonished to learn that in May 1940 the *Deuxième Bureau* estimated the strength of the Panzerwaffe at between

7,000 and 7,500 tanks, twice that of the French Army! The reality was that Germany had 2,439 tanks at the Front, including 523 PzKw Is, 955 PzKw IIs, 349 PzKw IIIs, 278 PzKw IVs, 106 PzKw 35(t)s and 228 PzKw 38(t)s. There was also a small reserve and 135 PzKw Is and IIIs which had been converted to armoured command vehicles, but nothing could conceal the fact that of the total no fewer than 1,478 were light tanks armed only with machine-guns.

Following the Polish campaign the 1st, 2nd, 3rd and 4th Light Divisions were re-designated respectively the 6th, 7th, 8th and 9th Panzer Divisions, so that the German order of battle now contained ten panzer divisions. For the campaign in the West these were equipped as follows: 1st, 2nd and 10th Panzer Divisions – 30 PzKw Is, 100 PzKw IIs, 90 PzKw IIIs and 56 PzKw IVs; 6th, 7th and 8th Panzer Divisions – 10 PzKw Is, 40 PzKw IIs, 132 PzKw 35(t)s or PzKw 38(t)s and 36 PzKw IVs; 3rd, 4th and 5th Panzer Divisions – 140 PzKw Is, 110 PzKw IIs, 50 PzKw IIIs and 24 PzKw IVs; 9th Panzer Divisions – 100 PzKw Is, 75 PzKw IIs, 36 PzKw IIIs and 18 PzKw IVs. This apparent imbalance in divisional strength was quite intentional and reflected the role these formations were to play.

Thus, on the southern flank of Army Group A's penetration and responsible for leading the drive to the coast, Guderian's XIX Panzer Corps contained no fewer than three divisions, the 1st, 2nd and 10th, each with a high proportion of PzKw IIIs and IVs; in the centre, Reinhardt's XLI Panzer Corps contained two divisions, the 6th and 8th, which were generously equipped with Czech 37mm-armed tanks; while on the northern flank was Hoth's XV Panzer Corps with one strong Czech-equipped division, the 7th, and one with a lower proportion of gun-tanks, the 5th. Together, these three corps made up a panzer group commanded by General Ewald von Kleist, the commander of the XXII Panzer Corps in Poland, who had received this appointment specifically to co-ordinate their advance, which in day-to-day terms meant keeping a rein on Guderian and preventing him from breaking away without due regard for what was happening to the rest of von Rundstedt's army group.

For its invasion of the Low Countries, von Bock's Army Group B was allocated two panzer corps, the larger of which, Höpner's XVI, contained the 3rd and 4th Panzer Divisions; the smaller, Schmidt's XXXIX, consisted of a single panzer division, the 9th, and was the most northerly of the German armoured formations. By comparison with Rundstedt, therefore, Bock had only three of the ten panzer divisions, and these contained a much lower proportion of the all-important 37mm and 75mm gun-tanks, but to balance this and reinforce the impression that it was his army group that was delivering the main German blow, he was also provided with most of the airborne resources and a heavy Luftwaffe participation.

The great offensive began at 0535 hours on 10 May. Everywhere Army Group B flooded across the frontier. The Belgian Army had intended to fight along the line of the Albert Canal but was soon forced to withdraw when its flank was exposed by a spectacular glider-borne attack which compelled the surrender of the allegedly impregnable Fort Eban Emael, dominating the junction of the canal with the River Meuse. Simultaneously, vital bridges and airfields in western Holland were seized by airborne and air-landing troops. Gamelin reacted promptly to the threat, and within hours the BEF and the best of the French armies were streaming north.

There now occurred one of those episodes which in other circumstances would have been hailed as remarkable but which was obscured by greater events at the time and has tended to remain so ever since. Von Bock's plan required the 9th Panzer Division, which had been recruited in Austria, to drive straight across Holland and relieve the paratroopers who had just taken the Moerdijk bridge over the Maas before the French First Army, advancing from the south, could recapture it. This was the weakest of all the panzer divisions, for although it was equipped with 229 tanks, 175 of these were PzKw Is and IIs. On the other hand its commander, Major-General Dr Ritter von Hubicki, who had served with great distinction in the old Austro-Hungarian Army, had a certain style and dash which was well suited to the occasion. In the event, his task was made easier by the French commander who, within striking distance of the objective, split his advance guard into a reconnaissance screen which was easily brushed aside, and then tamely withdrew. The 9th Panzer broke through to the paratroopers on 12 May and then swung north towards Rotterdam, the strategic effect of its drive being to isolate the Dutch Army before the Allies could reinforce it. On 15 May Holland surrendered.

Further south, Höpner's XVI Panzer Corps had crossed the Maastricht Appendix and then motored on across Belgium until it reached the Gembloux Gap, where, throughout 12 and 13 May, it fought a fierce encounter battle with Prioux's 1st Cavalry Corps, screening the deployment of the French First Army. The French formation consisted of the 2nd and 3rd DLMs and was equipped with 174 of the formidable Somuas, 87 Hotchkiss H.35s and 40

AMR light tanks, plus a small Belgian contingent, but the only German tanks able to engage on anything like equal terms were 100 PzKw IIIs and 48 PzKw IVs. However, the disadvantages of the French one-man turrets were immediately apparent in their erratic fire – sometimes with the wrong ammunition – and the awkward handling of the vehicles themselves. In contrast, the German three-man turret crews worked together as a team, as well as having the benefit of excellent optical gun-sights. Moreover, panzer commanders were able to use the flexibility conferred by good communications to direct several tanks against individual French machines and so whittle down the enemy's strength by degrees, while dive-bombing attacks also did much to further distract Prioux's crews. When the battle ended each side had lost more than a hundred tanks and both claimed victory. The 1st Cavalry Corps, having fulfilled its mission of permitting the First Army to settle into its positions on the Dyle, then withdrew, abandoning the battlefield so that the Germans were able to recover many of their vehicle casualties. For his part Höpner could draw satisfaction from the fact that, although his advance had received a temporary check, the scale of the fighting had served to concentrate French attention on central Belgium and divert it from the real threat which was beginning to unfold elsewhere. Gamelin clearly felt that the engagement confirmed Germany's intentions and despatched the 1st and 2nd DCRs north into the trap.

Meanwhile, on Army Group A's sector, Panzer Group Kleist was moving steadily through the Ardennes towards the Meuse, its columns stretching as far back as the Rhine. French cavalry units saw only the heads of those columns and were unable to estimate their strength, while overhead the Luftwaffe, which outnumbered the *Armée de l'Air* and the Royal Air Force contingent serving in France, as well as possessing more modern aircraft, flew a dense protective umbrella which kept prying eyes out of range.

By the evening of the 12th the three panzer corps had closed up to the river along a forty-mile (64 km) front running from Dinant in the north to Sedan in the south. Opposite them and straddling the boundary between the French Second and Ninth Armies were four Class B Reserve divisions composed of middle-aged soldiers recalled by the war from a comfortable civilian life. It had never been Gamelin's intention that these men should bear the brunt of the battle, and for this reason they had been selected to man what was anticipated would remain a quiet stretch of the line. Now they were to find themselves in the epicentre of a firestorm.

At 0900 on the 13th the bombers of General Hugo Sperrle's Third Air Fleet began subjecting the crossing sites to intense and continuous attack. This phase of the operation lasted six hours, paying particular attention to the largely unprotected French artillery. At 1500 the bombers left, and the motor rifle troops began crossing in their assault boats, only to meet determined resistance which caused serious casualties. This was suppressed little by little, largely as a result of energetic action by the German divisional commanders, who concentrated their tanks, anti-aircraft and anti-tank guns against centres of resistance. By dusk these methods had secured footings on the enemy bank for all three corps, but it seemed as though much hard fighting would be required before these could be turned into bridgeheads. Then, near Sedan, opposition suddenly collapsed. The French 55th Division commenced a disorderly retreat at about 1800 and was soon joined by the neighbouring 71st Division so that a yawning gap began to develop between the Second and Ninth Armies. The cause of this was a wild report from a shell-shocked artillery officer that German tanks were across the river and that his guns were limbering up to avoid capture. The rumour spread rapidly, generating more and more reports of enemy armour among the already shaken troops. Soon the roads to the rear were filled with crowds of panic-stricken infantry who saw no reason to stay if the guns had gone. The tragedy was that the tanks were real enough, but they were French and merely moving into position to support the defenders; not one German tank crossed the Meuse on 13 May.

While the German engineers worked like men possessed to complete their bridges, often under determined air attack which the Luftwaffe and a strong anti-aircraft defence successfully held at bay, Gamelin and his senior commanders conferred on how best to seal off the huge penetration which had broken their line. They decided to commit three *Divisions Cuirassées* in a converging attack, the 1st from the north, the 2nd from the west and the 3rd from the south, but each was to operate independently under *local* command without due regard for the obvious advantages of co-ordinating their counter-stroke. Speed was now critically important to both sides, a fact fully appreciated by the Germans, who strove to get as many tanks as possible across into their expanding bridgeheads ready to break out, while the French seemed unable to respond to the quickening pulse of the battle.

One German commander chafing at the bit was Major-General Erwin Rommel, the commander of the 7th Panzer Division.

Rommel was the sort of officer who feels most at home at the forward edge of the battle, his brilliant performance at Caporetto in World War I leading to the award of Imperial Germany's highest decoration, the *Pour le Mérite*. In some respects his character was similar to that of Guderian. He was, for example, restless, impatient and capable of driving his men beyond their normal limits, and he also owed much to having attracted Hitler's favourable attention at an opportune moment in his career. In the West he remains probably the best known of all the Third Reich's panzer leaders, but in Germany his undoubted abilities still do not serve to place him in the first ranks of merit, since a great deal of his success clearly stemmed from a highly developed sense of opportunism which occasionally lapsed into mere gambling.

The most important elements of 7th Panzer were its 36 PzKw IVs and 106 PzKw 38(t)s. However, while Rommel's division was moving up to the Meuse, its running mate, the 5th Panzer Division, was seriously delayed by congested roads, and Hoth, the corps commander, placed its leading armoured regiment, Panzer Regiment 31, under his command, so making 7th Panzer an extremely powerful formation. The attachment was intended to be a temporary one, but Rommel made a poor neighbour, and it is far from clear just when or how much of Panzer Regiment 31 he returned to its rightful owner. What is certain is that on 21 May his loss return includes six PzKw IIIs, tanks which did not form part of his own order of battle.

He began moving out of his bridgehead at 0800 on the 15th. An hour later his leading elements came across the demi-brigades of the 1st DCR, replenishing in close leaguer near Flavion, and the second major tank battle of the campaign began. Throughout the previous day the French division had run its fuel tanks dry as it attempted to reach the battlefield over roads clogged with refugees and the wreckage of broken units, so that many of its formidable Char Bs, known as *Kolosse* to the Germans, were unable to get into action. Rommel read the situation correctly and, calling up his dive-bombers to pound the French, swung round the enemy flank and set off for the west. 1st DCR had still not recovered from the shock when 5th Panzer arrived to continue the battle. A hard fight ensued during which the French claimed to have knocked out about a hundred of Hoth's tanks. For their part the panzer crews were shaken to discover that their 37mm guns were quite unable to make any impression on the stout armour of the Char Bs. However, these vehicles did possess vulnerable points in their tracks and their radiator louvres, the latter being located in the side of the hull, and the German gunners took these as their aiming points, slowly notching up a growing tally of kills. As the French were pushed slowly back, still more of their vehicles were destroyed by their own crews, having been abandoned because of mechanical failure or fuel shortage. These causes were ultimately to destroy 1st DCR, for when the division broke contact and withdrew at last light, it continued to shed vehicles, so that at dawn on the 16th this once-mighty formation was reduced to a mere seventeen tanks.

Reinhardt's XLI Panzer Corps also broke out on the 14th. If Gamelin's counter-stroke had gone according to plan it would have run straight into the 2nd DCR, but during the day this division had been subjected to such bewildering changes in its orders, to say nothing of uniquely bad staff work, that in due course its major components found themselves simultaneously travelling in opposite directions. At about 1700 Reinhardt's tanks overran part of the divisional artillery and the rest of the wheeled vehicles sought sanctuary south of the Aisne, leaving the armoured demi-brigades north of the river. The 2nd DCR was never able to re-assemble and was thus removed from the French order of battle with a minimum of effort on the Germans' part, although its tanks attached themselves to local infantry formations and fought under their control for as long as they were able without their supply and technical support echelons.

The same day the steadily expanding bridgehead of Guderian's XIX Panzer Corps at Sedan came under local counter-attack by French armour. Guderian mentions that twenty enemy tanks were destroyed at Bulson and a further fifty at Chémery. He does not refer to his own loss in this engagement, although whatever it had been was aggravated when a Stuka formation dived on a German concentration at Chémery, causing heavy casualties. Following this incident the 10th Panzer Division and the crack *Grossdeutschland* motorized infantry regiment were detailed to take the high ground at Stonne, thereby protecting the southern shoulder of the bridgehead while the 1st and 2nd Panzer Divisions prepared to move off westwards the following day.

Meanwhile the 3rd DCR had arrived and by 1600 was in a position to mount a counter-attack. Even if this had proved only partially successful, it could have caused very serious damage to Guderian's preparations, yet, incredible as it may seem, the counter-attack was cancelled by the responsible corps comman- der, General Flavigny, who then deployed the division's tanks as an eight-mile-long (13 km) line of static pillboxes along the southern edge of the German penetration. The 3rd DCR did re-assemble next morning but was then committed to several days of costly and intense attritional combat against 10th Panzer and *Grossdeutschland* at Stonne.

Von Rundstedt and his team had always been conscious that, as the forty-mile-wide (64 km) 'panzer corridor' began to open, it would become more vulnerable to counter-attack from the south than it was from the north, where constant and unremitting pressure by Army Group B was absorbing the Allies' entire attention on that sector. To guarantee the southern flank as it became daily more extended, therefore, Rundstedt arranged for General Gustav von Wietersheim's XIV Motorized Corps to follow directly in the wake of Guderian's XIXth Panzer Corps and assume responsibility for the newly captured ground until, in turn, it was relieved by marching infantry formations. The XIV Corps' first regiments began moving into position on 15 May, Guderian gladly placing 10th Panzer and *Grossdeutschland* under Wietersheim's temporary command until the situation at Stonne had been resolved, while he pursued his westward advance with his own corps.

In passing, it is worth mentioning that in May 1940 the German Army possessed eighty battalions of motorized infantry, but only two of these were equipped with the SdKfz 251 half-tracked APC. The campaign also witnessed the Sturmartillerie's baptism of fire, four six-gun batteries (640, 659, 660 and 665) being employed under various formations in all three army groups; 640 Battery particularly distinguished itself while fighting in support of *Grossdeutschland* at Stonne.

It was now apparent to senior German commanders that Sichelschnitt was working exactly as Manstein had prophesied it would. Brauchitsch and Halder became increasingly relaxed and confident of success as they watched each stage of the battle unfold as it had during the experimental war games; curiously Hitler, who had accepted the scheme with enthusiasm, was suddenly a prey to fears that an Allied counter-stroke would isolate much of the German armour in the west and wreck the entire plan of campaign. For their part, the panzer divisions were pushing onwards across northern France with a self-confidence that had not existed in Poland. Little in the way of determined resistance was encountered, and often a few bursts of machine-gun fire were sufficient to induce the surrender *en masse* of demoralized French survivors retreating from the earlier débâcles, or of bemused reinforcements moving up to form a fresh line only to find that the panzers had got there first. Often, tanks filled up at civilian petrol pumps, further fuel being landed by the Luftwaffe at captured airfields and collected by divisional transport echelons. When leaguers were briefly formed, the short time available was consumed in replenishment tasks and essential vehicle maintenance. Sleep became a precious commodity but its lack was compensated for by a mounting sense of elation.

On 20 May Guderian reached the sea, having also secured useful bridgeheads over the Somme at Peronne, Amiens and Abbeville, and the trap snapped shut on those Allied armies north of the corridor. The way west had not been quite without incident, for on the 17th France's newest armoured division, the 4th DCR under Major-General Charles de Gaulle, had counter-attacked the southern flank of the XIX Panzer Corps at Laon but had been driven off by units of the 1st Panzer Division. Of greater annoyance to Guderian were the checks imposed on his progress by von Kleist, the Panzer Group commander. These inevitably led to a blazing row during which he tendered his resignation. Rundstedt, however, despatched General List, the commander of the Twelfth Army, with a plan which not only endorsed Kleist's authority but also satisfied the operational needs of the moment; this involved Guderian's headquarters maintaining its position until released, while the rest of the XIX Panzer Corps continued on its way to the coast, performing what was described as a 'reconnaissance in force'.

The French realized that they had suffered a major defeat as early as the 16th but remained unable to read the battle correctly for several more days. Some officers believed that the German armour would wheel south behind the Maginot defences, others that its objective was Paris; few guessed its real destination until it was too late, and in any event all the reserves had already marched north into Belgium. Prime Minister Reynaud replaced Gamelin as Commander-in-Chief with General Maxime Weygand who, for all his seventy-three years, was still brisk and energetic. What he proposed was that the panzer corridor should be cut in two by converging thrusts from north and south. The southern thrust never really developed, but near Arras on 21 May the British 50th Division and 1st Army Tank Brigade broke into the 7th Panzer Division's line of march behind its armoured spearhead, inflicting serious loss on its two motor rifle regiments and causing a panic in the nearby SS motorized infantry division *Totenkopf*. The 37mm anti-tank gun, referred to by the troops as 'the door-knocker', proved incapable of penetrating either mark of British tank, and it was only by concentrating the entire resources of his artillery, including his 88mm anti-aircraft guns, that Rommel was able to halt the enemy's advance. His own Panzer Regiment 25, returning to counter-attack, ran into an anti-tank gun screen and was attacked in turn by the remnants of the 3rd DLM, receiving a rougher handling than Rommel cared to admit. Although the British withdrew that night, he had clearly been shaken by the encounter, his report that he had been attacked by 'hundreds' of tanks being a wild exaggeration, as was a needless and bewildering suggestion that the commander of the 5th Panzer Division had somehow contributed to his misfortune!

Nonetheless, the report was quickly transmitted from Hoth's headquarters to Kleist's, thence to Rundstedt's and on to OKH and OKW, where the Führer's worst fears seemed about to be realized. Reinhardt's XLI Panzer Corps, echeloned to the right-rear of Guderian's XIX and closer to the coast than Hoth's, was promptly ordered back along the corridor towards Arras in case the situation deteriorated further, and for the next twenty-four hours the final northward slice of von Manstein's sickle remained suspended. When it was resumed, it was against tougher and more resolute resistance, especially at Boulogne and Calais, but on 27 May the exhausted Belgian Army surrendered, making the position of the BEF and the trapped French divisions impossible. Their evacuation from Dunkirk continued from 28 May until 4 June.

Various reasons have been suggested as to why this was permitted when the two German army groups had it within their power to overrun the contracting Allied perimeter, thereby providing a classic finale to a campaign based on *Vernichtungsgedanke*. Hitler himself severely curtailed the participation of the panzer divisions after 24 May, to the intense annoyance of Guderian and others, leaving the final phase to be completed by von Bock's infantry and the Luftwaffe, which Goering had begged be allowed to administer the *coup de grâce*. There can be little doubt that Hitler's decision to call off his armour was the correct one and, although opposed by Brauchitsch and Halder, it was supported by Generals Wilhelm Keitel, the Chief of OKW, and Alfred Jodl, his Chief of Staff. As Jodl commented to one of his staff, Colonel von Lossberg, who expressed a contrary opinion, 'The war is won and all we have to do is end it — it is not worth losing a single tank when the Luftwaffe can do the job better.' Unfortunately, the Luftwaffe could not and began to incur serious losses as the RAF threw its modern Spitfire squadrons, flying from airfields in England, into the struggle. This was the first of several notable occasions on which Goering promised the German Army that which was not in his gift to deliver.

Understandably, many German officers found it inexplicable

that 336,000 Allied troops, one third of whom were French or Belgian, should be permitted to escape. It was Churchill's belief that, if Hitler had not halted his panzer divisions on the 24th, they would, despite the water obstacles and marshland surrounding Dunkirk, have overwhelmed the Allied resistance so quickly that as few as 45,000 men could have been lifted out. And yet Hitler's decision, which Rundstedt did much to influence, made sound sense in the light of the Army's priorities. Those who escaped had been forced to abandon all their heavy equipment, and the majority their small arms as well.

What happened inside the pocket became less important with every hour that passed. The real priority of the moment now lay in defeating the very considerable French forces lying south of the panzer corridor, and for that the panzer divisions urgently needed time to re-organize and re-group. They were now spread in an arc around the southern edge of the pocket with the 1st, 2nd and 10th on the coast, the 6th and 8th at Aire, the 3rd and 4th north-west of Bethune and the 5th and 7th approaching Lille; the only exception was the 9th, which had motored south from Holland and was deployed along the Somme. Panzer Group Kleist reported heavy losses in men and material and a reduction in its tank strength by more than fifty per cent. A breathing-space was essential not only to allow breakdowns and repairable battle casualties, which had been shed along the line of the advance all the way back to the Meuse, to catch up with their parent formations, but also to untangle lines of communication, carry out heavy maintenance and replenishment and deploy for the last act in the drama.

That this commenced on 5 June, the day after the last Allied soldier had been lifted off the Dunkirk beaches, confirms just how necessary such a pause was. Known as Plan Red, this saw a more even distribution of armour between the two army groups. On the right wing Army Group B contained Hoth's XV Panzer Corps, which would operate on its coastal flank, while the main effort would be made by Panzer Group Kleist, now consisting of von Wietersheim's XIV Panzer Corps (9th and 10th Panzer Divisions) and Höpner's XVI Panzer Corps. Guderian's earlier efforts were rewarded by his being given command of Army Group A's Panzer Group, which included Schmidt's XXXIX (1st and 2nd Panzer Divisions) and Reinhardt's XLI Panzer Corps. Each panzer corps now incorporated a motorized infantry division, either Army of Waffen SS.

The front line lay along the southern edge of what had been the panzer corridor and was known to the French as the Weygand

Line. There can be little doubt of the extent to which France had been traumatized by the events of the past three weeks, but somehow Weygand had managed to evoke something of the spirit of 1914 among his countrymen. He constructed a defensive zone several miles deep, based on towns, villages and woods rather than a continuously held line. Where possible, these strongpoints were mutually supporting, but in any event the areas between were turned into artillery killing-grounds. The French still possessed some tanks, although their numbers were now few in comparison with their opponents, and in quality they could not compare with the hundreds of fine machines squandered in Belgium and north-east France.

At first the Germans made little progress against incredibly tough resistance; in fact, von Kleist's panzer group was so seriously checked that its original axis of advance was abandoned and its point of attack shifted to a less obstinate sector further east. However, as the French defence was essentially based on artillery, the Luftwaffe made this their special target, so that the creation of breaches in the Weygand Line became as mathematically predictable as those of a Vauban siege. When the artillery had been silenced and the French tanks destroyed, the panzer formations flooded through into what was now, in effect, empty space.

On the coastal sector the first stages of Rommel's advance found him engaged against mainly British troops. He managed to trap a major part of the 51st (Highland) Division at St-Valéry but was unable to prevent the evacuation from Cherbourg of that portion of the 1st Armoured Division which had been sent to France. During subsequent operations by the XV Panzer Corps Hoth directed 7th Panzer to capture Cherbourg and 5th Panzer to move through Rennes against Brest. Paris, having been declared on open city, was entered by a token force of infantry on 14 June while Panzer Group Kleist roared on southward through Dijon to Lyons. Further east still, Guderian's group finally created the conditions envisaged by Count Schlieffen, trapping several French armies with their backs to the Swiss frontier and the Maginot Line, the latter coming under simultaneous attack from von Leeb's Army Group C; the huge pocket so formed yielded half a million prisoners.

Italy entered the war as an ally of Germany on 10 June, and two days later Weygand advised Reynaud that an armistice should be sought. This was granted on the 22nd, hostilities formally ending on the 25th. Seldom in history had so rapid and complete a victory been attained. Within a period of six weeks the armies of

France, the United Kingdom, Belgium and Holland had been decisively beaten at a cost to Germany of 27,000 killed, 111,000 wounded and 18,000 missing. France suffered 90,000 dead, 200,000 wounded and 1,900,000 missing or taken prisoner. British casualties (dead, wounded and missing) totalled 68,000, Belgian 23,000 and Dutch 10,000.

Most of the German loss fell on the two arms of service that had borne the brunt of the battle, the Luftwaffe and the Panzertruppen. The former lost 1,284 aircraft as against the RAF's 931 and the *Armée de l'Air's* 560. The latter's strength was reduced by half as a result of battle casualties, damage and mechanical failure, the highest proportion of loss falling on the light tanks. On the other hand, the tanks had been subjected to very hard usage indeed. For example, during the Sichelschnitt phase the 1st and 2nd Panzer Divisions covered 300 miles (480 km); this was immediately followed by a 200-mile (350 km) road-march to the divisional start-lines for Plan Red, and then a further advance of 300 miles (480 km). The vehicle recovery and repair organization had performed well enough, although during the final stages tanks had a lengthy and time-consuming journey from the heavy repair workshops in Germany back to their divisions, and there were ominous signs that the system would find difficulty in coping with the problems posed by a longer campaign. Yet for many years the myth of Germany's armoured might went unchallenged, for the Allies were simply unable to accept that they had been defeated by an army which fielded so few effective tanks.

Hitler continued to claim the credit for Manstein's brilliant plan, startling those around him by remarking that he had read de Gaulle's book on mechanized warfare, *Vers l'Armée de Métier*, 'again and again', and that he had learned a great deal from it. Albert Speer was later to comment that Hitler considered himself an instant expert on any book he picked up, but actually read very little. After the war Liddell Hart asked Guderian and von Thoma whether the methods employed by German armour had been influenced by de Gaulle, and both answered that they had not. If anything, the campaign was a justification of Fuller's Plan 1919 with overtones of *Vernichtungsgedanke*, but it had taken the genius of von Manstein to combine the two. It is probably fair to add that in May 1940 Hitler's Panzerwaffe was the only armoured corps in the world capable of fulfilling such a concept.

3. Poisoned Victories

In Germany the victory in the West was greeted with a sense of intense relief and unbounded joy that the war which all had dreaded was now apparently over. The church bells clanged for a week in celebration while Hitler received the adulation of the crowds, distributed decorations and took the startling step of creating twelve new field marshals; von Manstein's name was not among them. Some of the newly honoured senior officers even received *Dotationen* from the Führer's private funds or grants of land in the conquered territories, a custom revived from the days of the monarchy. Many of the troops returned to their home barracks, where they were welcomed as heroes, and some units were even demobilized. Everywhere there was cause for satisfaction that one of the great crises of the twentieth century had seemingly passed, leaving Germany untouched.

Yet, to Hitler's bewilderment, his peace feelers directed at the United Kingdom remained unacknowledged, and on 16 July he issued a directive: 'Since England, in spite of her militarily hopeless situation, shows no signs of coming to terms, I have decided to prepare a landing operation against her and, if necessary, to carry it out. The preparations for the entire operation must be completed by mid-August.' The operation was to be known as Sea Lion.

In spite of his definite instructions, there are grounds enough to question whether Hitler's heart was really in the project. The success of his Norwegian venture could not conceal the very heavy loss and damage sustained by the Kriegsmarine's surface fleet, so that never again did he feel quite at ease in questions involving the exercise of sea power. Moreover, the Navy's Commander-in-Chief, Grand Admiral Raeder, was far from enthusiastic about the idea, pointing out that he lacked the necessary units with which to escort the invasion fleet. Furthermore, short as it might seem, a crossing of the Channel was a very different matter from a river crossing. It involved consideration of tides which rose and fell, flowing first one way and then the other, limiting the landing periods to a number of tactical 'time windows' which were also governed by the type of light conditions required, yet it was still subject to imponderables such as wind-strength and barometric pressure. As if this was not enough, air superiority was vital, yet was proving impossible to obtain. Small wonder, then, that by October Sea Lion could be regarded as a dead duck. In the light of all the subsequent evidence, it seems likely that the Germans *would* have been able to establish a beachhead ashore and even break out of it, only to be forced into surrender by lack of resources when their cross-Channel links were severed.

During the planning stage of Sea Lion it was appreciated that the assault wave would require the direct support of tanks at the earliest possible moment. To examine this question the Panzerwaffe set up an amphibious warfare trials unit known as Panzerabteilung A, recruited from volunteers drawn from Panzer Regiment 2.

The unit's most important work involved trials of *Tauchpanzer* (diving tank) versions of the PzKw III and IV. All exterior openings of the vehicle were sealed with a water-tight compound, and the gap between the hull and turret was closed by an inflatable rubber ring. Rubber sheeting covered the commander's cupola, the mantlet and the hull machine-gun, but this could be blown away from inside the vehicle by means of an electrical detonator. Air was supplied to the engine by a flexible fifty-nine-foot (eighteen-metre) hose which was held on the surface by a buoy, exhaust gases being carried upwards through two tall vertical pipes fitted with non-return valves. Maximum safe diving depth was forty-nine feet (fifteen metres), and the crew's submerged endurance was set at twenty minutes. The intention was for the tanks to launch themselves from lighters and then drive ashore along the sea bed, direction being maintained by instructions passed through a radio link from the parent vessel. Another type of vehicle evaluated was the *Schwimmpanzer II*, based on the PzKw II. This, as its name implies, would swim ashore from its parent vessel using a kit of flotation tanks attached to the return rollers, powered by a propeller driven by an extension shaft from the engine. One advantage possessed by the *Schwimmpanzer II* over 'diving' versions of the medium tanks was that it could use its guns during the landing.

Although Panzerabteilung A did not see the results of its work used operationally against Britain this was not wasted as its personnel joined Panzer Regiment 18, which, the following year, carried out an amphibious crossing of the River Bug in Poland during Operation Barbarossa, using *Tauchpanzer* III and IV; it is unlikely that any of the *Schwimmpanzer II* were used as their bulky flotation tanks made these vehicles more suitable for landing across a beach than for a river crossing in which they would have to negotiate difficult banks on entry and exit.

One of the lessons arising from the tank battles of the recent campaign was that the 37mm tank gun could no longer be relied on as an armour-defeating weapon. In the case of the Czech tanks there was nothing that could be done, but Hitler personally gave instructions that the spare capacity left in the PzKw III design was to be absorbed by fitting the 50mm L/60 gun. This fired a 2.25kg armour-piercing round at a muzzle velocity of 1,189 metres per second, but there was also in the German armoury a less powerful 50mm L/42 gun which fired a 2.18kg AP round at 685 m/sec and, possibly because of supply difficulties, it was this weapon that was fitted.* When, the following April, Hitler learned that his specific instructions had been disobeyed, he flew into one of his fearful rages and never again quite trusted the Ordnance Department. Fortunately the re-fitting programme was far from complete, and subsequent conversions were armed with the L/60 weapon, but as a direct result of what had taken place the Panzerwaffe was to find itself in serious difficulties when faced with the Red Army's new 76.2mm tank guns.

Hitler's thoughts were already turning towards an invasion of the Soviet Union while Sea Lion was still officially alive. This was what he had always wanted, and his writings in *Mein Kampf* made his feelings perfectly clear. The difference was that Germany no longer stood in danger of a war on two fronts, so the time for such an undertaking could hardly be bettered. First, however, it would be necessary to expand the Panzerwaffe to a level at which it was capable of tackling the enormous task it was to be set. In the autumn of 1940, therefore, eleven more panzer divisions were formed, numbered from 11 to 20 inclusive and 23. This was achieved by reducing the number of armoured regiments in each panzer division to one, occasionally with three battalions but generally with two. In effect, such a step doubled the overheads of the Panzerwaffe without increasing the number of tanks available as the expansion required twice the motorized infantry, artillery and support units. Guderian, von Manteuffel and von Thoma all made it quite clear that they believed this to be poor business management and that the panzer divisions should have remained tank heavy. A quite contrary view was expressed

---

* In common usage German guns are usually described as an expression of calibre-length, i.e. in this case the weapons are 50mm × 60 and 50mm × 42.

by Nehring, who believed that even the actual strength of some 280 tanks possessed by the old divisions was too large and cumbrous. Other German senior officers took the view that the proportion of motorized infantry to tanks needed to be *increased*; later British and American experience tended to reinforce this opinion, as it did that of Nehring.

Nor was this to be the end of the Panzerwaffe's expansion. More and more armoured formations would be added to the Army's order of battle, and Himmler was to demand his share for the Waffen SS, as was Goering for his Luftwaffe ground troops. Thus, while tank production in 1940 was 1,460, doubling to 3,256 in 1941 and thereafter rising steadily to 8,328 in the final eighteen months of the war, this was barely enough to replace battle casualties, let alone equip new formations. The very real dangers of rapid expansion in late 1940 were first that, even after the Panzerwaffe's experience in France against the French Char Bs and the British Matildas, no consideration was being given to producing a second generation of battle tanks, and secondly that so much of the existing tank stock continued to consist of obsolete lights tanks with a very limited service life ahead of them. Again, of the twenty-one panzer divisions, no fewer than six (the 6th, 7th, 8th, 12th, 19th and 20th) were equipped with Czech vehicles, which had been regarded as being of substitute standard at the best of times. It was true that hundreds of French tanks had been captured in running-order but their one-man turrets did not fit the German tactical pattern so that in their original form they were of little use to the panzer divisions, although their chassis were later to be put to good use; in addition, some 180 Renault R.35s were modified slightly in 1941 and issued to occupation troops.

In other areas, neither the provision of self-propelled artillery (Panzerartillerie) nor of tracked tank-destroyers (Panzerjäger) for use within the panzer divisions was being treated with anything like the urgency demanded by the gigantic undertaking which Hitler was proposing. The motorized infantry had also undergone an expansion comparable with that of the armoured formations and by the spring of 1941 numbered ten divisions, but without any increase in the overall number of APCs available. This expansion was to continue until September 1943, when 226 infantry battalions were classed as mechanized, of which only twenty-six possessed APCs. By way of contrast, the Sturmartillerie expanded at a slow but logical pace dictated by the delivery of its purpose-built assault guns. The success of those batteries which had seen action during the campaign in the West had led to the idea – fully justified by events – that even better results could be obtained if assault guns were employed in battalion strength, and the Artillery School at Jütebog promptly set about training the first units of this size. Initially only two battalions were being produced every three months, but this was accelerated to three battalions every two months. The new battalions consisted of a headquarters battery which contained the commanding officer's assault gun, the battalion transport echelon, recovery, workshop and medical services, plus three assault batteries, each of three two-gun troops, battery echelon and fitters. The internal organization of the battery was later strengthened by adding one gun to each troop and by providing the battery commander with his own gun in place of the armoured command vehicle from which he had originally exercised control, so giving a total battalion strength of thirty-one assault guns.

While detailed planning for the invasion of the Soviet Union continued under the code-name Barbarossa, events in the Balkans began to exercise an influence which, in the long term, was to inflict serious damage on the German cause. Sensitive about the security of his southern flank, and concerned in particular about the vital Ploesti oilfields, Hitler had managed to bring Hungary, Romania and Bulgaria under his control by political means, simultaneously ensuring that Yugoslavia was governed by a pro-German faction. Over this apparently satisfactory situation a lengthening shadow was being cast by a succession of disasters which continued to befall his Italian ally, Benito Mussolini. The latter's pride had been deeply hurt when Hitler had occupied Romania without so much as mentioning the matter to him, and he peevishly declared that he would now himself 'occupy' Greece. This proved to be a piece of hopeless optimism, for the Greeks roundly defeated the invading Italians and chased them back across the frontier into Albania. Simultaneously, in North Africa a tiny British force of never more than two divisions utterly destroyed a 250,000-strong Italian army in eight weeks fighting. It was patently clear to Hitler that, unless he intervened, Mussolini faced a similar extinction in the Balkans which could see him swept from power in Rome, but of particular importance was the need to act before the British could send effective aid to the Greeks and establish themselves in this new theatre of war on the eve of Barbarossa. He therefore gave instructions for the planning of a German invasion of Greece from Bulgaria, the code-name for this being Operation Marita.

During the early hours of 27 March 1941, however, the Balkan apple-cart was overturned by a *coup* in which anti-German

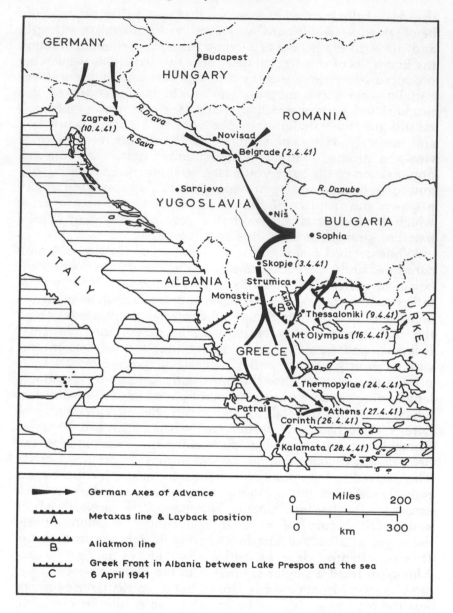

GERMANY

•Budapest

HUNGARY

ROMANIA

Zagreb
(10.4.41)

R.Drava

R.Sava

•Novisad

Belgrade (2.4.41)

R. Danube

•Sarajevo

YUGOSLAVIA

•Niš

BULGARIA

•Sophia

ITALY

ALBANIA

Skopje (3.4.41)

Strumica•

Monastir•

A

Axios

B

•Thessaloniki (9.4.41)

C

▲Mt Olympus (16.4.41)

GREECE

▲Thermopylae (24.4.41)

•Patrai

Corinth (26.4.41)

●Athens (27.4.41)

•Kalamata (28.4.41)

TURKEY

German Axes of Advance

A   Metaxas line & Layback position

B   Aliakmon line

C   Greek Front in Albania between Lake Prespos and the sea
6 April 1941

Miles
0   200

0   300
km

The Balkan Campaign, 6-28 April 1941

elements seized power in Yugoslavia. Hitler's furious reaction was that the new administration in Belgrade represented a threat not only to Marita but also to Barbarossa. This was something of an over-statement but in his rage he gave orders that Yugoslavia was to be 'beaten down with merciless brutality in a lightning operation'. This was to coincide with Marita and, such was the Führer's depth of feeling, it was named, with a degree of predictability, Operation Punishment.

By now, German staffs from OKW downwards were tuned to such a pitch of efficiency that only ten days were needed for the planning and movement of the troops. In the south the blow would be delivered by Field Marshal Sigmund List's Twelfth Army, which contained a panzer group commanded by General Ewald von Kleist, while in the north the invasion would be carried out by General Maximilian von Weichs' Second Army; simultaneously smaller operations would be mounted by the Italian Second Army on the coastal sector and by the Hungarian Third Army in the Banat. Altogether one third of the Panzerwaffe's tanks were to be employed in the subjugation of two countries whose powers of resistance had been considerably over-estimated.

The Luftwaffe struck Belgrade on 6 April, turning the centre of the city into an inferno. When the Yugoslav Air Force attempted to intervene, it provided a tragic commentary on the state of the country's armed forces as a whole, for instead of tackling the enemy's bombers its British-supplied Hurricanes engaged its German-supplied Messerschmitts in an untidy dogfight over the capital. On the ground, the Yugoslav Army was poorly armed and riven by racial, religious and political differences; the Croats, for example, had no intention of fighting for a country which regarded them as second-class citizens, while soldiers of German descent were only too pleased to welcome the invaders. Both the Yugoslavs and the Greeks placed the same sort of misguided reliance on their native mountains as a defence against armour as had the Poles and the French on 'tank-proof' forests.

Using their well-tried formula, the panzer divisions experienced no difficulty in effecting penetrations and advancing along the axes of the principal valleys, leaving the Yugoslavs' cordon defence isolated. There was little fighting, the German progress being subsequently described by Major-General von Mellenthin, who served as a staff officer in Second Army at the time, as 'virtually a military parade'. The terrain actually provided more problems than the enemy, but given the will to win and the application of skill, courage and determination, a tank can be made to negotiate apparently insuperable obstacles.

The interest in the panzer divisions' operations in Yugoslavia lies in the staggered timing of their assaults around the long frontier, the intention being to keep the enemy in a state of uncertain ferment with every fresh penetration, and in the way the country was quickly carved into sections by converging attacks on the main cities executed by different formations. On 6 April the southern sector of the front witnessed drives by the 9th Panzer Division on Skopje and 2nd Panzer Division on Strumica in the Axios valley, the intention being to eliminate the possibility of co-operation between the Greek and Yugoslav armies. Two days later the 5th and 11th Panzer Divisions broke clear of the Twelfth Army's right flank and headed north along the Morava valley towards Niš. Concurrently, on the Second Army sector the 8th and 14th Panzer Divisions were driving hard for, respectively, Zagreb and Belgrade. Zagreb was taken on 10 April and Belgrade fell two days later, the 14th Panzer Division effecting a junction with the 5th, the latter motoring north after its capture of Niš. Sarajevo fell on the 15th, and forty-eight hours later Yugoslavia agreed to surrender unconditionally. The fact that 345,000 of her soldiers marched into captivity while *total* German casualties amounted to a mere 558 undoubtedly confirms the suggestion that a sledgehammer had been used to crack a nut, yet this cannot disguise the sheer professionalism with which the panzer divisions carried out their mission.

The campaign in Greece was not to be quite such a walk-over, although the nature of the Greek Army's deployment made an Axis victory an eventual certainty, for of the twenty-one divisions which were available no fewer than fifteen were involved in the fighting in Albania and a further three were manning the defensive positions along the Bulgarian frontier known as the Metaxas Line. Behind this lay the sixty-mile-long (96 km) Aliakmon Line, running north-west from a point on the coast north of Mount Olympus to Mount Kaymakchalan on the Yugoslav frontier, into which a British, Australian and New Zealand expeditionary force in corps strength was actually moving when the Germans struck. The problem for Greece and her allies was that the left flank of both the Metaxas and Aliakmon Lines was wide open to attack from Yugoslavia, and that the yawning gap between these positions and the main body of the Greek Army in Albania was so lightly held that any thrust from the north was bound to achieve a deep penetration. Given that Greece had apparently nothing to fear from the direction of Yugoslavia, these dispositions nonetheless seemed perfectly sensible at the time.

When, on 6 April, the Twelfth Army's XXX Corps crossed the Bulgarian frontier and attacked positions in the Metaxas Line, it met the toughest resistance imaginable and was barely able to report progress. The same was true of General Böhme's XVIII Mountain Corps save that, having secured Strumica, its objective in Yugoslavia, the 2nd Panzer Division promptly swung south down the valley of the Axios, breaking through an over-extended Greek motorized division to reach the port of Thessaloniki during the night of 8th April, a brilliant application of the indirect approach which isolated the defenders of the Metaxas Line and led directly to their surrender next day.

Meanwhile, spearheaded by the 9th Panzer Division, General Stumme's XL Motorized Corps had taken Skopje and was now driving south to enter Greece through the Monastir Gap. A weak screening force was swept aside, thereby compelling the British to abandon the Aliakmon Line and take up fresh positions based on Mount Olympus. The same move turned the flank of the Greek First Army in Albania, which was forced to embark on a fighting withdrawal. At this point General Papagos, the Greek Commander-in-Chief, indicated to General Wilson, the commander of the British corps, that he could only see the campaign ending in a German victory but gallantly offered to go on fighting until the expeditionary force could re-embark, and actually held out until 23 April. Wilson conducted his own retreat with great skill, falling back initially on the famous Pass of Thermopylae, which presented as great an obstacle in 1941 as it had in Xerxes' time. On 24 April I/Panzer Regiment 31 (5th Panzer Division) unwisely tried to batter its way through in an attack along the road with nineteen tanks, made in file. This was not the sort of liberty to take with experienced troops, and inevitably the result was that every vehicle was either set ablaze or immobilized.

As their embarkation commenced, the British fell back into the Peloponnesus, and on the 26th the high bridge across the Corinth Canal was blown when German parachute troops came within an ace of seizing it with a daring *coup de main*. This meant that there was a delay in getting panzer units across the water into the Peloponnesus so that throughout the 27th the embarkation continued without molestation, save by the Luftwaffe. On the 28th, however, the 5th Panzer Division got across and broke into Kalamata on the south coast, capturing the port's naval embarkation officer. About 7,000 men, mainly line-of-communication troops, were waiting to be picked up and many were captured. The remainder counter-attacked with such vigour and ferocity that soon the German spearhead was itself overwhelmed and forced to surrender, but the scale of the fighting ashore convinced the commander of the approaching Royal Navy squadron that he was not justified in hazarding his ships for so few men, and he gave orders to turn away; thus, at the end of the day, the roles of captor and captive were again reversed.

The action at Kalamata ended the campaign in Greece. This had cost Germany 4,500 casualties and an acceptable number of tanks. More than 70,000 Greeks had been killed or wounded, and 270,000 were captured. Wilson's corps sustained nearly 12,000 casualties and the loss of all its heavy equipment, but eighty per cent of its personnel were lifted out.

Hitler's Panzerwaffe now stood at the very pinnacle of efficiency and self-confidence. From the Atlantic to the Aegean it had proved itself the weapon of decision again and again. Yet the past three weeks' campaigning were to have an immense effect on its fortunes and those of the entire German Army. After the hard running which had been demanded of them, the tanks needed three weeks of heavy maintenance before they were fit to take the field again. Even so, the effects of wear and tear on tracked fighting vehicles are cumulative and in this case were bound to increase the break-down ratio in Russia, where the panzer divisions would be required to cover greater distances than ever before.

Of yet further-reaching significance was the fact that the operations in Yugoslavia and Greece had led to the start of the Operation Barbarossa being postponed for five weeks, an extremely serious consideration since the lack of surfaced roads in Russia limited the full scope of mechanized warfare to the period between the end of the spring thaw and the start of the winter rains. Much of this priceless time had already been lost; an optimist might conclude that what remained might appear just sufficient, but a clear-sighted realist would conclude that there was absolutely no margin for error.

4. Barbarossa

In the years immediately following World War II the Soviet Union adopted an attitude of such belligerent intransigence towards its former allies that the United States Army commissioned a group of senior German officers, under the direction of Colonel-General Franz Halder, to write a series of pamphlets in which various aspects of warfare on the Eastern Front were examined by experts. The conclusions contained in one of these included the following note: 'One cannot provoke such a conflict and expect to carry it through in a spirit of adventure. The equipment of the soldiers and the total amount of material must meet the requirements of Russian terrain at all seasons. This is a question of industrial potential which, by applying the experiences gathered in the last war, is not difficult to solve.' Yet such was Hitler's belief in his own intuition and the ability of the Panzerwaffe to win him victories in the face of impossible odds that, when the bubble of his dreams finally burst during the winter of 1941, he complained bitterly to Guderian that, if he had known that the Russian tank-production statistics contained in the latter's book *Achtung – Panzer!*, published in 1937, were accurate, he would never have attacked the Soviet Union.

It is indeed difficult to reconcile this with his assertion, made shortly before the start of Barbarossa, that, 'We have only to kick in the front door and the whole rotten structure [i.e. the Red Army and the Soviet apparatus of government in general] will come tumbling down,' for the Kremlin has never made any secret of the fact that the primary task of its heavy industry was – and remains – the manufacture of swords rather than ploughshares.

In 1928 the USSR, still recovering from the effects of World War I and the Civil War, was a military power of no consequence with a mere ninety-two tanks in its armoury. But once Stalin's Five Year Plans began to take effect, the results were truly astounding: by 1935 Russia possessed 15,000 tanks and in June 1941 the figure had climbed to 24,000. It was, therefore, clearly apparent that, if the means of tank-manufacture survived the

German onslaught, the long-term prospects for Germany were bleak indeed, since she could never hope to equal the Russian output. It was true, of course, that, notwithstanding the Red Army's concentration hitherto on firepower as the most important element in AFV design, many of these tanks were hopelessly obsolete. In the heavy class, for example, there had been a fashion for multi-turreted land-battleships like the SMK, the T-100 and the T-35, machines as renowned for their mechanical failure as they were for their bizarre appearance, the latter prompting the nickname of *Kinderschrecken* (things to frighten children, i.e. bogeymen) conferred on captured examples by German tank crews; even Stalin managed to pierce the all-pervading Marxist-Leninist gloom with a wry sally to the effect that one of them looked like a department store! Further down the scale was the T-28, a multi-turreted medium, the T-26, which had been encountered in Spain, and the BT Christie-based cruiser series, very fast but lightly armoured. In the light tank class the T-60 was very similar to the PzKw II, being armed with a 20mm cannon, and unlikely to make much of a contribution. There was also a series of light amphibians – the T-37, T-38 and T-40 – but these were little better than tracked machine-gun carriers.

What German intelligence did not suspect – and nor did anyone else for that matter – was that all the effort involved and all the mistakes made in building this immense tank fleet had also produced two brilliant designers, named Mikhail Koshkin and Josef Kotin, whose teams respectively conceived the T-34 medium and the KV (Klimenti Voroshilov) heavy tanks. The T-34, now considered the grandfather of all modern tank designs, was armed with a 76.2mm gun, travelled on a high-speed Christie suspension, possessed mathematically angled hull armour which provided ballistic protection equivalent to twice that of the 45mm plate employed, and represented an ideal combination of firepower, protection and mobility. The KV-1 employed a conventional torsion bar suspension but was armed similarly to the T-34, its outstanding feature being its 90mm armour. Both designs were capable of being up-gunned and of further development, both were driven by the same type of high-performance diesel engine, both had wide tracks which enabled them to negotiate mud, sand and snow in a manner which the German tanks could not, and both were in quantity production and in the possession of active service units when the invasion began, as was the KV-2, an assault tank mounting a 152mm howitzer in a huge, slab-sided turret.

The Panzerwaffe therefore entered this new campaign not

simply confronting the sort of odds it had never faced before but also, as far as the newer Soviet tank designs were concerned, out-gunned and under-armoured as well, the basis of the PzKw III's and IV's armour being 50mm at this period. The Russians were, in fact, already experimenting with much larger tank guns (thanks to a quite unjustifed assertion by Stalin's Chief of Artillery, Marshal G.I. Kulik, that German tanks were now being fitted with 100mm armour plate) and were to maintain their lead in this field over both the German and Western armies for the remainder of the war and for some years after. Although this was not altogether a case of doing the right thing for the wrong reasons, it is worth mentioning that Kulik was an old Civil War crony of Stalin's who had been raised to his present exalted position because he was too stupid to be devious. With an abysmal ignorance of his profession, he was much given to making Olympian but quite groundless pronouncements similar to that above, another of which was that the use of mines was a sign of weakness! At length his inefficiencies led to his reduction in rank, and finally Zhukov, never one to suffer fools gladly, dismissed him into limbo. It is truly remarkable that the entirely negative influence of this humourless buffoon should have had such a profound effect on AFV armament for the next decade.

In addition to the enemy's equipment, other factors which would affect the Panzerwaffe's struggle in Russia were his command, control and communications apparatus, the morale of his troops and the terrain which was to be fought over. Insofar as the Soviet senior command echelon was concerned, most of its officers were some years younger than their German counter-parts, by whom they were regarded as capable professionals. However, in the middle and lower ranks of command there was a grievous lack of initiative and a willingness only to act upon specific orders from above; since the strata affected went as high as corps and divisional commanders, this was to have a paralysing effect on the conduct of armoured operations, most of which took place at the operative level. In part this stemmed from the flawed Communist tenet that there is only one correct solution to every problem and that this is decided upon by the Party. The consequence is a centralized decision-making process in which a display of initiative by or within individual units is far from welcome since it may prejudice some hitherto undisclosed grand design. In 1941, too, the chill legacy of fear left by the Great Purge of 1937-8 was such that most officers preferred to keep a low profile rather than suffer accusations of nascent Praetorian-ism which had led to the deaths of hundreds of senior officers and the imprisonment or disappearance of thousands more. The purpose of this massacre was to convince the Army that it existed by courtesy of Stalin and the Party hierarchy, the result to leave the survivors too cowed to argue.

The most famous victim of the Great Purge was Marshal Mikhail Tukhachevsky, who had established large armoured formations in the German manner. On his death the asinine Kulik succeeded to his post, confiscating all the Army's light automatic weapons on the grounds that these more properly belonged to the police (by which he presumably meant the NKVD, the ancestor of the present KGB) and putting a temporary stop to the manufacture of anti-aircraft and anti-tank artillery for reasons best understood by himself. As if this was not enough, when General D.G. Pavlov, the commander of the Soviet armoured contingent in Spain, unwisely regarded by some as a Russian Guderian, arrived home to announce that he no longer saw a future for large armoured formations and that henceforth the tank should be regarded as an infantry support weapon, Kulik seized the opportunity to disband the mechanized corps which Tukhachevsky had formed. During the Winter War against Finland and the occupation of Poland and the Baltic Provinces, the Soviet tanks were therefore deployed in infantry support battalions and brigades, which performed very badly; by way of contrast, in the Far East Zhukov employed Tukhachevsky's principles and used the concentrated mobility of his armour to inflict a signal defeat on the Japanese along the River Kalkhin. Quite possibly this would have been forgotten had not the Panzerwaffe demonstrated in Poland and France just what could be achieved. Very quickly the Kremlin decided that the mechanized corps must be re-formed at once, their order of battle being two tank divisions (each of two tank regiments with 200 tanks apiece, a motor rifle regiment and an artillery regiment) and one mechanized, i.e. motor rifle, division. These received a quota of the new T-34s and KVs but the bulk of their strength consisted of a hotch-potch of the older designs, a high proportion of which were always off the road with mechanical problems.

Naturally this combination of fear and uncertainty did nothing for the morale of the Soviet tank arm. Further, the size of the mechanized corps made them unwieldy and difficult to control, especially as the shortage of tank radios meant that it was rare for a command net to be established below regimental level. Formation commanders therefore had only slightly more control over their troops than their predecessors had in World War I, and they were therefore forced to rely heavily on rehearsals and drills.

Thus attacks tended to be made in straight lines with strictly limited objectives. The question of changing the direction of an attack once it had begun or the forming of *ad hoc* battlegroups in the manner of the Panzerwaffe did not arise. Nor had the vital administrative elements of the mechanized battle – replenishment with fuel and ammunition, vehicle-recovery and repair, the provision of spare parts, casualty evacuation and so on – been developed by the Soviets to anything like the degree that they had by the Panzerwaffe.

But whatever shortcomings the Red Army may have had, the Russian terrain was itself to have a profound effect upon the conduct of operations. Large areas of northern and central Russia were extensively covered in forest and swampland, movement off the road being difficult even in the dry season. In the south, conditions were much better, so that cross-country movement was possible almost everywhere, save in the wet season. Apart from the main motor route running west from Moscow, surfaced roads were almost unknown. Even major roads between cities had never been intended to support much more than horse-and-cart traffic, so that the combined impact of the winter rains and thousands of motor vehicles quickly turned them into bottomless mud-wallows.

As Halder's team comments in the Department of the Army Pamphlet 20-230:

The principle of establishing lanes of movement rather than routes of advance proved satisfactory for the Germans as well as the Russians; the same was true of the separation of lanes of movement for motorized and non-motorized units. Here, the German motorized troops had to be allotted the lanes with the best roads. The rate of progress of motorized troops could be roughly estimated in advance only if they were travelling on hard-surfaced roads. A rule of thumb was that on average dry roadways, motorized troops made from five to six miles (8-9.6 kms) per hour, and foot troops from one to less than three miles (4.8 kms) per hour. Terrain and road conditions in the East required, according to German experience, three to four times the amount of motor fuel needed under normal conditions in Europe. Sand, mud and snow impeded the advance of all types of troops and put great strain on motors. Lined up and jammed along one road, the troops slowly and painfully inched forward – a long snake crawling slowly over the difficult ground. Time-calculations, the most important factor in operations, had to be based on entirely new concepts. Frequently the time required for a movement could not be estimated even approximately. It continued to run far in excess of the expected maximum. No matter how easy it was for vehicles with cross-country mobility to cross great, open stretches in any direction during dry seasons, on long marches they were confined

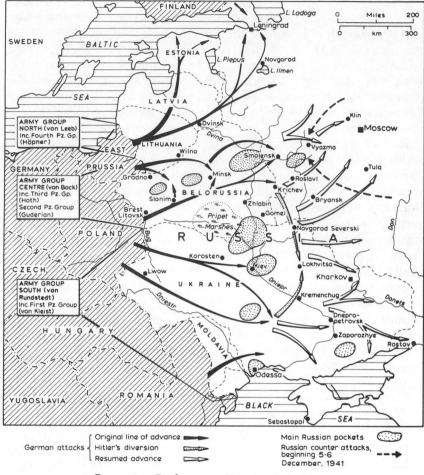

Operation Barbarossa, Russia, 1941

mostly to the existing roads, since the Russian terrain always confronted them with terrain obstacles which they were unable to overcome (swamps, watercourses, ravines, steep rises etc). Furthermore, it required considerably more time and fuel to move cross-country.

For the moment, however, most of these factors remained unknown to the OKW, which could only see that the German Army deployed along the Soviet frontier from the Black Sea to the Baltic on the eve of Barbarossa was undoubtedly the finest, the most experienced and the most self-confident in the world. Altogether, three army groups were to be involved in the invasion, the largest of which was von Rundstedt's Army Group South, consisting of fifty-two infantry divisions, including a substantial contribution from Germany's allies of two Romanian armies, the Third and Fourth with a total of fifteen divisions, a Hungarian motorized corps of two divisions and an Italian corps; leading Rundstedt's advance would be the five panzer divisions of Panzer Group I under von Kleist. Army Group Centre, under von Bock, contained forty-two infantry divisions and nine panzer divisions, the latter being divided between Panzer Group II (Guderian) and Panzer Group III (Hoth). Army Group North, commanded by von Leeb, was the smallest of the three since it was responsible for a comparatively narrow sector of front and contained only seven infantry divisions; on the other hand it had a difficult run to make through the Baltic states and was therefore allocated Höpner's Panzer Group IV of three panzer divisions.

When the offensive opened, the Panzerwaffe had seventeen divisions in the line and two more in reserve. Tank strength amounted to 410 PzKw Is, 746 PzKw IIs, 149 PzKw 35(t)s, 623 PzKw 38(t)s, 965 PzKw IIIs and 439 PzKw IVs. This produced a total of 3,332 tanks, most of which, even at this stage, were light tanks and ageing Czech stock. For the benefit of the marching infantry divisions which would be following in the panzers' wake, the Sturmartillerie initially supplied two battalions to each army group, plus a number of independent batteries, and steadily increased the number of units participating until approximately 250 assault guns were engaged in supporting the advance.

The overall objective set for Barbarossa was nothing less than a line running south from Archangel to Astrakhan on the Volga. This, it was calculated, would place targets in Europe beyond the range of the Soviet Air Force and in Hitler's opinion would ensure that Communism would wither and perish on the wind-blasted steppelands of inner Asia. He accepted the advice of his professional military experts that the key to this lay in securing

Moscow, the seat of the Soviet government and hub of the country's strategic rail network, without which not even the Red Army could function, and for this reason the bulk of the Panzerwaffe's resources had been concentrated under Army Group Centre, but it is very doubtful whether he understood that a 660-mile (1056 km) run in Russia – the minimum distance from the frontier to Moscow – was nothing like a journey over a similar distance in western Europe.

There were, too, a number of other considerations which were to become obsessions and which were to exert a baleful influence on the Panzerwaffe as it attempted to fulfil its incredibly ambitious mission. In addition to seizing Moscow, for example, Hitler wanted also to control the economic assets of the Ukraine and destroy Leningrad, a city which he detested because it had spawned Bolshevism, although it was manifest that the Wehrmacht's strength was not equal to further strain. For the moment, however, he was still prepared to listen to professional opinions, although he was greatly concerned from the outset that the enemy's armed forces should be destroyed in western Russia rather than be allowed to retreat intact into the country's endless hinterland in the manner of 1812, a point which he emphasized in his famous Directive No. 21, which was issued as early as 18 December 1940.

As planned, Operation Barbarossa had more in common with Fuller's Plan 1919 than with *Vernichtungsgedanke*, the deep penetration Phase I being the task of Army Group Centre with the Phase II holding-actions being executed simultaneously by Army Groups North and South. War games revealed that as the operation progressed the two flanking army groups would generate pressure for assistance from Army Group Centre to secure their own objectives and that, if these demands were not resisted, the consequences could be most serious.

Barbarossa began at 0315 on 22 June 1941. The Luftwaffe's four Air Fleets achieved complete strategic surprise, destroying 1,489 Soviet aircraft on the ground and 322 more in the air during the first day's fighting, the figure escalating dramatically to 4,990 during the next week. Russian positions close to the long frontier were quickly swamped under whirlwind bombardments and then bypassed as the Panzer Groups began pushing out into the hinterland.

The most serious resistance was encountered by Army Group South, which was directly opposed by Colonel-General Mikhail Kirponos' South-West Front. Kirponos was one of very few commanders who had done well during the Winter War, and he had been promoted rapidly as a result. Under his command were no fewer than six mechanized corps, IV, VIII, IX, XV, XIX and XXII, containing some of the best-equipped and most efficient tank divisions in the Red Army. It speaks volumes for his energy, drive and perception that by 25 June these were converging on the four panzer divisions (11th, 13th, 14th and 16th) which formed the spearhead of Kleist's Panzer Group 1 in the area of Brody. There ensued a fierce but untidy tank battle – the largest of the war thus far – which raged for the next four days. Much of the Russian numerical superiority was written down when the Luftwaffe pounced on the tank columns during their approach-march, and the rest was squandered in piecemeal and unco-ordinated attacks. More tanks were lost through poor tactical use of ground, too-numerous firing halts and inadequate driver training, all faults which were to plague the Russian armoured corps for the rest of the war. In this series of engagements the panzers concentrated on whittling away the older designs until the new T-34s and KVs were isolated; these were then destroyed by combined attacks involving tanks, the divisional medium artillery and 88mm anti-aircraft guns, and the Luftwaffe. In the end Kirponos was forced to extract what remained of his corps and retreat on Kiev, shedding still more tanks by the hour for lack of fuel or because of breakdown. His action had, however, inflicted on Kleist's group the heaviest losses the Panzerwaffe was to incur during Barbarossa, as well as imposing a check on Army Group South that was to contribute to the eventual failure of the operation. Halder noted in his diary that the forces opposing Rundstedt were being 'directed with firmness and vigour'.

The same was not true on Army Group Centre's sector, where von Bock was opposed by West Front under Pavlov, the Soviet tank specialist on whose views Stalin unwisely placed such importance. Pavlov had three mechanized corps (VI, XI and XIV) immediately available and a fourth (XIII) in reserve, but soon demonstrated that he lacked Kirponos' instinct for the game as both Guderian and Hoth cut swathes through his confused troops. By 27 June Panzer Groups 2 and 3 were 200 miles (320 kms) east of their startlines, their spearheads closing to meet east of Minsk, thereby emphasizing that, while the strategy of the campaign might follow Fuller's thinking, at the operative level it was a series of quickly executed *Vernichtungsschlachten* which was required to prevent the Red Army's escape into the Russian interior. The effect of this junction, therefore, was to create two major pockets, one at Bialystok and the other at Minsk itself, which were sealed off as the German infantry arrived and then slowly crushed. But far from being intimidated, the Russians demonstrated their fierce resolve to defend their homeland against the invaders, as they were to do throughout the war, revealing the terrifying fatalism with which they accepted death in attack or defence; and yet, when their ammunition was expended, their leaders were dead and there was nothing more to be done, that same fatalism could produce instinctive surrenders *en masse*.

When the last defenders of the pockets gave up on 3 July, 290,000 men marched into captivity, abandoning masses of equipment, which included 2,585 tanks and 1,449 guns. Furious at the scale of the débâcle, Stalin called Pavlov to Moscow and had him shot on the spot, appointing Marshal Semyen Timoshenko in his stead.

While Timoshenko attempted to construct a defence line along the upper reaches of the Dvina and Dniepr rivers in the hope of amassing sufficient reserves to mount a counter-offensive, Guderian and Hoth had resumed their advance with a view to isolating further large enemy forces in the area of Smolensk. The going was now extremely bad, involving great stretches of forest and swamp in which major roads were mere sandy tracks. These were sometimes mined by the Russians but would also become impassable after an hour or two's rain, and remain so until the sun had dried them out. However, an even greater source of delay was that after 3 July both panzer groups were placed under the direct command of Field Marshal Gunther von Kluge of the Fourth Army who, understandably worried about the yawning gap beginning to open between the armoured formations and his infantry divisions, repeatedly imposed checks on their progress. Both Guderian and Hoth resented this interference, the former particularly so, as he had served briefly under von Kluge during the opening phase of the war against Poland, but long enough for a clash of personalities to develop. Hoth was further aggravated by an order from Hitler himself to detach one of his panzer corps into the space between Army Groups Centre and North, which the Führer incorrectly believed to be vulnerable to Soviet counter-attack, giving vent to a disgusted aside that this was a first-class example of how not to conduct armoured operations.

As a result of these various factors, the average rate of advance, which had been forty miles (64 km) a day before the formation of the Minsk pocket, dropped to twelve miles (19.2 km) a day on the way to Smolensk. Even so, by 10 July Guderian was across the Dniepr near Mogilev, and Hoth was over the Dvina at Vitebsk. After several days of hard fighting, both panzer groups broke out of their bridgeheads and through into the rear of Timoshenko's armies; Smolensk itself fell on 16 July. The following day the armoured jaws all but encircled a huge pocket containing elements from up to twenty-five Soviet divisions, but unaided the panzer formations were unable to do more than form cordons around their catch. It was beyond their power to close a corridor which remained open to the east through which Timoshenko not only withdrew a number of battered units but actually inserted fresh troops into the battle, demonstrating that he did not intend being brow-beaten by his opponents' expertise. Gradually the walls of the pocket became more and more substantial as the German infantry marched up from the west, cutting the corridor on 27 July. Resistance finally ended on 5 August. This time the haul amounted to a quarter of a million prisoners, over 2,000 tanks and a similar number of guns. For the time being, this concluded offensive operations on Army Group Centre's sector.

Meanwhile, Army Group North, led by Höpner's Panzer Group 4, had made remarkable progress against Colonel-General F.I. Kuznetsov's North-West Front in its advance on Leningrad through the Baltic states. Here, although the going was as bad as anywhere in Russia and the axes of advance were channelled into two corridors between the coast, Lake Peipus and Lake Ilmen, only two mechanized corps, the III and XII, were present in the Soviet order of battle.

Höpner's panzer group consisted of two panzer corps, the XLI under Reinhardt with the 1st and 6th Panzer Divisions, 36th Motorized Infantry Division and 269th Infantry Division, and the LVI under von Manstein with the 8th Panzer Division, 3rd Motorized Infantry Division and 290th Infantry Division; detailed to follow up whichever corps made the better progress was the SS Motorized Division *Totenkopf*.

Shortly after it had crossed the frontier, Reinhardt's corps was counter-attacked by both Soviet mechanized corps in the area of Rasienai, between Tilsit and Shauliya, and immediately became involved in heavy fighting. With Luftwaffe assistance Reinhardt soon gained the upper hand while Manstein skirted the southern edge of the battle and headed straight for Dvinsk, covering the intervening 200 miles (320 km) in four days and seizing the town's bridges across the Dvina by *coup de main*. Thereafter, progress towards Leningrad became less dramatic as resistance stiffened but by mid-July Panzer Group 4 had penetrated the gap between Lakes Peipus and Ilmen. Voroshilov had now replaced Kuznetsov as Front Commander, and he used the fresh I Mechanized Corps to spearhead a counter-attack by the Soviet

Eleventh Army which isolated the LVI Panzer Corps for three days, cutting the 8th Panzer Division in two and separating it from its partner, the 3rd Motorized Division, near Zoltsy. Repeated Russian attacks on the encircled troops were held with difficulty until the situation was restored by the arrival of reinforcements. Elsewhere, Army Group North's leading elements reached the Luga, only sixty miles (96 km) from Leningrad. This was crossed on 8 August; a week later Novgorod fell. By the end of the month Leningrad was cut off from the rest of Russia, her fate to remain a prisoner of the Wehrmacht and the Finnish Army on the Karelian isthmus for the next 900 days. Simultaneously, 20,000 survivors of North-West Front, trapped in a pocket between the Luga and the developing siege lines, laid down their arms. Leeb had fulfilled his brief, the only army group commander to do so.

All three army groups had now advanced over 400 miles (640 km) into the Russian heartland, and a pause was necessary to allow their supply and administrative elements to catch up. This, then, was a good moment to take stock. It was only too clear that, despite its apparently limitless reserves of manpower, the Red Army had been very badly hurt, and although it had managed the remarkable feat of dismantling many of its armaments plants and transporting them lock, stock and barrel to the Urals, it would be many months before tanks, guns and aircraft would be coming on stream in anything like adequate numbers. On the other hand, German tank losses were fifty per cent higher than in previous campaigns, and the break-down ratio was equally high, especially among those units which had taken part in the Balkan campaigns. The centralized repair apparatus, quite unable to cope with the totally unexpected demands made upon it, was replaced by a system of field workshops. This involved the forward shipment of thousands of tons of spare parts, but as the system was new, teething problems arose as a matter of course and consignments went astray or were delivered to the wrong formation. The German motor transport fleet, which had been assembled from all over Europe and contained types too diverse to enumerate, also gave rise to serious concern as the unexpectedly hard usage to which it was put steadily eroded its strength, the more so since it proved impossible to establish a coherent supply of spares. Simultaneously, the further the advance penetrated, the greater was the demand for fuel and replacement tyres. Nor could horse-drawn transport be substituted at short notice; there were already half a million horses hauling guns and supply wagons into Russia, of which half would not survive the year. The

One of the four Assault Artillery batteries employed in the 1940 campaign in the West

A PzKw III belonging to Panzer Regiment 3, 2nd Panzer Division, heads south during the 1941 campaign in the Balkans. Participants commented that in Yugoslavia this had much in common with a military parade, although Greece proved a tougher nut to crack

The majority of the Third Reich's panzer leaders were educated in the spartan background of Imperial Germany's cadet academies. Here cadets give a demonstration of nerve and agility during a sports day at the famous Gross-Lichterfelde Academy near Berlin in the summer of 1912

By selective recruiting General Hans von Seeckt succeeded in making the 100,000-strong Reichsheer an army of leaders. He was adamant that the Army must remain above politics, yet ironically his leanings towards the now-defunct monarchy were to cost him his own position

Field Marshal Gerd von Rundstedt enjoyed not only the universal respect of the German officer corps, but also that of his opponents. His secret vice was detective novels, which he concealed within a drawer of his desk

Field Marshal Erich von Manstein, widely regarded within the Army as its best strategic brain

Field Marshal Ewald von Kleist commanded in succession the first panzer group to be formed, then the First Panzer Army, then Army Group A. Professional and efficient, he sought neither place nor publicity. He was dismissed by Hitler in March 1944

General Gustav Ritter von Vaerst commanded 15th Panzer Division for much of the campaign in North Africa and was subsequently promoted to the command of Fifth Panzer Army, being captured in Tunisia in May 1943

General Wilhelm Ritter von Thoma commanded the Condor Legion's tank unit in Spain and subsequently held a variety of senior appointments within the Panzerwaffe. He was captured during the closing stages of the Second Battle of Alamein

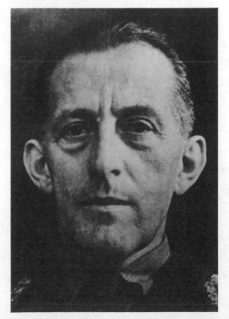

Regimental Headquarters' tanks of Panzer Regiment 25, 7th Panzer Division, France 1940. The tank nearest the camera is a PzKw 38(t) which has been fitted with additional radio equipment and a frame aerial appropriate to its function as a command vehicle

PzKw II and 38(t) halted by the roadside during *Barbarossa*. The vehicle markings indicate that they belong to Panzer Regiment 10, 8th Panzer Division

Forward tactical headquarters of 21st Panzer Division in the desert showing left, an SdKfz 250/3 communications half-track; centre, command version of the PzKw III; and right, the divisional commander's Horch staff car

General Hasso von Manteuffel commanded the Fifth Panzer Army during the Battle of the Bulge and it was on his sector that the Germans achieved most of their early successes. He is seen here during the period that he commanded the crack Panzergrenadier Division *Grossdeutschland*

Field Marshal Fedor von Bock commanded Army Group North in Poland, Army Group B in the West 1940 and Army Group Centre during *Barbarossa*

Field Marshal Wilhelm Ritter von Leeb commanded Army Group C in the West 1940 and Army Group North during *Barbarossa*

Obsolete tank chassis (in this case that of the PzKw II) provided an ideal mounting for the first generation of tank destroyers. This particular vehicle is known to have served with the 29th Infantry Division in Russia and the original print reveals more than 20 'kill' rings painted on the barrel. The face is that of Kohlenklau (The Coal Thief), a German music hall character who was the equivalent of the British spiv

The Nashorn (Rhino) Heavy Tank Destroyer was based on the PzKw IV chassis which provided a good platform for the 88mm L/71 gun but made concealment a difficult matter

Colonel-General Erich Höpner commanded XVI Panzer Corps during the 1940 campaign in the West and Panzer Group 4 (later Fourth Panzer Army) during *Barbarossa*. An energetic and aggressive panzer leader, he was also a difficult subordinate and was forced to retire in January 1942. He was hanged in August 1944 for his part in the Bomb Plot

Field Marshal Gunther von Kluge commanded the Fourth Army from 1939 to 1941, then Army Group Centre until 1943. He was Commander-in-Chief West when the Normandy front collapsed and then committed suicide because of his involvement with the July Bomb Plot. Guderian regarded him as his arch-enemy and at one point the two came close to fighting a duel

The most notable users of the PzKw 35(t) were Panzer Regiment 11, 6th Panzer Division, which retained them until the harsh winter of 1941–2, following which the division was withdrawn for refitting with more modern equipment. This pair were photographed during the early stages of the advance into Russia

The Panzerwaffe relied on deep reconnaissance to a far greater degree than its opponents. This heavy eight-wheeled SdKfz 232 armoured car was abandoned in deep sand near Gazala before being recovered by the British and towed to workshops in Tobruk. Note that the frame aerial mounting still enables the turret to be traversed in any direction

railways also presented problems of their own because of the break-of-gauge from the European standard of 4 feet 8½ inches to the Russian five feet. It would take time for the engineers to complete the change, during which the only solution was laborious trans-shipment between trains. A further source of worry was caused by the activities of partisan groups which were already beginning to prey on the German lines of communication in general. Operationally, the new Soviet tank designs had come as a severe shock, and some sort of answer would have to be found, but for the moment the Wehrmacht could collectively cope with the problem, thanks largely to the Russians' lack of expertise. On balance, the picture was less favourable than it had been when the campaign opened but von Bock, the commander of Army Group Centre, still believed that it lay within his power to capture Moscow. A German victory, therefore, continued to be a probability unless something untoward occurred.

That something was provided by the Führer himself. He had not interfered in the conduct of earlier campaigns because they had been short, but Barbarossa was a protracted affair, and ultimately he could not resist the temptation to leave his own imprint on events. On 19 July, while the fighting at Smolensk was still in progress, he issued his Directive No. 33, re-defining the entire strategy of the campaign. The drive on Moscow was to be suspended: Hoth was to be sent north and, in conjunction with Höpner, was to sever communications between the Russian capital and Leningrad: Guderian was to go south and assist von Rundstedt in his conquest of the Ukraine. This astonishing decision ran entirely contrary to the fundamental military tenet that the objective must be maintained throughout, for only the capture of Moscow could guarantee a German victory, and it was to that end that the Wehrmacht's entire effort should have been devoted. Further, Hitler did not seem able to grasp that, while the strategy of the campaign was based on the principles of Blitzkrieg, at the operative level it was *Vernichtungsgedanke* that counted; if the two were confused, it would be the former that would suffer, with sorry consequences for the whole campaign. So shocked were his senior officers by the enormity of the error that many, including von Brauchitsch, Halder, Jodl, von Bock, von Rundstedt, Guderian and Hoth, protested either strongly in person or formally through their superiors. Hitler, however, remained adamant, claiming that his generals had no understanding of the economic or political aspects of war.

Obduracy in high places also existed on the Soviet side of the lines. In the Ukraine Kirponos conducted a skilful withdrawal from the frontier, avoiding the sort of disasters that had overtaken first Pavlov and then Timoshenko further north, but he found himself hamstrung by Stalin's order that he must hold Kiev at all costs. Thus it came about that when, on 16 September, Guderian's panzer group, driving south-west from Smolensk in obedience to Hitler's *diktat*, met Kleist's advance guard moving north at a village named Lokhvitsa some hundred miles (160 kms) east of Kiev, a gigantic pocket was formed enclosing the major part of South-West Front. The Russians were slow to appreciate their danger, and by the time they did, Rundstedt had them held tight inside an iron ring. Kirponos died leading one of several frantic attempts to break out. When resistance finally collapsed on 26 September, the pocket yielded 900 tanks, 3,719 guns and no fewer than 665,000 prisoners. Such an enormous victory naturally gave rise to jubilation both within the Army and at home but in real terms it did not assist the German cause one bit; rather the reverse, in fact, since it provided a very superficial justification for Hitler's meddling. Many senior officers found themselves unable to share in the general euphoria, knowing the nature of the price that had been paid.

In early September, even before the Kiev pocket had been formed, Hitler decided that the emphasis must be returned to the Moscow axis as soon as possible. Unfortunately, the wheels he had set turning could not be put into reverse before the end of the month, but his confidence in the ability of his Panzerwaffe to attain victory during this, the last lap, remained unshaken. The beaten enemy, he told the German people, 'would never rise again!'.

The final drive on the capital was code-named Typhoon and began in the early days of October. Guderian and Hoth returned to the strategic centre-line, the latter angry because during the previous wasted month his tanks had achieved nothing save an unwanted increase in track-mileage, and were joined by Höpner. In the south Kleist was to spearhead a drive along the Black Sea coast, through Rostov and into the Caucasus, while in the north Leningrad was to be battered to rubble by heavy artillery and bombing.

For a while all went as before, and it seemed that the campaign could have no outcome other than another victory for the Wehrmacht. Hoth and Höpner sealed off a pocket at Viazma, as did Guderian and Kluge at Bryansk. By 20 October these had been eliminated, yielding 1,242 captured tanks, 5,412 guns and a further 663,000 prisoners. Apparently nothing was capable of halting the mighty juggernaut that smashed its way through every obstacle Timoshenko could place in its path, although the troops it encountered now were hastily raised levies and not the regulars who had been defeated only by skill and hard fighting further west; nor, ominously, could they be compared with the tough, experienced Siberian divisions which even then were entering European Russia.

Then, just as the leaves turned from green to gold without warning, the whole complexion of the battle changed. The first showers quickly became a downpour as the winter rains set in, the bottom fell out of the roads and progress slowed to a crawl. With whole army groups stuck fast in the thickening slough, the only vehicles which retained the ability to move were the tanks, often to be seen towing trains of five or six trucks through the mire in the manner of a railway locomotive. It placed an impossible strain on transmissions, but it was often the only way to get fuel, ammunition and food forward. By 14 November Guderian's panzer group, having crossed the frontier in June with 600 tanks, possessed only fifty operational machines. For a little while the ground hardened under heavy frost, and movement became possible again, but then came the first blizzards of the worst winter in living memory, accompanied by a screaming wind straight from innermost Asia and a deep, unimaginable cold. Temperatures were so low that track and firing-pins became brittle and snapped, ammunition refused to fire, oil thickened to the consistency of treacle and even the pneumatic links of the PzKw 35(t)s transmission became inoperable. No anti-freeze was available so it became necessary to light slow fires under vehicle sumps and start their engines every thirty minutes. Draught horses perished in their thousands unless they could be found shelter and fodder, while men who were unable to find winter clothing for themselves froze to death or suffered amputation because of frostbite.

In such circumstances Hitler's orders, based on maps and symbols studied in the cosy warmth of his East Prussian headquarters, provoked yells of derision when they spoke of objectives being seized by 'fast-moving battlegroups'. But they were orders, and von Bock did his best to see that they were obeyed. When Guderian and Reinhardt (who had replaced Hoth when the latter went to command the Seventeenth Army on 5 October) were finally halted by a combination of the Russian winter, sheer exhaustion and the rising tempo of the enemy's counter-attacks, they had already formed the jaws of a huge pincer that enclosed Moscow to the north and south; had those jaws been formed in September, the probability is that they could have been closed. German infantry broke into the capital's south-eastern suburbs on 4 December but were counter-attacked by local militia and pushed back. Guderian and Reinhardt also found themselves unable to hold their ground, while in the south Kleist had been forced to abandon Rostov as early as 28 November. It was clear that Barbarossa had run its course, and reluctantly Hitler admitted as much, simultaneously forbidding his troops to withdraw from their present positions.

This naturally ran contrary to his generals' advice, and soon German formations found themselves caught up and surrounded as the Russian advance gathered momentum. In this way, the 1st Panzer Division found itself isolated at Klin, thirty-five miles (56 km) north of Moscow, and was ordered to break out and enter the new German line at Nekrasino, some ten miles (18 km) to the west, abandoning its vehicles if necessary. This the divisional commander was reluctant to do, as he had about a thousand wounded whom he was not prepared to leave to the enemy because of earlier atrocities. He therefore ordered a dawn attack on the village of Golyadi, north of Nekrasino, by his armoured regiment and a motor rifle battalion led by an armoured infantry company, with the support of all the divisional artillery. Once Golyadi had been secured, the battlegroup would swing south, forcing all those Russian troops between Klin and Nekrasino to form a fresh front and meet this threat to their flank. This went exactly as planned but was only a diversion. The real break-out took place at noon along the Klin-Nekrasino road, led by the division's armoured infantry and motor-cycle battalions, joined as quickly as possible by some of the tanks from the diversionary force, all but one of the artillery battalions switching their fire to support this on receipt of a codeword. Strict traffic control was observed, all broken-down vehicles being pushed off the road into the deep snow. Still intact as a fighting force, the division broke through to Nekrasino without undue difficulty and was in action again twenty-four hours later. This interesting episode was to provide a model for the Panzerwaffe in the years that lay ahead.

Local successes such as this apart, for the first time in its history the Panzerwaffe was forced to accept the sour taste of failure, although the reasons for this obviously lay outside itself. It had lost through various causes 2,300 tanks, and of those that remained only the PzKw IIIs and IVs, always a minority, could be regarded as fit to retain their place on a modern battlefield. For a while offensive operations were out of the question but when they were resumed the Panzerwaffe would never again possess quite the self-confidence it had during the opening stages of Barbarossa. Notwithstanding, its achievements during the campaign have never been equalled. As Matthew Cooper points out in his book *The German Army 1933-1945*, it had not only carved out nine major pockets at Bialystok, Minsk, Smolensk, Uman, Gomel, Kiev, Briansk and Viazma and against the Azov coast, yielding over 2,250,000 prisoners, 9,327 tanks and 16,179 guns, the equivalent of 150 divisions, but had also been responsible for creating the conditions which resulted in thirteen smaller *Vernichtungsschlachten* ending in the capture of a further 736,000 men, 4,960 tanks and 9,033 guns. Some German authorities are now inclined to regard these statistics as being over-inflated by the Goebbels propaganda machine. On the other hand, the figures exclude the considerable quantity of booty and prisoners taken elsewhere, and the horrific but never accurately assessed total of Soviet dead. Again, the Russians themselves are unable to quantify their losses, and there can be no gainsaying the magnitude of the disaster which had befallen the Soviet Union; German casualties during Barbarossa amounted to approximately 800,000.

This, then, was the weapon which Hitler had wielded to the point of its destruction, and it remained to be seen whether it could be forged anew by the professionals he despised so much. Yet with typical perversity it was against many of those same professionals, the very men who for two years had won him one outstanding victory after another, that the Führer turned in his wrath when they counselled a withdrawal as being necessary for the survival of the Wehrmacht. As usual Brauchitsch, now seriously ill, was forced to endure the worst of his fury; Hitler screamed that he was 'a strawhead – a vain, cowardly wretch', then dismissed him and personally assumed his duties as Commander-in-Chief of the Army. Rundstedt and Leeb asked to be relieved of their commands rather than act contrary to their judgement; their request was granted. Bock went on sick leave and Kluge took over Army Group Centre; following further pointed disagreements with Guderian and some very frank speaking by Höpner, he reported both to Hitler and they were dismissed. And so it continued until almost all the higher-formation commanders had been replaced.

It might be thought that Germany already had troubles a-plenty to occupy her, but on 11 December Hitler chose to declare war on the United States.

5. Taking Stock

Notwithstanding Hitler's boast that it had been his no-withdrawal order that had saved the German Army in Russia during the winter of 1941-2, the sheer instinct for survival, coupled with the comparative weakness of their Soviets at this period, had a far more immediate effect on preserving the integrity of the front. The Germans stayed under cover in the more important villages and towns which lay along the principal road and rail links and very quickly devised numerous ingenious ways of keeping themselves alive and healthy and their equipment in working order, many of which are now included in survival manuals as a matter of course.

Starting tank engines in the extreme cold always provided problems but German crews were lucky in that the PzKw II, III, IV and 38(t) were fitted with a hand-operated inertia starter as well as an electric self-starting device. If the self-starter failed, or if it was inadvisable to use it because the sump oil had been chilled to a semi-solid state, recourse was made to the inertia starter, whose handle was inserted into the engine compartment through the stern plate. The handle was swung by two men until the flywheel reached a speed of 60 rpm, when the power was tripped to turn the main engine. The system was geared, but its operation in the depths of the Russian winter required a great deal of initial effort, although it was possible for the driver to eliminate the drag of the gearbox oil by depressing his clutch. Another system which was developed to assist cold starting was known as the *Kühlwasserübertragung* – cold water exchanger. When one tank had been started and had reached its normal operating temperature, the warm coolant was pumped from it to the next vehicle by the exchanger, in return for cold coolant. In due course the rise in temperature would permit the second vehicle to be started, and so on. For movement across packed ice and snow, a set of track extensions known as *Ostketten* were fitted to increase traction.

Getting about in winter, however, was not the Panzerwaffe's most serious worry, although it would never be able to compete with the legendary mobility of the T-34 which led to the Russian medium being named 'the Snow King' by the Germans themselves. What gave rise to the gravest concern was that both the T-34 and the KV were better armed and protected than anything Germany had available. Of these two designs, the KV made the greater impression at first, but it was the T-34 that came closest to the German operational concept and which von Kleist unhesitatingly described as the finest tank in the world. In November 1941 a team of ordnance officers, designers and manufacturers arrived at the front to evaluate the tank on the spot and decide what had to be done to restore the balance in Germany's favour. A number of hasty – and tactically ill-considered – suggestions were made that Koshkin's design should simply be copied but, pride apart, there were several technical reasons why this was impractical, the most important of which centred on the difficulty involved in manufacturing the aluminium diesel unit and on the general shortage of alloys resulting from the Allied blockade. The only complete answer lay in producing a new German medium tank with an even better performance.

The Ordnance Department's specification for the new vehicle, initially known simply as Project VK 3002, required a 75mm L/48 main armament, an armour arrangement comparable with the T-34, a weight range of 30-35 tons (30,480-35,560 kg) and a maximum speed of 35 mph (56.33 kph). The degree of urgency involved is emphasized by the fact that invitations to submit competitive designs were issued to Daimler-Benz and MAN (Maschinenfabrik Augsburg-Nürnberg) on 25 November, within days of the commission of enquiry's return from Russia. Both organizations were forced to incorporate a stream of modifications in their work, including the replacement of the 75mm L/48 gun with the more powerful L/70, but were able to submit their designs in the spring of 1942. Of the two Hitler preferred the Daimler-Benz candidate, which was slightly the better vehicle, but the Ordnance Department objected strongly on the grounds that the main armament had too long a frontal overhang and that the tank's overall appearance was *too* similar to that of the T-34 for peace of mind. Somewhat unexpectedly, Hitler gave way, and the MAN design was accepted, entering production in November 1942 as the PzKw V Panther. Hitler was to force the pace of production and commit the vehicle to action without the benefit of adequate user trials, with catastrophic consequences, but after most of its teething troubles had been cured, the Panther was to evolve into a fine medium tank.

Both the Daimler-Benz and MAN candidates incorporated features from another line of research in which their organizations had been involved, Project VK 3001, which was one of a series of experimental heavy break-through tank designs initiated in 1937. Encounters with the French Char Bs and the British Matildas had revived Hitler's interest in the heavy tank family, and he gave orders for a parallel line of development to begin on a tank with heavy armour, a high-velocity gun and a maximum speed of 24.5 mph (39.43 kph), to be known as Project VK 3601. Then, in May 1941, one month *before* the start of Barbarossa and *without* prior knowledge of the T-34 and KV, the remarkable decision was taken to arm the vehicle with a tank version of the redoubtable 88mm dual-purpose anti-aircraft/anti-tank gun while permitting an increase in weight to forty-five tons (45,720 kg). By now Daimler-Benz and MAN had dropped out of this race, leaving the field clear for the Henschel and Porsche organizations, who had been told that they should have their prototypes ready to demonstrate to the Führer on his birthday, 20 April 1942. This they achieved by incorporating what they believed to be the better features of their respective Project VK 3001 and 3601 designs. The trials were held at Rastenburg and the Henschel entry was adjudged the superior. Production of this commenced in August 1942, the tank being designated PzKw VI Tiger H, later amended to Tiger E, and continued for two years, in which time 1,350 were built, an average of fifty-six per month.

The Tiger was to become one of the legendary weapon systems of World War II but it should be remembered that each machine cost 800,000 Reichsmarks and 300,000 man-hours to construct; on balance it seems probable that the money, time and resources would have been better spent elsewhere. The Tigers were formed into Heavy Tank Battalions (Schwere Panzer Abteilungen – sPzAbt) whose theoretical establishment included battalion headquarters with three tanks and four companies each with two company headquarters tanks and three four-tank platoons, giving a total of fifty-nine Tigers. In practice, battalions thought themselves lucky if they possessed sufficient vehicles to form their third company. Hitler was to comment that each Tiger battalion was worth a panzer division to him, although the former could never perform the duties of the latter, nor was it ever the intention that they should. The Tiger was a tactical weapon system, and its influence was purely local; it won most of its battles but failed to influence the course of a single campaign. The Porsche entry, commonly known as the Elefant – and occasionally as the Tiger (P) or Ferdinand after its designer, Dr Ferdinand Porsche – was eventually developed as a 67-ton (68,000 kg) tank destroyer with 200mm frontal armour and a maximum speed of 12 mph (19.2 kph). Of the ninety produced, seventy-six were issued to Heavy Tank Destroyer Battalions 653 and 654, taking part in the great tank battle at Kursk in 1943.

Although they had exceeded their specification target weight by a wide margin, the Panther and Tiger represented the Panzerwaffe's long-term answer to the problems of the Russian Front, but in January 1942 an immediate and effective short-term solution was a desperate necessity. That could be achieved only by a drastic re-organization of assets and a new approach to the question of equipment. The nub of the matter was that any weapon of less than 75mm calibre was now inadequate, and although the PzKw IV and the assault gun were armed with the 75mm L/24 howitzer, this fired high-explosive shells at low velocity which were unable to penetrate the armour of the new Russian tanks. The situation was partially corrected by the issue of shaped-charge ammunition during the year, but it was apparent that kinetic energy still remained the real tank-killer and what was required, therefore, were guns capable of producing the high muzzle velocities that would enable conventional armour-piercing round to destroy their target. Fortunately, both the PzKw IV and the assault gun possessed sufficient spare internal space to accommodate the recoil of a high-velocity weapon and permit the handling of larger ammunition, and both were up-gunned first with the 75mm L/43 gun and then with the more powerful 75mm L/48. Throughout the year increasing numbers of these vehicles, including older models which had been modified, began reaching the front. The Sturmartillerie, anxious that the anti-tank aspect of their new armament should not detract from their primary purpose – the close support of infantry with direct gunfire – compensated for the loss of the 75mm L/24 howitzer by introducing the 105mm Assault Howitzer 42, which accounted for one-eighth of subsequent assault gun production.

Although the performance of the 50mm L/60 models of the PzKw III was now well below the required standard, it was necessary to retain them in order to keep up the strength of the panzer divisions. In fact, between December 1941 and the spring of 1943 a total of 1,969 PzKw IIIs of this type were built, and manufacture of the tank did not cease until August 1943; even then, the chassis continued to be used in the construction of assault guns. The final version of the PzKw III was the Model N, armed with the 75mm L/24 howitzer, which provided organic fire support for the motorized divisions and also served for a while in the heavy tank battalions. After the experiences of 1941, both the PzKw III and IV were up-armoured to the extent their designs would permit, initially using *appliqué* plates which were bolted to the existing frontal armour.

For some tanks, however, the end of Barbarossa also meant the end of their active service careers in the Panzerwaffe. Those PzKw Is that survived, for example, were returned to Germany, where they were stripped down to their chassis and used for primary driver training, having been adapted to burn wood-gas as a fuel. The PzKw 35(t) remained in front-line service with Germany's allies for a while longer, notably with the Romanian 1st Royal Armoured Division and the Slovak Fast Division, but its best-known German users, the 6th Panzer Division, lost their last tank, named *Anthony the Last*, when it broke down near Klin on 10 December.

The PzKw II and PzKw 38(t) were also finished as gun-tanks but this proved to be a blessing in disguise as their chassis could be converted quickly for use as self-propelled gun mountings, as could those of a number of captured French tanks, including the R.35, H.35, H.39 and FCM, and the Lorraine tracked carrier. In this way, by mounting different versions of the German 75mm PaK 40 anti-tank guns and captured Russian 76.2mm anti-tank guns re-chambered to take German 75mm ammunition in fixed, open-topped superstructures, it proved possible to deliver quantities of simple but well-armed tank-destroyers very quickly, so restoring the technical balance on the Eastern Front. The majority of these vehicles were named Marder (Marten), the Marder I being based on the Lorraine carrier, the Marder II on the PzKw II and the Marder III on the PzKw 38(t). Simultaneously, work began on a heavy tank-destroyer known as the Nashorn (Rhino) which combined the 88mm L/71 PaK 43/1 and the PzKw IV chassis, but this did not enter service until 1943. Notwithstanding the speed and ingenuity of the German response, these designs were regarded as being of a stop-gap nature, and even while conversions were in hand plans were being drawn for a second generation of tank-destroyers which was to enter service some eighteen months later.

As well as benefiting the Panzerjäger troops, the acquisition of so many redundant tank chassis also assisted the provision of equipment for the Panzerartillerie, using the same expedient approach of a fixed, open-topped superstructure of lighter armour plate enclosing the weapon mounting and crew. The field batteries of the panzer divisions began receiving the Wespe (Wasp) 105mm self-propelled howitzer, based on the PzKw II, in 1942, and several French chassis were also converted to this role, but the medium batteries had to wait until 1943 for their Hummel (Bumble Bee) 150mm self-propelled howitzers, which employed the chassis of the PzKw IV.

As far as the motorized infantry were concerned, the experience gained during Barbarossa led directly to a number of organizational changes. Within the panzer divisions the motor-cycle battalions had suffered very serious casualties and were disbanded, their survivors being posted to the divisional armoured reconnaissance battalions. It was also realized that, just as mechanized infantry were complementary to tanks, the reverse was also true and, starting in 1942, each motorized division was augmented by its own organic tank battalion; in practice, the general shortage of tanks meant that many of these battalions were equipped with assault guns manned by the Sturmartillerie.

On 5 July 1942 Hitler officially recognized the élan, efficiency and flexibility of the panzer divisions' mechanized infantry by conferring on them the prestigious title of Panzergrenadier, and in March the following year this was extended to the motorized divisions as a whole, both Army and Waffen SS. At the regimental level, however, soldiers can be cantankerous in the extreme when it comes to accepting honours conferred by distant politicians, and many units continued to refer to themselves by the more ancient titles of Grenadier or Fusilier which had been intentionally preserved by the old Traditionskompanie.

The establishment of each mechanized infantry regiment included an infantry gun company, several of which were equipped with the 150mm heavy infantry gun mounted on a PzKw I chassis. This pre-war conversion was not only top-heavy but also overloaded the suspension so that its cross-country-performance was poor, but during 1942 a very successful combination was achieved by mounting the same weapon on the PzKw II chassis; later, two further versions were produced using the PzKw 38(t) chassis, one with the engine forward, the other aft.

Meanwhile, despite the equipment crisis and the fact that the Wehrmacht was stretched to its limits, Hitler continued to raise yet more panzer divisions. The 21st was formed for service in North Africa in February 1941, and the 22nd was raised in September of that year. The 24th and 25th followed in February 1942, the former being recruited from the 1st Cavalry Division, the German Army's last mounted formation; the 26th and 27th were formed in the autumn of 1942. *Grossdeutschland*, always a favourite of Hitler's and now expanded to divisional strength, was designated a panzergrenadier division in May 1942 but actually possessed more tanks than the average panzer division. At the higher level the four panzer groups which had taken part in Barbarossa retained their numbers but changed their title to Panzer Army, the 1st and 2nd on 5 October and the 3rd and 4th on 31 December 1941. In practice the change meant little save that rather more infantry was placed at the disposal of the army commanders.

It was against this background that the gigantic struggle in Russia continued, although for the first half of 1942 it was a kind of broken-backed warfare that the combatants pursued, with neither side quite strong enough to inflict a critical defeat on the other. When the year opened, the Red Army had about 4 million men under arms and approximately 2,000 tanks. As the re-sited factories began production and the first shipments of British Matildas and Valentines arrived, the Soviet tank strength grew slowly, but it would be months before Russian crews began to show the first glimmerings of expertise. For the moment, too, Soviet commanders had completely lost confidence in their ability to handle large armoured formations and concentrated on gaining experience with fifty-strong independent tank brigades.

Although Germany and her allies had over 5 million men serving in Russia and could still field 1,400 tanks, Stalin decided to expand the local counter-attacks which had halted the German advance near Moscow into an all-out attritional offensive that was to last throughout the remainder of the winter and until the great thaw halted movement. This began with attacks on the German salients north and south of the capital by Koniev's Kalinin Front and West Front, now commanded by Zhukov, and was then taken up by Volkhov and North-West Fronts in the north, and Bryansk and South-West Fronts in the south. The effect of this was to disperse the Russian effort along the entire line when more could have been achieved by a concentrated blow against Army Group Centre. Even so, as might be expected when the possession of villages and towns ensured the survival of those who held them, the fighting was bitter in the extreme. Somehow, the Germans preserved a sense of humour, referring to their local counter-attacks and relief operations as 'snail offensives', the ability to preserve movement at any speed being regarded as a major achievement. The Soviets made better progress on the northern and central sectors of the front, removing the immediate threat to Moscow and advancing up to 200 miles (320 km) in some areas. In the final analysis, this was also of benefit to the Germans as it enabled them to establish a stronger and more natural defence line than that on which Hitler had insisted they stand fast. In addition, it brought them closer to their railheads and workshop facilities, so expediting the recovery of the panzer divisions.

Whenever Russian armoured formations broke through the German defence zone, they tended to drive on into the void and were soon isolated and dealt with in detail. Set-piece attacks were poorly co-ordinated and repeated regularly over the same ground that had witnessed earlier failures. The Germans quickly learned to use artillery and automatic weapon fire to separate the Soviet infantry from their armour, to the detriment of both, and since the Red Army failed to develop an armoured personnel carrier until after the war, it was never able to solve this problem. Lacking radios, the Soviet tanks bunched around their company and battalion commanders, watching their hand and flag signals. The latter's vehicles therefore became primary targets, and once they had been knocked out, the remainder of the units, which at this period had been trained scarcely beyond the level of manning its tanks, tended to mill aimlessly around the objective. This era therefore witnessed a staggering total of tank kills recorded by individual German anti-tank guns, tanks, assault guns and Panzerjäger, a phenomenon that would seldom be equalled again in this theatre of war and never attained in others.

This was something Dr Goebbels' Propaganda Ministry, now faced with selling the prospect of a long, hard war to the public, seized upon eagerly, creating the tank or assault gun ace to answer the need for inspiring acts. This was a concept which did not find favour with Western armies as, unlike the air or submarine ace, the individual concerned did not always produce results unaided. A tank crew in action act as a team, but a tank commander may well work with several crews over a period of weeks, and it is manifestly unfair that he should inherit the entire credit for their combined efforts. Again, so many outside factors, including luck, are at work concurrently during a land battle that the tank ace cannot *always* be said to have created the conditions which led to his victories. Conversely, it must be freely admitted that the German tank and assault gun aces were first-class soldiers with a highly developed tactical sense who never failed to take advantage of a favourable situation.

Although few of the tank aces' names reached the West, in Germany their actions were as widely reported as those of the Luftwaffe's most successful pilots and the Kriegsmarine's

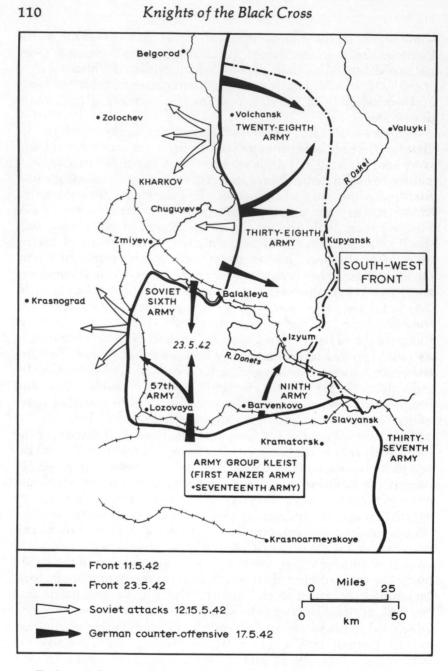

Defeat of the Soviet spring offensive and the German response –
Operation Fredericus, May 1942

top-scoring U-boat commanders. The Panzerwaffe's most decorated regimental officer was Colonel Count Strachwitz von Gross Zauche und Camminetz who, in addition to winning the lower grades of the Iron Cross, was awarded the Knight's Cross on 28 August 1941 and Oakleaves on 13 November 1942, both while serving with I/Panzer Regiment 2, Swords on 28 March 1943 while commanding Panzer Regiment *Grossdeutschland*, and Diamonds on 15 April 1944 while commanding a battlegroup on Army Group North's sector. Strachwitz, originally a cavalryman, belonged to an old military family with estates in Silesia and as a young man had seen active service during World War I and with the Freikorps. An individual who clearly relished action, he excelled as a small battlegroup commander. His exploits would fill a book on their own, proving the point that fact is often far more exciting than fiction. On one occasion he laid an ambush with four of his panzers deep inside Soviet lines, destroying 105 enemy tanks in less than an hour, without loss. Wounded no fewer than fourteen times, he survived the war to become a prisoner of the Americans.

Equally renowned was Wachtmeister (Sergeant) Hugo Primozic of Assault Gun Battalion 667. Primozic was a veteran of the selectively recruited Reichsheer and was noted for his quick reactions, clever tactical use of ground and the icy nerve which in tense situations enabled him to hold his fire until his opponent had closed to point-blank range, so ensuring a first-round kill. In September 1942 he became the first NCO in the history of the German Army to be awarded the Knight's Cross when his three-gun troop, fighting in isolation, routed a determined Russian attack on the Rzhev sector, destroying a total of twenty-four enemy tanks. By January 1943 Primozic had sixty personal kills to his credit and after an equally gallant action on the 28th he was awarded the Oakleaves, being simultaneously commissioned with the rank of Lieutenant.

Confronted by this sort of expertise, coupled with good shooting and the flexibility conferred by a universal radio net, the inexperienced Russian tank brigades were clearly no match for their opponents so that, when operations were brought to a standstill in March by the *rasputitsa* (the wet season), they had, for the moment, been fought very close to destruction. As a direct result of the losses it inflicted, the Panzerwaffe recovered much of the confidence that had been shaken loose by the failure of Barbarossa. Some of its members doubted whether the Russians would ever be able to master the mechanics of the tank battle, however brilliant some of their designs might be. Such a view discounted the enemy's legendary stoicism, patience and the degree to which he was now motivated, as time would reveal.

By the beginning of May the Wehrmacht was itself preparing to return to the offensive with Army Group South, a preliminary move being Operation Fredericus, intended to eliminate the large salient based on Izyum, south of Kharkov, and seize a bridgehead over the Donets which could be used as a springboard for the projected drive into the Caucasus. This salient, nearly sixty miles (96 km) deep and about the same distance across, represented the sole success of Timoshenko's South-West Front during Stalin's January offensive. The Soviet intention had been to break away southwards towards the Sea of Azov, so containing the right wing of Army Group South inside a pocket, but this proved wildly ambitious and was stopped in its tracks by a battlegroup based on III Motorized Corps and named after its commander, General Eberhard von Mackensen; simultaneously the combined efforts of First Panzer and Seventeenth Armies, known collectively as Army Group Kleist, wore down the momentum of the Russian attacks until by the beginning of February this area of the Front had settled down to relative quietude again.

In April, however, Stalin decided that South-West Front would strike north out of the salient and re-capture Kharkov, partly to disrupt German preparations for the forthcoming offensive and partly because the objective itself held enormous propaganda value. Having used the operational pause during and after the *rasputitsa* to build up his strength, Timoshenko had available 640,000 men and 1,200 tanks. By now, having acquired some command experience with its small tank brigades, the Red Army had again begun forming tank corps, although these bore no relation to the unwieldy pre-war organizations and were really tank-heavy armoured divisions containing three tank brigades with a total of 180 tanks, a motor rifle brigade, a motor-cycle battalion and a reconnaissance battalion; a group of two or more such corps, with additional troops, was known in Soviet parlance as a tank army, which had approximately the same strength as a panzer corps. For its drive on Kharkov, South-West Front had two of the new tank corps, the XXI and XXIII, and thirteen tank brigades.

Timoshenko struck on 12 May, six days before the scheduled start of Fredericus, breaking through the front held by von Paulus' Sixth Army to a depth varying between fourteen and twenty miles (23-32 km). He was aware that Army Group Kleist was ready for action and had assembled around Kramatorsk, some miles below the southern shoulder of the pocket, yet to

Stalin he was openly dismissive of this fresh and powerful counter-attack force, as was his senior political officer, Nikita Khrushchev.

The reaction of German officers on the spot was that Fredericus would have to be abandoned and all efforts concentrated on a static defence of Kharkov. Hitler and Halder, for once in complete accord, took a quite contrary view: what the situation demanded was the counter-attack that had already been planned – far from being cancelled, Fredericus would begin a day early. When, on 17 May, Kleist smashed his way through the southern wall of the salient, he possessed a local superiority of 4.4 to one in tanks, 1.3 to one in infantry and 1.7 to one in artillery weapons. Timoshenko still failed to read the situation correctly and at first sent back a single tank brigade to deal with the threat, but once the full enormity of what had taken place dawned upon him, both tanks corps followed in rapid succession. On the 18th, realizing that his armies had entered a trap, he requested permission to abandon the drive on Kharkov. Stalin refused, but the following day changed his mind. It was too late, for Paulus' Sixth Army was already attacking south from Balakleya through the northern wall of the salient, effecting a junction with Kleist's armour on 22 May.

The encircled troops fought hard but in vain to break through the ring of fire, numerous senior officers dying in the attempt, including Kostenko, the Deputy Commander of South-West Front, Gorodniansky and Podlas, respectively the commanders of the Soviet Sixth and Ninth Armies. Every Russian armoured formation inside the pocket was wiped out and over 250,000 prisoners were taken. But perhaps even more serious than the physical damage sustained by the Red Army during Stalin's abortive Kharkov offensive was the shattering blow to its confidence, so painstakingly nurtured over the past six months.

6. Disaster and Recovery

While Operation Fredericus was recognizably a product of *Vernichtungsgedanke* in the traditional mould, the same could hardly be said of Case Blue, the major German offensive planned for the summer of 1942. It was certainly true that in many respects Blue was a product of Blitzkrieg thinking, but the problem lay not only in identifying which phase was intended to induce strategic paralysis and which was a holding action, but also in identifying the objectives themselves and the very reasons why they had been chosen.

On 1 April – All Fools' Day to a large part of the world – Hitler had told von Kleist that he intended to seize the oilfields at Maikop, Grozny and Baku in the Caucasus 'because Germany could not continue the war without them'; in fact, she survived for a further three years. Yet to Halder the Führer explained that the capture of the oilfields represented a master-stroke of economic warfare which would cripple the Soviet Union's ability to fight, accepting OKH's point that the vulnerable left flank of this deep penetration should be protected by a defensive front along the Don from Voronezh to Stalingrad on the Volga. He then became so absorbed by the possibilities of eliminating the industrial capacity of Stalingrad that this began to assume equal weight with the drive into the Caucasus while planning was actually taking place, so repeating the previous year's mistake in which he had improperly understood the relationship of Army Groups North and South to Army Group Centre.

Fuller was to describe the concept of Blue as being radically unsound, pointing out that the capture of Saratov, two hundred miles (30 km) upstream from Stalingrad, would have yielded better results for less effort, as the loss of this vital rail junction and river transport centre would, properly exploited, have placed a stranglehold on the Soviet supply of oil from the Caucasus fields, greatly restricted the flow of Allied aid reaching Russia via Persia and the Caspian, and unhinged the entire southern sector of the Soviet line. Hitler, however, was not given to such subtle considerations of the Indirect Approach nor, now that he had assumed the mantle of the Army's Commander-in-Chief, had he the patience or ability to pursue the traditional German objective of securing a crushing victory before the first shot was fired. Instead, he opted for a flashy but impractical political solution to his problems, proclaiming his ultimate intention of seizing all the Middle East's oil-producing areas with a twin drive through the Caucasus and Egypt aimed at Iraq and Persia; at one stage, even India was on the agenda.

According to Manstein, the one thing Hitler lacked as a Supreme Commander was *'military ability based on experience –* something for which his "intuition" was no substitute ... He failed to understand that the objectives and ultimate scope of an operation must be in direct proportion to the time and forces needed to carry it out – to say nothing of the possibilities of supply. He did not – or would not – realize that any long-range offensive operation calls for a steady build-up of troops over and above those committed in the original assault. All this was brought out with striking clarity in the planning and execution of the 1942 summer offensive'.

With the exception of local activity around the Leningrad perimeter, the strategic planning for Blue required Army Groups North and Centre to remain on the defensive. Army Group South was divided into two new Army Groups designated A and B, of which the former, under List, would make the deep penetration into the Caucasus while the latter, commanded by von Bock, whose health had improved somewhat, acted as flank guard and established the projected defensive front along the axis Voronezh-Stalingrad. Army Group A consisted of the First Panzer Army (three panzer, two motorized, seven German and four Romanian infantry divisions), still under the command of the veteran von Kleist; and Group Ruoff with the Seventeenth Army (one panzer, one motorized, six German and four Romanian infantry divisions) and the Eighth Italian Army (six infantry divisions). Army Group B contained the Fourth Panzer Army (three panzer, two motorized and six infantry divisions), now under the command of Hoth; von Paulus' Sixth Army, with two panzer, one motorized and fifteen infantry divisions; von Weichs' Second Army, with one motorized, four German and two Hungarian infantry divisions; and the Second Hungarian Army with four infantry divisions.

The tank regiments of the nine panzer divisions directly involved in the offensive had each been expanded to three battalions, the average divisional tank strength being approximately 140 vehicles. A total of 1,495 tanks would take part in the offensive, of which 133 were up-gunned PzKw IVs; in addition, the total of 75mm-armed tank-destroyers and improved assault guns reaching the front was rising steadily. This accretion had been obtained at the expense of the ten panzer divisions serving with Army Groups North and Centre, which had not been re-equipped and were operating with tank battalions reduced to between forty and sixty vehicles each.

Superficially, therefore, the situation looked more favourable than it had on the eve of Barbarossa, for after the run-down or defeat of her recent counter-offensives the Soviet Union was weaker than at any time since the war began. Conversely, as Matthew Cooper points out in his book *The German Army 1933-1945*, the real German assets were not as well organized as they had been a year earlier. These, the panzer and motorized infantry divisions, amounted to only one-fifth of the total force employed and were all below their mechanical transport establishment. Furthermore, one third of the panzer divisions were serving in a subordinate role in infantry armies, a state of affairs which the original architects of the Panzerwaffe had always striven hard to prevent, and a similar dispersion of effort affected three of the seven motorized infantry divisions available. Again, more than half the formations which themselves constituted the panzer armies remained entirely dependent on the *horse* as a prime mover, a grouping quite incompatible with the task in hand.

A clever deception plan succeeded in convincing the Soviet *Stavka* (the General Staff) that the German blow would again be directed at Moscow, but on 19 June a Fieseler Storch light aircraft carrying a Major Reichel, the Staff Officer (Operations) of the 23rd Panzer Division (XL Panzer Corps) was shot down between the lines, killing its occupants. A Russian infantry patrol reached the wreckage first and recovered Reichel's briefcase, containing a set of corps orders for the opening phase of Blue, with a map and other documents outlining German intentions. These indicated that the XL Panzer Corps would attack along the axis Volchansk-Novy Oskol towards Voronezh on 22 June and were taken directly to General Golikov, the commander of the Bryansk Front, who viewed them very seriously since they confirmed the assessment built up by his Intelligence staff from other sources; Stalin and *Stavka*, on the other hand, regarded the documents as a German plant, and when the 22nd came and went without incident, this opinion seemed justified. In fact, Hitler's anger at this careless attitude to security was such that the commander of the XL Panzer Corps, General Georg Stumme, and the officer commanding the 23rd Panzer Division, Major-General von Boineburg-Lengsfeld, were both instantly dismissed and subsequently court-martialled.

The start of Case Blue had actually been postponed for a week, but Golikov retained his suspicions and when the storm broke over his Front on 28 June he promptly set his I and XVI Tank Corps in motion. *Stavka*, shaken, not only despatched the IV and XXIV Tank Corps from South-West Front but also contributed the XVII Tank Corps from its own operational reserve and ordered that one of the first Tank Armies be formed – Lizyukov's Fifth, composed of the II and XI Tank Corps – into action. Over, 1,200 KV-1s, T-34s and light T-60s and T-70s were now converging on Army Group B's spearhead, setting the scene for a major tank battle which would undoubtedly have taken place had not the Russian command and control apparatus fallen victim to its own inherent faults. The essence of the Soviet difficulty was that there were too many people issuing orders and too few receiving them.

Golikov's position was made extremely difficult by the arrival of Fedorenko, the Chief of Armoured Troops, with instructions from Stalin to supervise armoured operations in person. To do this he set up a command post at Kastornoye, although this description was purely nominal, since it possessed neither a staff nor asignals system. For a while it remained unclear whether Golikov or Fedorenko was in command, and each continued to issue orders to the other over a shaky radio link; the ultimate judgement could hardly be described as helpful as it placed the armour under Fedorenko and the rest of the troops under Golikov. Nonetheless, it was to Golikov that *Stavka* directed a stream of signals regarding *armoured* operations. Simultaneously, both Stalin and Colonel-General Vasilevskii, the Chief of General Staff, bombarded the hapless Front commander with unwanted advice and needless criticism. At lower levels the all out complete breakdown of communications left troops without orders from their commanders, and commanders without the slightest idea where their units were; one army staff was forced to commandeer a squadron of elderly biplanes to go and look for them!

Needless to say, in such a climate of black farce the German armoured formations were able to beat their opponents in detail with an almost contemptuous ease. Even the counter-stroke by the Fifth Tank Army, a concentration of 600 tanks which was in theory capable of striking a hammer-blow at the German advance, was bungled badly. For some reason Lizyukov, instead of advancing *en masse* to the attack, decided to disperse his units in *columns*, whose heads were easily shot away with direct gunfire while the remainder of his army was harried by the Luftwaffe to the point of dispersion. If one episode encapsulated the opening of the Germany offensive, it was the 24th Panzer Division roaring through the field headquarters of the Soviet Fortieth Army, whose general and staff were forced to abandon their command caravans and take to their heels.

A forty-mile (64 km) gap was torn open between the Bryansk and South-West Fronts, but the Russians had learned the previous year's lessons and quickly retreated out of danger before the panzer spearheads closed behind them; such pockets as were formed yielded little by comparison with the staggering captures of Barbarossa. This annoyed Hitler, who felt that the German armour should be used more aggressively to prevent the escape of the Soviet armies across the Don. Much of his anger was directed at von Bock, who was taking longer than the Führer was prepared to allow to consolidate his hold on Voronezh; on 13 July this veteran senior commander who had served Germany well in Poland, in the West in 1940 and in Russia the previous year, was summarily dismissed after criticizing an OKH directive, his place being taken by von Weichs.

As originally drafted, Case Blue required Hoth's Fourth Panzer Army to lead the advance on Stalingrad, followed by von Paulus' slower Sixth Army, and if this had been adhered to, it is certain that this straggling industrial city on the right bank of the Volga could have been taken by the end of the month, and probably without a fight. But on 17 July Hitler made a decision that was to have even more disastrous consequences than his diversion of the panzer spearheads before Moscow in 1941. He decided that Hoth's army would drive south along the Don and assist von Kleist's First Panzer Army in securing crossings over the lower reaches of the river as a prelude to a great battle of encirclement with which he planned to destroy the Soviet South Front against the coast. No such battle would ever take place, for South Front was already retreating out of the trap as fast as it could march, leaving long stretches of the Don quite undefended. Thus, many of Kleist's men were able to swim and sunbathe while the engineers put in their bridges almost unmolested. The arrival of Hoth and his tens of thousands of vehicles on this peaceful, ordered scene could hardly be described as welcome since it jammed the roads behind both panzer armies, ensured that neither could be supplied properly and prevented the re-organized vehicle recovery and repair system from functioning. Further north, the shortage of fuel and hard fighting brought the

Sixth Army to a standstill on the Don at Kalach.

By the end of July the position had been clarified somewhat, and Army Group A was on its way into the Caucasus. On 1 August the Fourth Panzer Army reverted to Army Group B and, having crossed the Don at Tsimlyanskya, received orders to advance north-east along the Novorossisk-Stalingrad railway while Paulus' Sixth Army resumed its offensive from Kalach. At first both armies made reasonable progress, but the closer they got to Stalingrad the tougher resistance became until, by the third week of August, they had been fought to a standstill. Terror raids made by the Luftwaffe throughout 23 and 24 August failed to break the enemy's resolve, and it became obvious that the Russians intended throwing the rule-book out of the window by fighting a battle of extermination among the ruins with a wide river at their back.

Entrusted with the defence of the city was the commander of the Soviet 62nd Army, General Vasili Chuikov, who received an unimpressive but uncharacteristic first impression of the Panzerwaffe at work, noted by Douglas Orgill in his book *T-34 Russian Armour*: 'The German tanks did not go into action without infantry and air support. On the battlefield there was no evidence of the prowess of the German tank crews, their courage and speed in action, about which foreign newspapers had written. The reverse was true, in fact: they operated sluggishly, extremely cautiously, and indecisively.'

The reason for this was that Army Group B had actually fulfilled its mission by reaching the Volga at Stalingrad while Army Group A was driving ever deeper into the Caucasus against minimal opposition – on 9 August the First Panzer Army reached the Maikop oilfields; on the 22nd *Gebirgsjäger* hoisted the swastika on the summit of the 18,500-foot (5,640 metre) Mount Elbruz; on the 25th Mozdok was captured, and on 6 September Novorossisk, the last Russian naval base on the Black Sea, fell. Case Blue was apparently working, and total defeat of the enemy seemed imminent. In such circumstances the physical possession of Stalingrad had little relevance; few soldiers would willingly risk death or injury in the sort of pointless street fighting to which all the lessons of Warsaw pointed that tanks should never be committed, let alone at the moment of victory.

Such optimism, while understandable, was unfounded. For some time Hitler had apparently attached as much importance to the capture of Stalingrad as he had to that of the Caucasus oilfields, and now that the Red Army clearly intended denying him the former, he must needs have it, the more so as the city bore the name of his arch-enemy. All of von Paulus' Sixth Army, and a large part of the Fourth Panzer Army as well, was committed to the struggle whose mounting ferocity sucked in reserves and supplies originally earmarked for Army Group A. The story of this terrible battle, a Second World War re-enactment of Verdun set in a landscape of rubble mountains and gutted, skeletal buildings, was to become an epic of endurance for both sides.

For the Panzerwaffe and Sturmartillerie the holocaust meant that immediate consideration had to be given to the production of armoured vehicles which were purpose-built for street-fighting or the reduction of fortifications, although none was completed in time to take part in the campaign. Of these the most successful was the Grizzly Bear (Brummbär) assault howitzer, based on the PzKw IV chassis. This vehicle possessed 100mm frontal armour and was armed with a 150mm L/12 howitzer, giving it a far heavier punch than the standard assault artillery weapon systems. The Grizzly Bears began reaching the front in April 1943, serving in the heavy infantry gun companies of Panzergrenadier regiments or forty-five-strong assault battalions which remained at the disposal of army commanders. An outgrowth of the same idea employed a 380mm naval rocket projector mounted on a Tiger chassis and known as the Sturmtiger. The weapon was capable of firing a 761-lb spin-stabilized missile up to 6,000 yards. Very few were built, and by the time they appeared in 1944 the German Army was engaged in defensive battles and had little use for such equipment. Hitler is also said to have recommended construction of a Ramtiger intended to bulldoze buildings to the ground with their defenders still inside, but that particular fantasy was never given substance.

In the Caucasus, too, the early promise of the German offensive proved illusory. As the open steppe gave way to the wooded foothills of the main range, resistance became stiffer the further the Germans advanced. By the end of August Kleist's First Panzer Army of eight divisions was outnumbered by five to one and was still over 300 miles (480 kms) distant from its final objective of Baku. List, concerned that Army Group A was already over-extended, declined to comply with a directive from the Führer that would have aggravated the situation still further, and on 6 September was dismissed for his trouble. Hitler, already Supreme Commander of the German Armed Forces and Commander-in-Chief of the Army, now added personal command of Army Group A to his list of responsibilities until 21 November, when he handed over the army group to Kleist, appointing Mackensen to command the First Panzer Army.

Despite his difficulties, Kleist believed that he could have reached all his objectives had his forces not been weakened by the demands of Army Group B at Stalingrad, coupled with an acute shortage of fuel. This left entire armoured formations stalled for days on end, dependent on the long, trudging lines of camel trains, heavily laden with jerricans on their panniers.

In September, following the failure of a determined attempt to take Stalingrad by storm, Halder advised Hitler that the Sixth Army should be pulled out of the city. He was promptly relieved of his post. His replacement was General Kurt Zeitzler, a staff officer who had shown exceptional ability during the Polish and French campaigns and had served as Kleist's Chief of Staff during Barbarossa.

One of the points which Halder had been trying to get across to the Führer, unsuccessfully, was that the Sixth Army was itself in mortal danger of encirclement, as its flanks were covered by the over-extended and under-equipped Third Romanian Army to the north and by the equally stretched Fourth Romanian Army to the south. Manstein, who had returned to the Leningrad sector after his Eleventh Army had cleared the Crimea and taken Sebastopol, had little regard for the soldierly qualities of Germany's allies and believed that the Russians would soon recognize Hitler's fixation on Stalingrad and turn it to their own advantage.

And so it transpired. While Hitler's attention was held by the struggle at Stalingrad and by a diversionary attack on the Rzhev sector of the front, Zhukov and Vasilevskii set about preparing their strategic response, which they code-named Operation Uranus. In the north this involved South-West Front, now commanded by General Nikolai Vatutin, breaking out of the bridgeheads which it had retained on the right bank of the Don with the Fifth Tank Army (I and XXVI Tank Corps) and Twenty-First Army, including the IV Tank Corps, while in the south General Andrei Yeremenko's Stalingrad Front went over to the offensive with three armies, spearheaded by the IV and XIII Mechanized Corps; simultaneously, Rokossovsky's Don Front would mount holding actions between these major thrusts.

At 0730 on 19 November a hurricane bombardment heralded the attack of South-West Front, which burst through the Third Romanian Army, leaving five of its divisions isolated in a pocket. The following morning Stalingrad Front swamped or brushed aside the resistance of the Fourth Romanian Army. Sweeping on across the snow-covered landscape, the waves of T-34s from both Fronts converged on Kalach, were they effected a junction on 23 November, having fended off local counter-attacks by the 16th

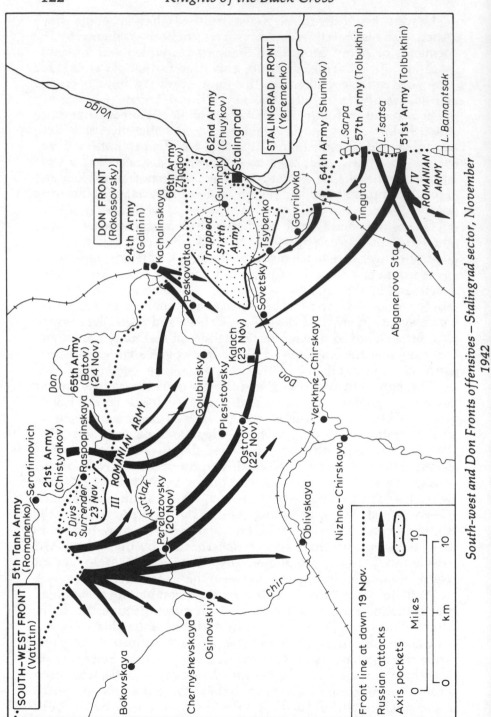

South-west and Don Fronts offensives – Stalingrad sector, November 1942

STALINGRAD FRONT (Yeremenko)

DON FRONT (Rokossovsky)

SOUTH-WEST FRONT (Vatutin)

Volga

62nd Army (Chuykov)
Stalingrad
66th Army (Zhadov)
24th Army (Galinin)
Kachalinskaya
Gumrak
Peskovatka
Trapped Sixth Army
Sovetsky
Tsybenko
Gavrilovka
64th Army (Shumilov)
L. Sarpa
57th Army (Tolbukhin)
L. Tsatsa
51st Army (Tolbukhin)
L. Bamantsak
Tinguta
IV ROMANIAN ARMY
Abganerovo Sta.

65th Army (Batov) (24 Nov)
Don
Golubinsky
Plesistovsky
Kalach (23 Nov)
Verkhne–Chirskaya
Don

21st Army (Chistyakov)
Raspopinskaya
5 Divs Surrender 23 Nov
III ROMANIAN ARMY
Kurtlak
Perelazovsky (20 Nov)
Ostrov (22 Nov)
Nizhne–Chirskaya

5th Tank Army (Romanenko)
Serafimovich
Bokovskaya
Chernyshevskaya
Osinovskiy
Chir
Oblivskaya

Front line at dawn 19 Nov.
Russian attacks
Axis pockets

Miles
km
0   10
0   10

and 24th Panzer Divisions on the way. With startling ease Zhukov had managed to throw a ring around the German Sixth Army, and part of the Fourth Panzer Army as well.

Paulus requested permission to break out to the west and was supported in this by Weichs, the commander of Army Group B, and Zeitzler, the Army's new Chief of General Staff. For a brief moment it seemed as though Hitler would give his approval, but at this point the braggart Goering announced that the Luftwaffe would supply all of Paulus' requirements by air. This was an absurd boast, since these were set at 600 tons (609,600 kg) per day whereas the total lift available by transport aircraft amounted to only 300 tons (304,800 kg), but it was enough for Hitler to declare that the Sixth Army would hold all its ground while operations to relieve it were organized. In the event, the average amount flown into the Stalingrad perimeter amounted to less than a hundred tons (101,600 kg) tons per day despite the suicidal courage of the air crews.

The officer Hitler sent for to control the relief operations was von Manstein, who was instructed to take under command the Sixth Army, the Fourth Panzer Army and the Fourth Romanian Army, thereby forming Army Group Don. But not even Manstein could make bricks without straw, and as most of these forces were either besieged or had been badly mauled by the Russian offensive, he was forced to wait until such reinforcements as could be scraped together reached the front; these included the LVII Panzer Corps, drawn from Army Group A, and 17th Panzer Division, released from OKW reserve. In due course a force of thirteen divisions was assembled, and these, commanded by Hoth and spearheaded by the 6th, 17th and 23rd Panzer Divisions, were to penetrate the seventy-five miles (120 kms) which separated the restored German line from the Stalingrad perimeter, the code-name for the operation being Wintergewitter (Winter Storm); concurrently, the besieged garrison was to break out and advance towards the relief force on receipt of the key signal Donnerschlag (Thunderclap).

Hoth began his advance on 12 December and at first made good progress but by the 18th had been brought to a halt on the line of the Myshkova river by the Second Guards Army, rushed into the area for this purpose by *Stavka*. Manstein instructed Paulus to implement Donnerschlag but the latter chose instead to interpret literally a recent Führer Directive to the effect that he must remain in his existing positions. Only thirty-five miles (56 km) now separated the two groups but there was nothing more Manstein could do.

Few harboured any doubts that the situation would get much worse before it got better. There was, however, some comfort to be drawn from a series of dashing actions fought by General von Knobelsdorff's XLVIII Panzer Corps on Hoth's immediate left, which demonstrated in no uncertain manner that the Panzerwaffe had lost none of its expertise. This formation, lying in reserve behind the Third Romanian Army, had got off to a very bad start during Uranus, the counter-attack of the 13th Panzer Division and the 1st Romanian Armoured Division starting late and making no impact. The commander of the former provided an interesting excuse for the delayed advance of his panzer regiment, alleging that mice, seeking a comfortable winter home, had taken up residence in the tanks and started eating the electrical wiring! Be that as it may, the affair cost the then corps commander and his chief of staff their jobs, although the two armoured formations were eventually able to cover the withdrawal of the shattered Romanian army back to the line of the Chir, a tributary of the Don, remaining under its control until it was replaced by an *ad hoc* collection of German formations known as Operational Group Hollidt. The XLVIII Panzer Corps was reconstituted under Knobelsdorff with the 11th Panzer Division, drawn from OKH reserve, 336th Infantry Division and a Luftwaffe Field Division.

At this period the 11th Panzer Division possessed a brilliant commander in Major-General Hermann Balck, a former light infantryman and veteran of World War I and the Reichsheer. Balck was a firm believer in 'saddle-orders', taking his place with whichever of his groups was to make the main effort and visiting the regiments involved several times a day. While operations were in progress, he maintained contact with his staff through a radio link to divisional headquarters, which remained static some miles to the rear. He was also a convinced advocate of the value of night marches. 'For weeks on end the division moved by night and before dawn was at the very spot where the enemy was weakest, waiting to attack him an hour before he was ready to move. Such tactics called for unheard-of efforts, but saved lives, as the attack proper cost very few casualties, thanks to the Russians having been taken completely by surprise.'* The hallmark of Balck's battles was an attack directed into the enemy's rear, often while he was making his own attack. On one occasion the twenty-five tanks remaining to Panzer Regiment 15 destroyed sixty-five Russian tanks without loss to themselves in this manner, the

* Balck's comment to Major-General von Mellenthin, contained in *Panzer Battles*.

latter being under the impression that the Germans were their own second wave. The Soviet Fifth Tank Army, which had crossed the Chir full of confidence after its easy victory over the Romanians, was similarly savaged by 11th Panzer on 8th, 12th, 17th and 19th December until its offensive capacity was, for the moment, written off.

The XLVIII Panzer Corps was to have joined in the final phase of Hoth's advance to the Stalingrad perimeter had this proved successful. However, on 16 December South-West Front and Golikov's Voronezh Front opened Operation Saturn, a major offensive aimed at the Eighth Italian Army, holding the line north of Operational Group Hollidt. After three days the Italians were routed and Soviet armour began streaming west and south-west through the gap, rendering the Chir salient untenable; simultaneously Hoth came under intense pressure and by 29 December had been forced back to Kotelnikovo, from whence his relief attempt had started.

Suddenly the stakes in the game were higher than ever before, for if Zhukov could close the Rostov bottleneck, it would not only be the Sixth Army which found itself inside an iron ring but the whole of Army Group A as well.

Manstein's primary task, therefore, had become one of holding open a corridor through which von Kleist's troops could be hurriedly withdrawn from the Caucasus. This was no easy matter and involved constant use of his mobile formations to shore up one crumbling sector of the front after another.

Typical of these actions was that fought by the 11th Panzer Division on 25 January 1943 at Manutchskaya, a village located at the junction of the River Manich with the Don, only twenty miles (32 km) from Rostov. Here the Russians had seized a bridgehead which it was essential to eliminate, but a probe on the 24th revealed that they had dug in and concealed their tanks among the houses in the southern half of the village, where they were difficult to spot and deal with. Balck therefore decided to flush them out with a simulated tank attack on their northern perimeter, using his armoured cars and half-tracks under cover of a smoke screen. This had the desired effect, and once the Russian tanks were moving, the divisional artillery, less one battery which continued to fire smoke shells to mask the diversion, concentrated the weight of its fire on a pre-selected break-in point at the southern edge of the village. Through this gap burst Panzer Regiment 15, destroying its opponents in a sharp little battle among the houses. The rest of the defenders took to their heels but were pursued by the Panzergrenadiers and cut down. German

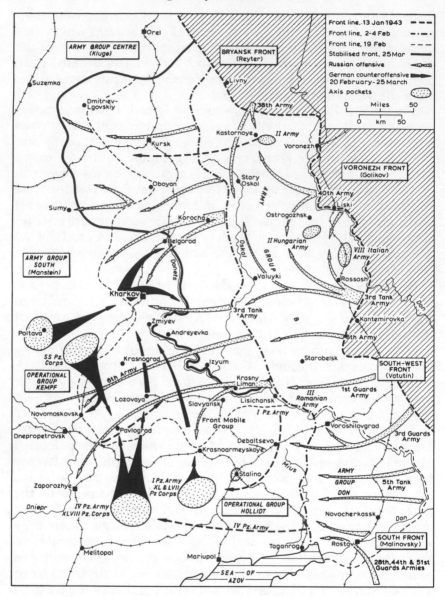

Russian winter offensive 1942-3 and Manstein's counter-stroke

losses amounted to one killed and fourteen wounded; Russian casualties exceeded 500, and twenty of their tanks were destroyed. Further local successes were gained by the first Tigers to enter service in southern Russia, manned by sPzAbt 503, but the strategic pattern of the campaign was beyond salvation.

Hitler was now reconciled to the loss of the Caucasus, and while the First Panzer Army streamed steadily through Rostov, the Seventeenth Army retired into the Kuban peninsula, whence it was evacuated by sea to the Crimea. And still the hammer blows fell. On 15 January Voronezh Front began a fresh offensive, this time against the Second Hungarian Army, to the north of the routed Italians. A gap 175 miles wide was ripped in the front through which two Soviet Fronts rolled westward across the steppe, turning the flank of the Second German Army and compelling it to abandon Voronezh itself on the 26th. On 2 February the inferno of Stalingrad was finally extinguished when von Paulus surrendered. About 120,000 of his men had died in the fighting but the human tragedy did not end there, for of the 91,000 who marched into captivity only 5,000 saw Germany again, and that after many years. Equipment losses during the siege and as a result of the Russian counter-offensives included approximately 3,500 tanks and self-propelled mountings of various types, 3,000 aircraft, 12,000 guns and mortars and 75,000 vehicles. Three panzer divisions, the 14th, 16th and 24th, were lost in the general surrender but were re-formed in France later in the year.

The only crumb of comfort was that, if the Russians had not directed so much of their effort into storming the embattled fortress, they could probably have eliminated Army Group A as well, but not even the versatile Dr Goebbels could hope to minimize the scale of the defeat sustained by Germany and her allies. A period of national mourning was ordered by a chastened Hitler, who admitted personal responsibility for the disaster, simultaneously expressing anger that the ungrateful Paulus, so recently elevated to the rank of field marshal, had not committed suicide.

Army Groups A and B were unified as a new Army Group South under Manstein, who flew to see Hitler on 6 February. To his surprise, the Führer sanctioned the abandonment of the Don basin and Rostov, albeit with the greatest reluctance, and approved the establishment of a defensive shoulder based on the line of the Mius, behind which the army group could re-organize and re-deploy.

Manstein was to comment that the extent of a general's ability could be measured by his capacity to divine his opponent's intentions, the further ahead the better. In the present circumstances he could see that the objective of Golikov's Voronezh Front was Kharkov, and he also guessed that once Vatutin's South-West Front had reached the Dniepr it would swing south towards the coast along the left bank of the river, isolating Army Group South in a huge pocket with the sea at its back. Bold as it was, the Russian plan was still subject to an inescapable rule of warfare, namely that the power of an offensive decreases in proportion to the distance it covers. Furthermore, while Soviet infantry formations were able to dispense with the sort of logistic backing enjoyed by their German and Western counterparts, this was obviously not true of their tank corps, and in this area lay the Achilles heel of the Red Army. Thus, although by the third week of February both Golikov and Vatutin had come a very long way against light opposition, they were now beginning to encounter tougher resistance so that, together, battle damage, breakdowns and fuel starvation had whittled away the strength of their tank spearhead. Vatutin's advance, for example, was being led by a mere 145 tanks, all short of fuel and dispersed over a wide area, while Golikov's condition was somewhat worse.

In contrast, although Manstein's First and Fourth Panzer Armies had been worn down by the recent fighting, reinforcements were beginning to arrive on his sector in the form of the Panzergrenadier Division *Grossdeutschland* and Waffen SS General Paul Hausser's SS Panzer Corps, consisting of the 1st SS Panzergrenadier Division *Leibstandarte Adolf Hitler*, 2nd SS Panzergrenadier Division *Das Reich* and 3rd SS Panzergrenadier Division *Totenkopf*, which, like *Grossdeutschland*, were panzer divisions in everything but name. Mellenthin mentions in his memoirs that all four newly arrived formations contained a Tiger battalion in their order of battle, but these were simply heavy companies which had been added to their existing panzer regiments, equipped with up to fifteen tanks.

This is not the place to debate the venomous reputation acquired by the Waffen SS, much of it by unfortunate if incorrect association with the Allgemeine SS who ran the concentration camps, although the taint of atrocity quite justifiably stuck to some formations. Nonetheless, at the time the majority of commanders were glad to have Waffen SS divisions placed at their disposal and Manstein himself referred to them as 'good comrades'. From the purely military standpoint, however, this creation of an armed Nazi élite denied the Army countless recruits

Colonel-General Georg-Hans Reinhardt commanded XLI Panzer Corps during the 1940 campaign in the West and Panzer Group 3 (later Third Panzer Army) during *Barbarossa*. In October 1944 he was appointed commander of Army Group Centre

Much of the Panzerwaffe's inherent strength lay in the initiative of its battlegroup leaders. It was, for example, thanks to the prompt counter-measures taken by General Walther Nehring that the Allies failed to capture Tunis in 1942. Nehring later commanded XXIV Panzer Corps, Fourth Panzer Army and First Panzer Army

Following his capture of Tobruk, the newly-promoted Field Marshal Erwin Rommel became a prisoner of his own ambition without making due allowance for the unresolved aspects of the Mediterranean sea-war

Panzergrenadier battlegroup on the move, 1943. The late model PzKw III is equipped as a command vehicle and mounts the splayed antenna which replaced the clumsy frame aerial

Profile of the PzKw IV after the 75mm L/24 howitzer had been replaced by a high velocity weapon. The continuing process of up-gunning and up-armouring left the foward suspension leaf-springs permanently bowed, causing the tank to yaw

General Heinz Guderian provided a stimulus for the development of the Panzerwaffe although his memoirs tend to denigrate the part played by several of his superiors if their opinions did not coincide with his own

Colonel-General Erich Raus began his military career in the Austro-Hungarian Army. His appointments included 6th Panzer Division in 1942, XLVII Panzer Corps in October 1943, Fourth Panzer Army the following month, First Panzer Army in April 1944 and Third Panzer Army in August 1944. Although virtually unknown in the West, he earned the reputation of being an energetic yet capable and steady panzer leader

Guderian produced amusing crew manuals for use with the Tiger and Panther. This page from the *Pantherfibel* (Panther Primer) deals with the problems of tank recognition

r Troja — wie's das Schicksal will —
af einst auf freiem Feld Achill
e Königin der Amazonen.
Zweikampf, denkt er, könnt sich lohnen.
wundernd, aber dennoch kalt,
sieht er ihre Wohlgestalt.
och da kein Mensch ein ganzer Engel,
um hatte selbst die Fürstin Mängel.
och davon muß — um die zu sehn —
an wie Achilles was verstehn.

Historie bringt uns Kleist in ernstem Gewande
r geklehtert jedoch sie als Histörchen erscheint.

Es gilt bei jedem Panzertyp
Genau das gleiche Grundprinzip.
Als erstes lernt schon der Rekrut:
Bleib klar im Kopf! Hab ruhig Blut!
Als zweites: Laß den Gegner ran,
Bis man ihn sicher knacken kann!
Doch kneift der Kerl, dann immer feste,
Dann rück ihm schleunigst auf die Weste.
Was ist's für einer? Schau gut hin!
Wann kann er Dich, wann kannst Du ihn!
Steckbrief und: Wo ist er zu packen?
Die schwachen Stellen mußt Du knacken!
Ein jeder Panzer ist zu brechen,
Kennst Du den Typ und seine Schwächen.
Dazu sieh Dir die Panzerbeschuß- und Erkennungs-
tafeln an, die am Schluß der Fibel eingeheftet sind.

Colonel-General Hans Hübe is best remembered for the skill with which his trapped First Panzer Army fought its way through the encircling Soviet formations in the spring of 1944. He was killed in an air crash only days after completing this extremely difficult operation

Field Marshal Walter Model was Hitler's favourite trouble-shooter in 1944, serving in succession as commander of Army Groups North, North Ukraine and Centre before taking over from von Kluge as Commander-in-Chief West. He believed that no German field marshal should be captured alive and committed suicide when his Army Group B was encircled in the Ruhr Pocket

General Hermann Balck displayed the same brilliance at the tactical and operative levels of war that von Manstein did at the strategic. He drove his troops hard and gained numerous victories on the Eastern Front, but real success eluded him in the West

The up-gunning of the assault gun gave the vehicle a valuable anti-tank capability. This troop are seen in action on the Eastern Front in 1943

The Jagdpanzer IV, otherwise known as 'Guderian's Duck', was issued to the tank destroyer units of the panzer divisions. It was based on the PzKw IV chassis and armed with a 75mm L/70 gun; the *Saukopf* or Pig's Head mantlet is clearly visible

The Brummbär (Grizzly Bear) was based on the PzKw IV chassis and armed with a 150mm L/12 howitzer. It served in the Heavy Infantry Gun Companies of Panzergrenadier Regiments as well as in 45-strong Assault Battalions which were committed at the discretion of senior commanders. This example was captured in Italy

This photograph of a Tiger E captured in Tunisia is of interest in that it shows the Feifel air filter system, evolved for use in hot, dusty climates

Saddle Orders. The German Army placed more reliance on verbal as opposed to written orders than its opponents. In addition, panzer leaders were given 'long distance tickets' and permitted to use their own initiative as to how they secured their objectives

Lieutenant-Colonel Dr Franz Bäke commanded a unique Heavy Tank Regiment which inflicted shattering losses on its opponents. The regiment consisted of one Tiger and one Panther battalion, plus supporting arms

Waffen SS Colonel-General Josef Dietrich was once described by von Rundstedt as being 'decent but stupid', although neither adjective is entirely apposite. His Sixth Panzer Army took few of its designated objectives during the Battle of the Bulge, although during the operations near Lake Balaton in 1945 he executed a difficult re-deployment of the army with some skill

The Tiger B, otherwise variously known as the King or Royal Tiger, was armed with an 88mm L/71 gun and represented a determined attempt to put Germany ahead once and for all in the gun/armour race with Soviet designers, but the vehicle's size and weight of 68.7 tons imposed serious constraints on its operational use

The sleek Jagdpanther provides an interesting contrast in tank destroyer design with the American M36, although the latter possessed the advantage of all-round traverse of NCO calibre, while the self-sacrificial style of fighting adopted by the Waffen SS invariably led to severe personnel casualties and heavy loss of equipment at a time when it could be afforded least.

In October 1943 *Leibstandarte, Das Reich* and *Totenkopf* were all officially declared panzer divisions, as were four more SS Panzergrenadier divisions: 5th *Wiking*, 9th *Hohenstaufen* (the family name of the first German emperors), 10th *Frundsberg* (a notable freebooter from the Landsknecht era) and 12th *Hitlerjugend*.

On 16 February Golikov captured Kharkov. Hitler had given orders that it should be held to the last man by the SS Panzer Corps but Hausser was not seeking the sort of martyrdom which had befallen Paulus at Stalingrad and pulled his men out. Very probably anyone other than an SS general would have paid for such an act of heresy with his life, but the very fact that it was a favoured Nazi officer who had committed this sin showed how thin confidence in the Führer's military judgement had become.

The following day Hitler paid a personal visit to Manstein's headquarters at Zaporozhe, demanding to know what was going on. Manstein explained to him that, now Hausser's corps was free of its defensive role, it would form a most welcome addition to his own counter-stroke force, which would deliver its blow when he was satisfied that Golikov and Vatutin had run themselves into the ground; *Stavka* would then rapidly discover that the great prize of Kharkov was untenable. He then went into the detailed planning of what was to be the German Army's last successful application of *Vernichtungsgedanke* of the war. The right flank would be protected by Operational Group Hollidt, which would continue to resist the attacks of Malinovsky's South Front along the line of the Mius; likewise, on the left flank Golikov's probes west of Kharkov would be contained by another *ad hoc* formation known as Operational Group Kempf. Within this framework the operation would proceed as follows:

Phase I. The SS Panzer Corps and XLVIII Panzer Corps, operating under the control of Hoth's Fourth Panzer Army, were already assembling respectively at Krasnograd and Zaporozhe and would converge on Pavlograd, isolating the heads of Vatutin's columns. Further east, the XL and LVII Panzer Corps, under the command of von Mackensen's First Panzer Army, would advance northwards into the Russian flank, driving South-West Front back across the Donets.

Phase II. Both Panzer Armies would then drive into the flank of Voronezh Front, recovering Kharkov in the process.

Phase III. The offensive would continue in a northerly direction, eliminating those Russian forces remaining in the Kursk area and effecting a junction with Schmidt's Second Panzer Army, which would be committed by Army Group Centre at the appropriate moment.

Manstein's plan, simple yet as comprehensive in its scope at Sichelschnitt, ensured a major German victory before a single soldier crossed the start-line, for although only 500 tanks remained to the Panzerwaffe along the entire Front, 350 of these were under his immediate control and would give him a superiority of seven to one at the point of contact, while the Luftwaffe had three times as many aircraft available locally as had the Red Air Force. There was nothing Hitler could add, and on the 19th he left. Next day, with Vatutin's tanks only twenty miles (32 km) from his headquarters, Manstein gave orders for the offensive to begin.

'The terrain was almost completely open,' wrote von Mellenthin, still with the XLVIII Panzer Corps, 'slightly undulating and cut here and there by narrow brooks which were then completely frozen. It resembled the area west of Stalingrad, and was very much like the North African desert. Russian columns streaming back to the north were visible at a distance of eight to twelve miles 10.8-19.2 km and were taken under effective artillery fire at that range.'

More columns were stalled for want of fuel, while those that did fight back quickly exhausted their ammunition and were ridden over in the best cavalry tradition. By the end of February all that remained of Vatutin's command had fled across the Donets, leaving behind 615 tanks, 400 guns, 23,000 dead and 9,000 prisoners. Golikov had already contributed his Third Tank Army in a vain attempt to retrieve his neighbour's fortunes, but this was caught re-deploying onto its new axis and pounded into scrap-iron by the Luftwaffe's ground-attack wings. Desperately he tried to establish a defensive front south of Kharkov as Hoth's panzer corps swung into Phase II without pause, but to no avail. The city was isolated on 11 March and on the 15th was once more in German hands. Operational Group Kempf had now also gone over to the offensive and, spearheaded by Panzergrenadier Division *Grossdeutschland*, had re-captured Belgorod on the 18th. By this time Golikov had lost 600 tanks, 500 guns and 40,000 of his men. Only the arrival of the *rasputitsa*, turning good, hard, frozen going to deep, clinging mud, prevented the implementation of Phase III, and this left a huge salient in the line, a hundred miles wide and seventy deep (160 × 112 km) centred on Kursk.

Both sides were now completely exhausted and welcomed the

break in operations as a chance to renew their strength. The disaster which had overtaken South-West and Voronezh Fronts had taken the edge off the Russian victory at Stalingrad and had again caused *Stavka* to doubt its ability to sustain deep penetration operations in the German manner. The German propaganda apparatus made much of Manstein's success in restoring the integrity of the Eastern Front, while von Mellenthin did no more than speak for a great body of professional opinion when he commented that, 'It may be questioned whether any achievement of generalship in World War Two can approach the successful extrication of the Caucasus armies and the subsequent riposte to Kharkov.'

Yet if there was indeed cause to celebrate in Berlin, there were also uneasy moments when the thoughts of those who knew turned to North Africa, where the successes of the previous summer had also curdled. The difference was that Germany did not have a Manstein in Africa, and every day the news grew worse.

7. The Aeschylus Factor

On 24 October 1940 Major-General Wilhelm Ritter von Thoma reported to the Führer on his return from a fact-finding mission to North Africa. The previous month Germany's Italian allies had launched an invasion of Egypt from Libya but had terminated their advance at Sidi Barrani, sixty miles (96 km) short of the main British defensive position at Mersa Matruh, and there dug themselves in. The offensive, though virtually unopposed, had done much to restore Italian morale which had hitherto suffered seriously at the hands of the British 7th Armoured Division, and while there was no suggestion at this stage that German troops be committed to the campaign, the possibility was certainly open for discussion, at least at OKW.

In von Thoma's opinion the overriding consideration was that of logistics, a particularly difficult question since the Royal Navy controlled the Mediterranean, and one which made it impossible to support a large German contingent as well as a major portion of the Italian Army in North Africa. If Germany was to send a contingent, the general concluded, it should be drawn from the Panzerwaffe and consist of four divisions; anything smaller could not guarantee success, and anything larger could not be maintained in the field. As events transpired, this was to prove a remarkably accurate assessment. For the moment, however, Hitler was prepared to place only one panzer division on standby for service in North Africa, and since the attitude of the Italians to German participation was distinctly lukewarm, even this was stood down after a few weeks.

On 9 December the British went over to the offensive. Commanded by Lieutenant-General Richard O'Connor, the grossly outnumbered Western Desert Force promptly initiated a series of startling victories that, during the next two months, utterly destroyed an Italian army of ten divisions, took 130,000 prisoners and captured huge quantities of equipment, including 380 tanks and 845 guns. The whole of Cyrenaica fell into British hands and all that remained between O'Connor's advance guard and Tripoli was a single Italian division. Whether the British

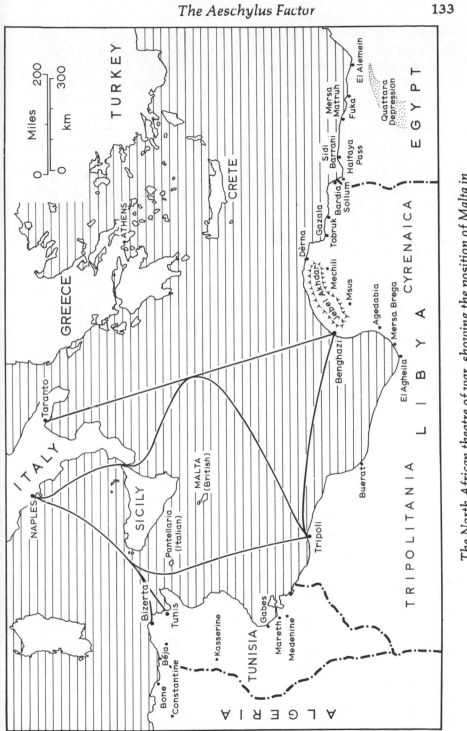

The North African theatre of war, showing the position of Malta in relation to the Axis sea communications

should have gone on to occupy the remainder of Libya has remained a subject for discussion ever since. At the time this did not seem necessary as the rout of the Italians and the occupation of one of their provinces as a buffer zone seemed to have removed the threat to Egypt; moreover Churchill, who could be almost as great a burden to his commanders as Hitler and Stalin were to theirs, was constantly urging General Sir Archibald Wavell, the Commander-in-Chief Middle East, to send a goodly proportion of his slender resources to the aid of the Greeks.

On 5 February Hitler, not being privy to British thoughts on a continued advance on Tripoli, again offered Mussolini military assistance, and this time the Italian dictator accepted. A small force was despatched with the strictly limited objectives of containing the British within their advance positions at El Agheila, providing a stiffening and technical expertise for the Italian troops and ultimately recovering the province of Cyrenaica for Italy in conjunction with the Italians.

The first German troops to arrive in Africa landed at Tripoli on 14 February 1941 and belonged to the 5th Light Division, a formation based on units drawn from the 3rd Panzer Division and which itself became the 21st Panzer Division in October. This was followed in April by the 15th Panzer Division, and together these two formed the Deutsches Afrika Korps. A motorized infantry formation known as the *Afrika* Division was raised locally from independent units in August and on 27 November was re-named the 90th Light Division, despite the fact that it lacked an armoured element. These formations were known collectively as Panzer Group Africa from 15 August, being elevated to the status of Panzer Army Africa on 30 January 1942 by the addition of six Italian divisions, one of which was armoured. The only other German formations to serve in the desert phase of the North African war were the 164th Light Division, consisting of infantry drawn from the garrison of Crete, and the Ramke Parachute Demonstration Brigade, which arrived in the summer of 1942. This represented about two per cent of the German Army's overall strength, and five to ten per cent of that of the Panzerwaffe.

The officer appointed to command this force was forty-nine-year-old Lieutenant-General Erwin Rommel, who had commanded the 7th Panzer Division with such dash during the campaign in France. Rommel had basked in Hitler's favour ever since the Führer had read and enjoyed his textbook *Infanterie Grieft An (Infantry Assault)*, and at one stage had even commanded his personal bodyguard, the Führerbegleitabteilung. None of this did much to endear him to Brauchitsch and Halder, especially as he displayed much the same sort of impatience with authority as did Guderian; Halder actively disliked him and made no bones about it, calling him a *parvenu*. No doubt relying on the strength of his own position at Court to protect him, Rommel decided from the outset that he would not only act independently of his nominal superior, Marshal Gariböldi, the Italian Commander-in-Chief in North Africa, but also set aside the limitations already set by OKH if he thought fit.

Before describing the course his operations were to take, it is necessary to emphasize a number of considerations that were peculiar to the conduct of this campaign. There were indeed large areas of hard, level going that were ideal arenas in which the major armoured formations of both sides enjoyed complete freedom of manoeuvre, but the desert also contained a wide variety of landscapes which inhibited the progress of mechanized forces, including treacherous saltmarshes, deep wadis, boulder fields, shifting dunes and the ancient sea cliffs which formed escarpments. Certain areas of this apparent wilderness were of critical importance, and it was in and around these that most of the decisive fighting took place. These included El Alamein, where the frontage between the coast and the impassable Qattara Depression was limited to forty miles (64 km), Halfaya Pass and Sollum on the Libyan/Egyptian frontier, which provided means of climbing the escarpment from the coastal plain, and the deep-water harbour of Tobruk, the best available between Tripoli and Alexandria, possession of which eased the logistic burden of either side. Particularly significant was the Benghazi Bulge: British possession of its airfields allowed convoys to run through the Mediterranean Narrows to Malta, but the Bulge was only too vulnerable to outflanking along the cross-country route Agedabia-Msus-Mechili and was therefore untenable in itself. Both armies operated from distant bases and consumed huge quantities of fuel and water, but the further they advanced the less reached them. Victorious armies had their advances terminated as much by supply difficulties as by enemy action; conversely, the closer an army retreated to its source of supply, the more troops it was able to maintain in the field. After a major engagement the defeated army could be pursued with only a fraction of the forces that had fought in the battle, and then only by stripping the transport from the formations left behind. Shortage of fuel haunted the thoughts of both sides and dictated the tempo of operations, which took the form of short but intense periods of action and much longer periods during which the level of hostilities was confined to patrol actions.

In Berlin, Brauchitsch had forbidden Rommel to take offensive action before the end of May; in Cairo, Wavell, whose intelligence sources had kept him briefed regarding the scale of the German build-up in Tripolitania, doubted whether he would be capable of it before then. Neither had allowed for the restless energy of the new German commander who was directing every unit of the 5th Light eastwards as soon as it landed, together with as many Italian units as he could muster.

Holding the British forward positions was Major-General M.D. Gambier-Parry's 2nd Armoured Division, recently arrived and completely inexperienced, equipped with the same worn-out light and cruiser tanks that had recently taken part in the defeat of the Italians; one of its armoured regiments was even equipped with wretched M.13s – otherwise known as 'tin coffins' – which had formed part of the spoils. In immediate reserve and with brigades based in Benghazi and Tobruk was another formation new to the desert, Major-General Leslie Morshead's 9th Australian Division. In overall command of the British troops holding Cyrenaica was Lieutenant-General Sir Philip Neame, O'Connor having returned to Egypt on sick leave.

Of course the 5th Light was also new to Africa but many of its men, particularly those manning the tanks of Panzer Regiment 5, were veterans of the Polish and French campaigns, and although the division's various units had not fought together before, they were soon to learn what Rommel expected of them. On 24 March an attack was made on the British position blocking the defile between the sea and the saltmarshes at El Agheila. The British withdrew to a similar defile at Mersa Brega, and this, too, was attacked on 31 March. This time the Germans were held by 2nd Armoured's infantry and artillery and would probably have been thrown back with some loss if Gambier-Parry had acted on a suggestion that his armoured brigade should mount a counter-attack. Instead, he relied too literally on standing orders which instructed him to fight a delaying action, and abandoned the position.

The 5th Light streamed through the defile, and Rommel immediately split the division into three battlegroups, using their mobility as a weapon in the best tradition of Blitzkrieg. The reconnaissance battalion drove north along the coast road, entering Benghazi unopposed on 4 April. Inland, two groups converged on Mechili, one by way of Sceleidima and Msus, which were also hastily evacuated, and the other through Ben Gania along a desert track which an Italian general histrionically described as a 'death trap,' although the Ariete Armoured Division also used it without coming to undue harm. Overhead flew Rommel in his Fieseler Storch, frequently landing beside the heads of his columns to tongue-lash officers who were not pushing on fast enough. By the time the 5th Light reached Mechili on 6 April the 2nd Armoured Division, fragmented, shedding broken-down tanks by the hour and suffering from communication and command difficulties, had ceased to exist as a fighting formation and although many of its individual units managed to work their way through the chaos, it was never re-formed. Gambier-Parry and his staff were surrounded and forced to surrender. On 7 April Neame was picked up by a German motor-cycle patrol; perhaps worst of all was the fact that sharing his unescorted car was O'Connor, sent forward by Wavell to retrieve the situation. O'Connor had declined to take over in the middle of a lost battle, although he agreed to act as Neame's adviser, and his capture at this juncture was most unfortunate for the British, most of whose senior commanders had yet to acquire his intuitive grasp of mechanized war at the operative level.

Meanwhile, the 9th Australian Division had withdrawn inside Tobruk's fortified perimeter and by 13 April had been cut off. The following day the 5th Light effected a penetration but ran onto a well-sited tank killing-ground, being forced to withdraw with the loss of seventeen tanks it could ill afford. On the 25th Halfaya Pass was taken, followed shortly after by Sollum, but a second attempt to capture Tobruk was repulsed after heavy fighting which reduced the German tank strength from seventy to thirty-five machines within a day. For the moment, the 5th Light had shot its bolt.

There remained the question of Rommel's flagrant disobedience. Brauchitsch was dumbfounded by the scale of his insubordination; Halder described him as a dangerous lunatic who had to be stopped, and even Hitler sent him a note advising caution. He could hardly be punished for recovering Cyrenaica and restoring Axis fortunes in the Middle East at such little cost, but Halder was determined that he should be reminded of his position and sent over his deputy, then von Paulus, to exercise a restraining influence for a while. Among his peers Paulus was known by the perceptive cognomen of *Cunctator*, and indeed his capacity for temporization was an important factor contributing directly to the catastrophe of Stalingrad, but in this instance he was undoubtedly right in persuading Rommel that he must remain on the strategic defensive. Rommel was to complain bitterly henceforth that OKH repeatedly denied him the resources which would have enabled him to obtain victory, forgetting that by definition his role was that of supporting actor in a secondary theatre.

For the British, the overwhelming priority now became the relief of Tobruk. A weak attempt to break through was made on 15 May and succeeded in re-capturing Halfaya Pass but was otherwise easily contained, although from Rommel's point of view a disturbing feature of the fighting around Fort Capuzzo was an evident reluctance on the part of his crews to engage the enemy's Matildas, whose thick castings could keep out anything the German tanks fired at them. When, on 27 May, he mounted an operation which re-captured the pass, he used the greater part of his tank strength to do so, although the armoured element of the tiny British garrison consisted of a single nine-tank Matilda squadron. The German gunners managed to put six of these out of action with damage to their tracks and running gear, but the squadron nonetheless inflicted startling loss and at one stage caused a retrograde movement in the German ranks when it instituted a local counter-attack of its own. This enraged Rommel to the extent that, whatever their previous achievements, he immediately sacked the commanders of the 5th Light Division, its panzer regiment and the tank battalion most affected, the last-mentioned also being court-martialled for his pains.

Having been substantially reinforced, Wavell made a further relief attempt on 15 June. By now Halfaya Pass had been fortified, its defences including a battery of 88mm dual-purpose anti-aircraft/anti-tank guns which shot an attacking Matilda squadron to pieces. Further south, Fort Capuzzo was captured but the anti-tank gunners holding Hafid Ridge more than held their own against the cruiser tanks of the 7th Armoured Brigade.

Rommel decided that next day he would send both his armoured formations round the enemy's exposed desert flank and strike into his rear, but near Fort Capuzzo Panzer Regiment 8 of the 15th Panzer Division ran straight into the Matildas of the 7th Royal Tank Regiment and was forced to withdraw after fifty of its eighty tanks had been knocked out in a furious exchange. The 5th Light had better luck against the 7th Armoured Brigade, which was losing cruisers through breakdown at such an alarming rate, especially the recently arrived Crusaders, that it would have to retire the following day. This put an end to Wavell's hopes of relieving the embattled fortress, and throughout the 17th he withdrew his troops from the frontier area, covered by two Matilda squadrons which held off attempts by the 5th Light and 15th Panzer to drive north to the coast, so trapping his most advanced units inside a pocket. British tank losses during the three days of fighting amounted to twenty-seven cruisers and sixty-four Matildas, the majority through break-down; the total would have been lower but for one commander's muddled understanding of the administration of a tank battle, which resulted in the abandonment of vehicles requiring minor running repairs. The Germans retained the battlefield and, although approximately one hundred of their tanks had been put out of action through various causes, the vast majority of these were recovered, only twelve being completely written off.

It was now Churchill's turn to be extremely angry. The senior British commanders involved in the fiasco were relieved of their posts, among them Wavell, who was replaced as Commander-in-Chief Middle East by General Sir Claude Auchinleck. With the benefit of hindsight it is possible to see that the Afrika Korps' successes stemmed not simply from the ability of its commander, nor even from the undeniable expertise acquired by the Panzerwaffe as a whole, but also from the fact that its opponents were as inherently flawed as any of the armies encountered by the Wehrmacht thus far, for after O'Connor's virtuoso performance against the Italians the British lapsed into a period of unorthodoxy which lasted over a year, thereby compounding their inexperience of fighting at the operative level. This manifested itself most obviously in the practice of dispersion as advocated by Lawrence of Arabia, and especially dispersion of divisional artillery and anti-tank resources in quasi-independent columns, the result being that it was generally the Germans who were the stronger at the point of contact, since they fought together and in balanced formations. Yet notwithstanding the faults of their commanders, the British excelled in the virtues of regimental soldiering, being courageous, tough and incredibly stubborn fighters with a high *esprit de corps*. Those who had fought them before knew that, while military logic might dictate that an engagement must end in their inevitable defeat, the reality was that the result could never be guaranteed. For their part, the British long suspected that they were being outgunned in the tank battle, although it was the Panzerwaffe's sword-and-shield combination of tanks, anti-tank guns and tank-destroyers that was really causing the damage. Not until the late summer of 1942 did the first up-gunned versions of the PzKw IV arrive in the desert, followed by the shipment of 88mm-armed Tigers to Tunisia at the end of the year, but neither were present in sufficient numbers to affect the issue. It was in anti-tank guns that the Germans possessed a marked superiority, although the British 25-pdr also proved to be an outstanding tank killer, despite the fact that it had not been designed for this role.

Following the June battle there was little further activity along the frontier for the next five months. In September Rommel led a reconnaissance in force into Egypt to ascertain the extent of British preparations for a renewed offensive. He failed to discover anything significant and on his return set about preparing an attack of his own which was to be mounted against the eastern perimeter of the Tobruk defences.

Meanwhile, the Royal Navy continued to wreak such havoc in the sea lanes that barely sufficient supplies reached North Africa to keep pace with the daily consumption of the Axis armies. On the night of 8/9 November this activity reached its climax when an entire convoy of seven ships was sent to the bottom by Force K, based at Malta, although its escort heavily outnumbered the attackers. The indirect influence of sea-power on the land battle was felt at once, as only 2,500 (2,540,000) tons of fuel were delivered that month. Strict rationing was immediately introduced and the attack on Tobruk was postponed; worse still, when Auchinleck struck on 18 November, Rommel remained critically short of fuel during the ensuing battle.

Auchinleck's forces in the Western Desert were now known as the Eighth Army and were commanded by General Sir Alan Cunningham. Two corps took part in the offensive, which was code-named Crusader, the XIII under Godwin-Austin and the XXX under Norrie. The XIII Corps consisted of two infantry divisions and a tank brigade, its function being to contain the Axis garrisons of the fortified positions on the frontier and proceed along the coastal route towards Tobruk. Further south the XXX Corps, including the 7th Armoured and 1st South African Divisions, was to sweep across the desert and into the rear areas of the enemy's siege lines, writing down the Axis armour as it did so. Simultaneously the Tobruk garrison, now consisting of the British 70th Division and a tank brigade – the 9th Australian Division having been relieved by sea some time previously – was to effect a large-scale break-out towards the relief force, British tank strength, excluding light tanks, of which there were still a few about, amounted to 724 vehicles, of which 201 were heavily armoured infantry-support Matildas and Valentines, and while the remainder included a proportion of rickety old cruisers, this was more than balanced by the presence of the 165 brand-new and entirely reliable American M.3 Stuarts which equipped the 4th Armoured Brigade. To meet this threat

Rommel had available only 139 PzKw IIIs and 35 PzKw IVs, plus 50-60 PzKw Is and IIs and the 146 M.13s of the Ariete Armoured Division, which were inferior to the British cruisers.

The opening tank battle was one of the most confusing in history. At the outset the British felt confident of victory, but Rommel's postponed assault on Tobruk meant that his two panzer divisions were already deployed in the right place. Furthermore, the 7th Armoured Division's three armoured brigades (the 4th, 7th and 22nd) were widely dispersed and unable to support one another, so that the concentrated German armour fell upon each in turn and defeated it in detail, the epicentre of the battle being the desert airstrip of Sidi Rezegh. By the evening of 23 November the 7th Armoured Division was in complete disarray, the moral of the battle being later encapsulated by Rommel for the benefit of one of his senior prisoners to the effect that the British numerical superiority counted for nothing when employed in such a manner. The Germans, too, suffered an inevitable erosion of their strength and – a portent of things to come – at one stage the 21st Panzer Division actually ran its fuel tanks completely dry and was forced to remain in a position of stationary impotence until a convoy reached it during the hours of darkness. Such was the fluidity of the situation that the field headquarters of Major-General Ludwig Crüwell's Deutsches Afrika Korps was overrun, although the general himself was absent.

Elsewhere, the British XIII Corps continued its advance, and the Tobruk garrison's break-out made good progress in spite of tough opposition from the *Afrika* Division. The significance of these events was underestimated by Rommel who, on 24 November, instituted a drive of his own towards the Egyptian frontier with both panzer divisions and the Ariete, hoping that this indirect pressure applied to the British lines of communication would force them to abandon their offensive. Auchinleck's resolve, however, remained implacable, and when Cunningham became nervous about the wisdom of continuing Crusader, he was promptly replaced as the Eighth Army's commander by Major-General N.M. Ritchie. During the night of 26 November the 2nd New Zealand Division, spearheaded by the Matildas of the 1st Army Tank Brigade, effected a junction with the Tobruk garrison at Ed Duda. Horrified, Rommel raced back from the frontier only to find that the 7th Armoured Division had used the pause it had been granted to re-organize and refit and was now ready to renew the contest. It was this sort of gambling which was to keep Rommel out of the foremost ranks of panzer leaders, for all that had been achieved apart from the temporary re-assurance of the Axis frontier garrisons was the loss of yet more irreplaceable tanks in pointless skirmishes and the consumption of much priceless fuel.

Now Rommel strove simultaneously to keep the 7th Armoured Division at bay while he severed the link between the New Zealanders and Tobruk. Incredibly, he managed to achieve both for a period, but his strength was now failing with every day that passed. On 29 November the commander of the 21st Panzer Division, Major-General von Ravenstein, was captured; on 3 December two relief columns despatched to the troops still holding Bardia, Sollum and Halfaya Pass were ambushed and destroyed; two days later an attempt to mount a concentrated counter-attack against the 4th Armoured Brigade at Bir el Gubi was cancelled, partly because Ariete failed to turn up and partly because of mortal wounds sustained by Major-General Neumann-Silkow, commanding the 15th Panzer Division.

Rommel now reluctantly accepted the fact that to remain in the area of Tobruk was to invite the annihilation of his army, and on 7 December he began to withdraw westwards towards Gazala, the first step of a rapid but well-conducted retreat that would take him out of Cyrenaica. On 16 December an attempt by the 4th Armoured Brigade to cut him off at Tmimi was foiled by a combination of difficult going and the Stuart's greedy fuel-consumption, so making a replenishment necessary. A second attempt at Mechili almost caught the tail of his column, but once again petrol shortage inhibited a close pursuit. On 13 December forty-five reinforcement tanks were sunk during the crossing from Italy, but on the 19th twenty-two were landed at Benghazi and twenty-three more at Tripoli. With these and the few that had survived Crusader, Crüwell struck back at the 22nd Armoured Brigade near Agedabia on the 28th and again on the 30th, inflicting sharp checks which enabled the Afrika Korps to slip through the El Agheila bottleneck, assisted by worsening weather.

There was, however, no point in attempting to deny that Crusader had been a British victory, despite the fact that it had achieved its object only after a far harder fight than had been anticipated. Three hundred German and Italian tanks had been lost, but while the British loss amounted to a comparable 278, the majority of the latter were recoverable. Personnel casualties totalled 18,000 British and 38,000 Axis, including the now-isolated frontier garrisons, which were forced to surrender.

History now revealed its capacity for repeating itself. Just as a year earlier Wavell had been forced to send some of his best units to Greece, so now Auchinleck was compelled to strip his command and despatch urgently needed reinforcements to the Far East, where Japan had just entered the war as Germany's ally. A further convoy reached Tripoli on 5 January, bringing fifty-five tanks, twenty armoured cars, replacement anti-tank guns and more supplies than the Axis divisions in Libya had seen for months. Rommel's thoughts immediately turned to the offensive, and on 21 January, contrary to the orders of his immediate German and Italian superiors, he attacked with 110 tanks, gaining an immediate local superiority over the scattered units of the 1st Armoured Division, so that within a week he had recovered the Benghazi Bulge. This time the British reacted more quickly and were able to contain him along a line running south from Gazala to Bir Hacheim. Both sides began laying extensive minefields to protect their front and for four months prepared for the next round of the fighting.

In the meantime, on 2 December 1941 Hitler had appointed Luftwaffe Field Marshal Albert Kesselring Commander-in-Chief South, his primary task being 'to secure mastery of the air and sea in the area between Southern Italy and North Africa in order to secure communications with Libya and Cyrenaica and, in particular, to keep Malta in subjection'. Kesselring took the view that, for the present, the despatch of further mechanized formations to North Africa would be counter-productive since they could not be supplied, the principal thorns in the Axis' side being the British naval and air units based on Malta. He therefore persuaded Hitler, Goering and Rommel that, once Tobruk had been taken during the next offensive, all efforts should be directed to the capture of the island fortress, for in his opinion the possession of Tobruk without Malta made poor strategic sense if the intention was to defeat the British in the Middle East. Detailed planning for the invasion went ahead under the code-name Operation Herakles. This was to take the form of limited parachute drops to secure beachheads for a much larger sea-borne landing; for this the Panzerwaffe was required to form a special-purpose battalion equipped with captured KVs and heavily up-armoured PzKw IVs. The first phase consisted of an all-out air attack against the island, commencing in January 1942 and growing steadily in intensity until May, when the demands of the Russian Front and the need to provide air support for Rommel's fresh offensive absorbed much of the Luftwaffe's resources.

Rommel began his attack during the night of 26-7 May by sweeping round the open desert flank of the British line with both panzer divisions, Ariete and the 90th Light. His tank strength amounted to 560, of which 228 were Italian M 13śs and fifty the useless PzKw IIs. Of the remainder, 223 were up-armoured 50mm L/42 PzKw IIIs, plus nineteen newly arrived 50mm L/60 PzKw III Model Js, the most powerful tanks in his armoury, and forty 75mm L/24 PzKw IVs. Ritchie's Eighth Army, on the other hand, could field almost a thousand tanks, its two tank brigades possessing 110 Matildas and 166 Valentines between them while its armoured divisions, the 1st and the 7th, were equipped with 167 Grants, 149 Stuarts and 257 Crusaders, and a further armoured brigade was moving into the line with seventy-five Grants and seventy Stuarts. That the majority of these tanks were armed with either the obsolete 2-pdr or its equivalent the 37mm were offset by fact that the Grant – a British variant of the American M.3 Lee Medium Tank – was additionally armed with a 75mm gun in a sponson which, while it prevented the vehicle going hull-down, was for the moment the most powerful tank gun on the battlefield. It can thus be seen that neither numerically nor technically did Rommel's offensive apparently stand much chance of success.

Nonetheless, the German attack did achieve tactical surprise and was rewarded with a number of encouraging local victories, but by the afternoon of the 27th the situation had changed radically. The memoirs of Major-General von Mellenthin, then a major serving as Rommel's principal intelligence officer, tell of the Grant being a far more formidable fighting machine than anything the Afrika Korps had thus far encountered, of serious casualties inflicted on German tank units, of motor rifle regiments being overrun, of supply columns being cut off and pursued across the desert by marauding armoured cars, and of the British armour's counter-attacks being pressed to the very muzzles of the anti-tank guns. Rommel, who narrowly escaped capture while trying to visit the 90th Light, frankly admitted that he had not allowed for the Grant in his calculations and that his plans had misfired badly. When the two panzer divisions went into close leaguer near Bir el Harmat at last light, the Germans had lost more than a third of their tanks; the 15th Panzer Division was almost out of petrol and ammunition and had been reduced to twenty-nine fit tanks, although the fitters were working frantically on fourteen more; 21st Panzer was slightly better off with eighty tanks, but Ariete was still entangled in the minefields surrounding Bir Hacheim.

In the days that followed, Rommel found himself pinned back against the British minebelt and a fortified position held by an infantry brigade. Starved of supplies, including water, he told a captured British officer that unless supplies got through very quickly he would have to ask Ritchie for terms. It was, in fact, the despised Italians who came to his aid, when the Trieste Division succeeded in breaking through the minefields. Even so, inside 'the Cauldron', as the Afrika Korps' position had become known, there was nothing to be done except dig in, site the *PAK-fronts** to the best advantage and wait for Ritchie to administer the *coup de grâce*. Elsewhere Crüwell, who had handed over the DAK to Lieutenant-General Walther Nehring in March and was now commanding the static sector of the front, was captured when his Storch was shot down behind British lines on 29 May. Kesselring was visiting his headquarters at the time, and von Mellenthin, for the moment acting as Crüwell's operations officer, asked him to take over. 'Smiling Albert', who had served for many years in the artillery before transferring to the Luftwaffe, was amused to be offered a job by the major but commented that it would be improper for a field marshal to place himself at Rommel's disposal, even if the latter had recently been promoted to Colonel-General! Nevertheless, he consented to act as a temporary stop-gap when the worried von Mellenthin pointed out that the alternative was to appoint a senior Italian officer, although he and Rommel inevitably disagreed over a number of tactical issues.

The Afrika Korps' troubles were solved for it by its opponents. At the highest level the Eighth Army's conduct of the battle was marked by discussion and delay just when decisive action was needed, while lower down the scale the British were still suffering from the same fundamental faults that had troubled them during Crusader, namely dispersion and the apparent inability to co-ordinate their efforts. One of the options open to Ritchie is detailed in an interesting sketch-map contained in von Mellenthin's memoirs and headed 'Alternative Cauldron Plan'. This reveals the manner in which the Panzerwaffe would have handled the situation and shows the British XIII Corps (2nd South African and 10th Indian Divisions, plus 32nd Army Tank Brigade) mounting a holding attack against the northern shoulder of the Cauldron while the XXX Corps (1st and 7th Armoured Divisions and 5th Indian Division) swept round the southern end of the line and attacked Rommel's perimeter from the West, through the 150 Brigade box in his rear. This was not, apparently, a course which Ritchie found attractive, and no sooner had Rommel's re-supply been effected than most of the German

* Anti-tank gun screens; PAK = Panzer Abwehr Kanone

resources were devoted to the elimination of this position, which was stormed after intense fighting on 1 June.

It took until 5 June for Ritchie to mount two major but unconnected attacks against the Cauldron. To the north the 32nd Army Tank Brigade ran over an extensive minefield and was then engaged by anti-tank guns in unfavourable light and finally counter-attacked by the 21st Panzer Division, losing sixty Matildas and ten Valentines. On the eastern perimeter part of the 5th Indian Division secured a lodgement through which passed the 22nd Armoured Brigade, pushing Ariete off Aslagh Ridge. Once again, however, the German anti-tank gun screen held and the British were forced to retire with the loss of sixty more tanks. Sensing instinctively that he had now regained the initiative, Rommel counter-attacked with the 15th Panzer Division, overrunning the Indians' penetration and capturing their divisional artillery.

Next day he invested the Free French contingent in its fortified box at Bir Hacheim; this proved too hard a nut to crack, and the garrison executed a successful break-out during the night of 10 June. On the 11th the concentrated Afrika Korps again defeated Ritchie's armoured brigades in detail, inflicting losses that eliminated the British numerical superiority. During the next few days a series of fierce actions took place around the fortified box held by the 201st Guards Brigade known as Knightsbridge. These still further wrote down the British armour to such an extent that, in order to save what remained of his army, Ritchie was forced to retire into Egypt, leaving Tobruk to be garrisoned by the 2nd South African Division, the 201st Guards and 11th Indian Infantry Brigades and 32nd Army Tank Brigade, the last being equipped with Valentines, a handful of Matildas and five Grants.

At 0520 on 20 June the fortress perimeter was breached in the same area Rommel had selected for his cancelled attack the previous November, and soon both panzer divisions were flooding through the gap. The British response was too slow and unco-ordinated to have much hope of success, and although the 32nd Army Tank Brigade fought bravely to the last tank and beyond, by 1800 the Germans were driving into Tobruk town. Major-General Klopper, the South African officer in command of the defences, agreed to a general surrender, and more than 30,000 British and Commonwealth soldiers marched into captivity. Together, the battles of Gazala/Knightsbridge and the capture of Tobruk represented the pinnacle of the Panzerwaffe's achievement in Africa, and on 22 June Hitler rewarded Rommel with his field marshal's baton.

Private armies were rare in the German service but one such unit, known variously as Sonderverband 288 or Combat Group Menton, had its baptism of fire during these engagements. Its broad function was to operate anywhere in the oil-producing areas of the Middle East, and to this end its ranks were filled with linguists, technicians and Brandenburgers, i.e. the German equivalent of the British commandos. It was equipped with a variety of weapon systems, including three assault guns, one of which fell into Piraeus harbour while being shipped to Africa. Of the two survivors, one wandered into the British lines and was captured just before the start of the offensive. These were the only assault guns to see active service in the desert, although a handful were later shipped to Tunisia. Sonderverband 288 served mainly under the command of the 90th Light Division, and many of the unit's adventures are described by Wolf Heckmann in his book *Rommel's War in Africa*.

Final preparations should now automatically have been made for Operation Herakles, the invasion of Malta, but Kesselring and Rommel disagreed fundamentally on what should be done next. Rommel argued that Herakles should be set aside while Ritchie was pursued and denied the time and space in which to recover from his defeat. This made good sense in the short term but Kesselring was quick to point out that Rommel lacked the resources, and especially air support, which would enable him follow through and seize the strategic objectives of Cairo and the Suez Canal. As was his wont, Rommel took matters into his own hands and set off into Egypt on the 23rd, confident that he would receive the Führer's blessing; given the latter's board-game approach to such matters, nothing was more certain, although Hitler was later to claim that it was his lack of confidence in the Italian Navy which had led him to opt against Herakles. Some of Rommel's apologists have suggested that both he and his men were doomed by Hitler's decision, but he was himself better acquainted with the economics of desert warfare than most and was in an ideal position to impress them on the Führer, had he chosen to do so. Rather, Germany's newest field marshal found himself subject to the classic formula of Aeschylean tragedy, in which the hero is destroyed by the very forces that have brought him greatness. Driven on by burning ambition that was itself fuelled by victory and his apparent ability to overcome every obstacle in his path, he seems never to have considered that the consequence of such *hubris* was always *áte* – utter ruin.

For a while all went well. Huge quantities of captured stores and fuel that the Eighth Army had stockpiled for its own pre-empted offensive were now used in its inexorable pursuit; at one stage eighty-five per cent of the trucks being used by the Axis armies had been paid for by the British taxpayer. During the night of 26-7 June the DAK, now reduced to a mere fifty tanks, effected a penetration between the British X and XIII Corps south of Mersa Matruh, thereby causing a disorderly and acrimonious withdrawal to El Alamein. Both sides were utterly exhausted, and from this point the fortunes of the Afrika Korps began to decline.

Auchinleck had assumed personal command of the Eighth Army during the retreat, and since the British were now operating so close to their base facilities, their strength recovered rapidly. Throughout July the front was stabilized in the series of hard-fought actions referred to as the First Battle of Alamein. In August Auchinleck was relieved as Commander-in-Chief by General Sir Harold Alexander, while Lieutenant-General Bernard Montgomery took over the Eighth Army. This resulted in an immediate return to orthodox methods, particularly as they affected the artillery, and a restoration of the army's confidence in itself.

For his part, Rommel was soon aware that he had tempted the gods once too often, but by the end of August he had amassed 203 German tanks, including seventy-four 50mm L/60 PzKw IIIs and twenty-seven 75mm L/43 PzKw IV F2s, plus 243 Italian tanks belonging to the Ariete and Littorio Divisions. The overall situation was unlikely to improve and he decided on one last desperate attempt to throw the Eighth Army off balance, breaking through the southern minefields during the night of the 30th-31st and swinging north-east towards the coast. But not only did the Eighth Army have 700 tanks available to meet the attack, it was also a changed organization which soon brought his advance to a standstill with a co-ordinated defence in which tanks, artillery, anti-tank guns and ground-attack aircraft all played a part. By 2 September he had cancelled the operation and retired behind his own minebelt. This engagement, which took its name from Alam Halfa ridge, cost the Afrika Korps forty-nine tanks, sixty guns and 400 trucks; Major-General von Bismarck, commanding the 21st Panzer Division, was killed by mortar fire in minefields during the first night.

Rommel and his army were now effectively prisoners of their earlier success. The captured stores had all been used up, and the RAF was making supply through the ports of Benghazi, Derna, Tobruk and Bardia almost impossible. The only 'safe' port was Tripoli, a thousand miles (1,600 km) to the west, so that the quantity of fuel reaching the front was barely enough at times to take care of day-to-day administration. To advance further was clearly impossible, yet to retreat would be to provoke the sort of mobile contest the Axis armour simply could not afford and which would certainly end in its destruction. The one bright spot was that, following the final rejection of Herakles, Kesselring gave Rommel all the support in his power. Some of the troops which were to have taken part in the invasion, including Ramcke's Parachute Brigade and the Italian Folgore Parachute Division, were shipped across, and the 164th Light arrived from Crete, but none of these formations possessed their own transport. Rommel, tired out and ill, departed for home on sick leave on 23 September, and temporary command of Panzerarmee Afrika devolved on General Georg Stumme, another former commander of 7th Panzer Division.

Meanwhile, Montgomery's thorough preparations for the Eighth Army's counter-offensive continued apace. When this opened, at 21.40 on 23 October, the British had immediately available 252 recently arrived Shermans, 170 Grants, 78 6-pdr Crusaders, 216 2-pdr or Close-Support Crusaders, 119 Stuarts and 194 Valentines; there were 200 tanks of various types held in reserve, plus a further thousand in workshops, a grand total of over 2,200. By way of contrast, Panzerarmee Afrika possessed thirty-one PzKw IIs, eighty-five 50mm L/42 PzKw IIIs, eighty-eight 50mm L/60 PzKw IIIs, eight 75mm L/24 PzKw IVs, thirty 75mm L/43 PzKw IVs and 278 M-13s, with twenty-two tanks (mainly PzKw IIIs) in workshops. In other areas the discrepancy was equally marked, making a British victory an eventual certainty, but lack of fuel kept the Axis armour virtually grounded, reducing its potential to that of intervention where a breakthrough seemed probable. Knowing this, Montgomery deliberately fought what he described as a 'crumbling' battle, switching the emphasis of his attack from one sector to another, thereby compelling the Germans to burn priceless fuel as they responded to each new threat.

Stumme was killed during a visit to the front on the 24th, and von Thoma, the commander of DAK, took over until Rommel returned the following evening. Rommel calculated that during a day's fighting his panzer army consumed about sixty miles' (96 km) worth of fuel and that he had about two days' supply in hand. On 26 October torpedo bombers of the Desert Air Force sank the Italian tanker *Proserpina* on passage with over 3,000 tons of fuel aboard, and the *Tergestea*, with 1,000 tons each of fuel and ammunition, was also sunk entering Tobruk. Another tanker, the *Luisiano* with 1,459 tons of petrol, fell victim to the

RAF off the Greek coast on 28 October, and on 1 November the *Tripolino*, with a mixed cargo of petrol and ammunition, was similarly sunk north-west of Tobruk. Small wonder, then, that when a senior liaison officer arrived at his headquarters from *Comando Supremo*, Rommel wiped the floor with him because of the Italian Navy's apparent inability to protect its shipping.

Just sufficient petrol got through to replace such daily use as there had been. The Axis armour was forced to react to events, being engaged in defensive fighting or local counter-attacks first in the Miteiriya and Kidney Ridge areas to prevent a break-out by the 1st and 10th Armoured Divisions, then on the coastal sector where part of the 164th Light was in danger of being isolated, and finally in the climactic tank battle against the 1st Armoured Division at Tel el Aqaqir on 2 November. The British sustained the greater loss, but it was one they were prepared for and could easily afford; furthermore, the Sherman's 75mm gun could fire a high-explosive round which enabled them to eliminate the Afrika Korps' anti-tank gun screens at long range, thereby discounting the sword-and-shield tactics which had been so effective in the past. Rommel, knowing that unless he withdrew his army it would be destroyed, had already initiated the thinning-out process, delayed for twenty-four hours by a pointless Führer-order to stand fast. He was able to extricate his mobile units on 4 November, but those formations without access to transport – notably the Italians – were forced to take their chances.

The Afrika Korps' disengagement from the Alamein position was covered by a handful of tanks commanded personally by von Thoma, who was captured when this flimsy screen was overwhelmed. That night, over dinner at Montgomery's headquarters, the German tank veteran suggested ruefully that Rommel might once again be able to work the oracle at El Agheila. It was not to be, for on 8 November the British and American landings took place in Algeria and Morocco, changing the whole strategic significance of the war in North Africa. On this date the Afrika Korps had about twenty tanks, and although this number increased fourfold by the time it had assembled all its assets at Mersa Brega the following week, the only course open to Rommel was to retreat through Libya to Tunisia, a distance of 1,500 miles (2,400 km), fighting only such rearguard actions as were absolutely necessary. There he could buy time behind the defences of the Mareth Line which, ironically, had been constructed by the French to keep out the Italians, and perhaps arrange for the evacuation of his men to Europe.

Yet Hitler and Mussolini were determined to maintain a military presence in Africa and commenced shipping a steady stream of fresh formations and ample supplies across to Tunisia. These included the 10th Panzer Division, the Tigers of sPzAbt 501 and 1/sPzAbt 504, the independent Panzerabteilung 190, two motorized infantry formations (one of them the élite Luftwaffe *Hermann Goering* Division), a number of independent units initially grouped together as the Division von Broich and later as the Division von Manteuffel, and finally, in the spring of 1943, the 999th Light Africa Division, a penal formation consisting of military criminals and men whose political differences with the Nazi establishment tended to merit suicidal employment rather than a trip to the extermination camp. Known collectively as the Fifth Panzer Army, these troops were commanded by Colonel-General Hans-Jurgen von Arnim, a former Footguard officer who had in turn commanded the 17th Panzer Division and XXXIX Panzer Corps in Russia. A scion of an old Prussian military family, von Arnim was conservative by nature and cautious by instinct. He was, therefore, the antithesis of Rommel, with whom it is unlikely that he would have got on even if the latter's anger at Hitler's interference with his withdrawal from Alamein had not been understandably tinged with bitterness at the sudden ability of OKW and *Comando Supremo* to supply everything he had once asked for, yet been denied.

The first task of the newly arrived German troops was to prevent the Allies seizing Tunis by *coup de main*. Between 1 and 3 December an *ad hoc* armoured battlegroup, including sPzAbt 501's first three Tigers ashore, engaged in scrappy fighting around Tebourba against the Crusaders and Valentines of the British 6th Armoured Division and the Stuarts of the American 1st Armored Division, bringing the Allied advance to a standstill and gaining time for a defensive line to be established in the mountains. During the course of these engagements the commander of 1/501, Captain Nikolai Baron von Nolde, was killed by shell splinters while directing his vehicles from an open *Kübelwagen*, the German equivalent of the American jeep.

Although the immediate threat was removed, von Arnim still believed that the danger was acute, and on 13 January Rommel was forced to detach the 21st Panzer Division and place it under his command. Further spoiling attacks were mounted by the Fifth Panzer Army during the next week, the weight of these falling on the weak French XIX Corps near Robaa, eliminating its small group of ancient tanks and most of its artillery so that in future it required constant assistance from the British in these areas.

When Rommel's last rearguards finally quitted Libya on 13 February, the Axis tank strength in Tunisia had risen to 280, and both German commanders felt capable of going over to the offensive. There was agreement that the inexperienced First Army should be the first target and that following its defeat their combined resources should be turned against Montgomery's advancing Eighth Army. As to the initial phase, Rommel envisaged a smaller version of von Manstein's Sichelschnitt, breaking through the US II Corps at the southern end of the line and then heading north-west through Kasserine Pass and Tebessa towards Constantine, Bone and the coast; this thrust deep into First Army's interior would sever its communications over a road system that had never been designed for the requirements of a mechanized war and compel its hasty withdrawal. Arnim simply wanted a disruptive attack that would penetrate some miles into the enemy's rear areas and eliminate his offensive capacity for a while, and it was his view that prevailed with *Comando Supremo*.

Thus it was that US II Corps, commanded by Major-General Lloyd R. Fredendall, became the first American formation to become involved in a major battle with the Panzerwaffe. Neutral until December 1941, the US Army had put to good use the lessons of the war to date in both the design of its tanks and the constitution of its armoured divisions, which contained three Combat Command headquarters around which battlegroups could be constructed to meet the needs of the moment. Unfortunately, during the inter-war years the Army had been even smaller than that of the United Kingdom, and the fact that it had expanded so rapidly meant that its formations were completely green. Nor, for the same reason, did it enter the war with any more experience of war – let alone mechanized war – at the operative level than had the British. II Corps was certainly not going to learn much of the art from Fredendall, who despised his allies and enemies with a fine impartiality, confused his subordinates and embarrassed his staff with his odd manner, and lived in subterranean splendour in a bunker built for him by his engineers *sixty* miles (96 km) behind the front.

Fredendall had one formation in the line, Major-General Orlando Ward's 1st Armoured Division, and on 14 February the Fifth Panzer Army struck its forward positions at Sidi Bou Zid in a whirlwind demonstration of Blitzkrieg. One combat command was cut off, and during that and the next day two more were cut to pieces as they mounted recklessly brave but unscientific counter-attacks against a sword-and-shield defence conducted with the instinctive ease of veterans, losing eighty-four Lees and Shermans.

Among the defeated Americans there were acts of heroism and

ugly scenes of panic as they were bundled westwards through
Sbeitla. Simultaneously the DAK under Rommel had burst
through Gafsa and Thelepte and on to Kasserine, where it was
joined by the 10th Panzer Division before storming the pass.
Fredendall's assessment of the situation was based on information
that was clearly out of date, so that few of the orders he issued
had much relevance to the rapidly changing scene. Luckily for the
Allies, Alexander had assumed command in Tunisia and quickly
detected the strategic menace inherent in Rommel's original idea,
moving Anglo-American blocking forces into position on the
Thala and Sbiba roads, where they halted, respectively, continued
thrusts by the 10th and 21st Panzer Divisions, while the rallied
1st Armored Division checked further progress by DAK east of
Tebessa; some of the American units which took part in these
battle had driven non-stop from Morocco to arrive in time.

Having inflicted serious damage, most of which fell on the II
Corps, Rommel then withdrew so skilfully on the night of 22
February that at first the Allies did not realize he had gone. The
booty captured was put to good use, prompting the thought that,
if he had been allowed to develop his original idea and compelled
the First Army to withdraw into Algeria, it would have been
immense and provided substantial reserves for his forthcoming
attack on Montgomery. On the 23rd he was appointed overall
commander of what was now known as Army Group Afrika, in
which those units which had fought in the desert, less DAK,
became known as the First Italian Army, commanded by General
Giovanni Messe, who had seen active service in Russia.

While Rommel re-deployed against Montgomery, von Arnim
mounted a series of holding-attacks against the British V Corps in
northern Tunisia. One element in this operation, known as
Ochsenkopf (Bull's Head), was the seizure of the important road
junction at Béja by an armoured battlegroup under the command
of Colonel Rudolph Lang. This consisted of 1/sPzAbt 501 with
fourteen Tigers and II/Panzer Regiment 7 with twelve new PzKw
IVs, eight old PzKw IVs and forty PzKw IIIs, plus supporting
artillery and panzergrenadiers. Many felt that this battlegroup
would have been better employed almost anywhere else, for its
route took it along the floor of narrow valleys in which its armour
could not deploy. Early on 26 February it ran into a British
outpost at Sidi Nsir, held by the 5th Battalion The Hampshire
Regiment and 155th Battery, Royal Artillery. This took a day's
hard fighting to overcome, and at one period as many as forty of
Lang's tanks were out of action, although some were repaired
during the night. The delay imposed also gained time for the

defenders of Béja to prepare a tank killing-ground onto which the German armour rolled next day, losing tanks to mines, hull-down Churchills, anti-tank guns, low-level fighter-bomber attacks and well-handled artillery concentrations. 1/sPzAbt 501 found itself the specific target of the British medium artillery and lost seven of its Tigers to this and other causes, subsequently referring to Béja in the battalion history as 'the Tiger Graveyard'. The rest of the German armour suffered even more seriously, and when Lang withdrew, it was with only a handful of tanks; this episode was to earn him the scornful soubriquet 'Tank Killer', a little unfairly, since many of the circumstances had been beyond his control.

On 6 March all three panzer divisions attacked the Eighth Army's positions at Medenine. The British held their fire until the German armour was within point-blank range before unmasking their anti-tank guns, while simultaneously artillery concentrations fountained among the stalled ranks. Montgomery conducted a textbook defence before which the Germans were eventually forced to retire, leaving fifty precious tanks on the battlefield. Medenine was the last straw for Rommel. Immediately after the battle he flew to see Hitler and demand evacuation. His request was turned down and he was sent on indefinite sick-leave. Von Arnim took over as army group commander, and von Vaerst, who had commanded the 15th Panzer Division for much of the campaign, assumed command of the Fifth Panzer Army.

Montgomery manoeuvred the First Italian Army out of the Mareth Line during a week-long series of operations commencing on 20 March, forcing it to fall back to the next series of defensive positions, based on the Wadi Akarit. While these battles were taking place, the US II Corps, which had recovered quickly from its experiences at Sidi Bou Zid and was very different in outlook now that Fredendall had been replaced as its commander by Major-General George S. Patton Jr, strove to get across Messe's communications with probes at Maknassy and El Guettar by the 1st Armored and 1st US Infantry Divisions. These were forestalled by the 10th Panzer Division and a hastily assembled battlegroup formed by Lang, including a dozen Tigers, which knocked out forty-four American tanks on the 24th alone. 10th Panzer then counter-attacked the 1st US Infantry Division at El Guettar but after some initial success was brought up short by a minefield and forced to retire in turn after being subjected to the fire of tank-destroyers and concentrated artillery, the encounter doing much to restore American self-confidence.

The Akarit defences were stormed by the Eighth Army on 6 April, Messe's troops being almost cut off during their subsequent withdrawal when the First Army's IX Corps fought its way through the Fondouk Pass against the toughest possible opposition put up by the convicts of the 999th Light Afrika Division, who had been promised remission of their sentences if they fought well. After this, Army Group Afrika found itself confined to an enclave in the north-eastern corner of Tunisia, suffering the same sort of supply shortages Rommel had experienced at Alamein. It was now accepted philosophically that the war which had begun in the barren fastness of the desert over two years earlier would end soon among rolling green hillsides and cultivated fields similar to those of southern Europe.

The final Allied offensive began on 22 April. Its most important phase concentrated on breaking the German hold on the Medjerda valley, and here thick-skinned but under-gunned Churchills of the British tank brigades surprised everyone by their ability to crawl up slopes that experts had declared tank-proof. On the 28th the Panzerwaffe mounted its last major attack in Africa when a composite battlegroup under the command of Colonel Irckens, containing elements from Panzer Regiments 5, 7 and 8, sPzAbt 501 and some Italian tanks, re-captured the key feature of Djebel Bou Aoukaz after a fierce struggle with the 24th Guards Brigade. The hill could not be held for long, however, and soon two British armoured divisions, the 6th and 7th, were streaming out of the Medjerda defile onto the coastal plain and on towards Tunis; to the north the US II Corps, now on the left of the Allied line, had also broken through and was heading for Bizerta.

Von Arnim surrendered on 12 May. In terms of prisoners taken, the Allied victory was comparable with that of Stalingrad, three months earlier, and, like the disaster on the Volga, it cost Germany three panzer divisions. All that remained was the glamour and the wistful attraction of what might have been, had not logistics imposed their iron grip.

8. Tigers, Panthers and Cauldrons

Although most of the major events of the war in Russia took place in the south, the rest of the front was seldom quiet for long, and around the encircled city of Leningrad the ferocity of the fighting sometimes reached a pitch of intensity equalled only at Stalingrad. It was here that Hitler insisted the Tiger should receive its baptism of fire in circumstances which proved premature and totally unsuitable. De-training at Mga on 29 August 1942, Major Richard Marker's 1/sPzAbt 502, consisting of four Tigers, one PzKw IIIN, a small echelon and fitters' section, went into action only hours later. Officers arriving at the daily OKW and OKH briefings the following morning looked forward with interest to learning the result of the engagement but were stunned to learn that every single one of the Tigers had been knocked out.

What had happened was that the tanks had been committed along narrow forest tracks bordered by close coniferous trees and were unable to give each other mutual fire support. The Russian anti-tank gunners facing them were battle-hardened, knew the range to a metre from experience and had refused to be intimidated by the monsters bearing down on them. They had aimed for the vulnerable tracks and when the Tigers had ground to a halt had sent round after round at the frontal armour. However, they had *not* succeeded in effecting a penetration, although the photographic evidence reveals the use of heavy-calibre ammunition, very possibly 122mm. The German crews had escaped but returned after dark, recovering three of the tanks; the fourth proved immovable and was blown apart with demolition charges to prevent its secrets falling into Russian hands.

On 12 January 1943 the Russians launched Operation Iskra (Spark), intended to break the siege of Leningrad. The next day 1/sPzAbt 502, now numbering four Tigers and eight PzKw IIIMs and Ns, received a frantic call for assistance from the 96th Infantry Division, part of which had been overrun by the Soviet 61st Independent Tank Brigade, equipped with twenty-four

T-34s and T-60 light tanks. In a temperature of 28° below zero, the four Tigers, commanded by Lieutenant Bodo von Gerdstell, were sent to the infantry's relief, quickly destroying half the Russian tanks and chasing the rest back to their own lines.

The battle continued to rage, and on 17 January the company lost a Tiger near Settlement No. 5 when an anti-tank gun penetrated the thinner armour of its engine compartment. Zhukov happened to be visiting the headquarters of Meretskov's Volkhov Front when news of the incident was received and he gave orders that the wreck was to be recovered, whatever the cost, which it was that night. Nonetheless, on 5 February 1/sPzAbt 502 received three new Tigers and six days later accounted for thirty-two of the forty-six tanks destroyed on the Leningrad sector, while between 19 and 21 March it knocked out forty T-34s. By the time the spring thaw brought fighting to an end, the company had been credited with 163 kills, including T-26s, T-34s, T-60s and KVs, approximately one-quarter of the total Soviet AFV loss. Iskra had not quite succeeded in its object, but the Leningrad and Volkhov Fronts had managed to effect a junction, creating a narrow corridor some eighteen miles (29 km) long, still within range of the German artillery, through which supplies began to flow regularly into the city.

Examination of the captured Tiger led directly to the production of a Soviet heavy tank destroyer, the SU-152, armed with a 152mm gun-howitzer mounted on a KV chassis. This followed the layout of the German assault gun, the prototype being complete in only twenty-five days, while manufacture began on 1 March 1943. Because of its ability to knock out Tigers and Elefants, the SU-152 earned itself the nickname of *Zvierboy*, (Animal-Killer). It would probably be wrong, however, to over-emphasize the impact of the Tiger on Soviet design for the remainder of the war; rather it accelerated a trend which was already present if not actually manifest. There was, for example, a feeling that the KV-1 provided nothing that was not already available from the T-34 and that it had really become a case of too much tank for too little gun. On the other hand, the long 75mm guns now arming the German PzKw IVs, assault guns and tank-destroyers had eliminated the technical superiority possessed by Soviet armour at the beginning of the war and there was a necessity to regain this by up-gunning the T-34 and producing a heavy tank which afforded some sort of comparison with the Tiger. These vehicles, plus their companion tank-destroyers and assault guns, would continue with their development throughout 1943.

It would have startled Russian design teams to learn that even as they evaluated the captured Tiger a much improved version armed with the 88mm L/71 KwK 43 gun had started its production run a month earlier. This, officially the PzKw VI Model B, more popularly known in Germany as the Königstiger (King Tiger) and to the western allies as the Royal Tiger, represented a determined attempt by the German Ordnance Department to establish a decisive lead over the Soviets in the gun-armour spiral. The vehicle, built by Henschel, was protected by 185mm armour, had a maximum speed of 23.6 mph (37.98 kph) and weighed 68.7 tons (69,800 kg), making it the heaviest tank to enter general service during World War II. The prototype was delivered in November 1943, the first production models reaching units the following February. The total number of Royal Tigers built by the war's end was 484, compared with 1,350 of the earlier Tiger Model Es, production of which ceased in August 1944.

For all its size, the Royal Tiger was not the largest German tank projected during this phase of the war. Much precious time and material were wasted on building prototypes of such monsters as the 140-ton (148,470 kg) E-100 and the 188-ton (191,000 kg) Mouse, which were to have been armed with a 150mm gun, plus a 75mm gun mounted coaxially. Nor was this the ultimate, since a proposal put forward by two engineers named Grote and Hacker for a mechanical nightmare weighing 1,500 tons (1,524.000 kg), to have been powered by U-boat diesels, actually received a degree of serious consideration. Where such a machine of clearly enormous dimensions could have fitted into the tactical picture remains a mystery; any attempt to parade it down the Charlottenburg Chaussee must inevitably have resulted in the wholesale destruction of the municipal infrastructure! Hitler certainly had a fascination for unusual weapon systems, but his interest in projects such as this cannot have been more than passing, for he had instinctively grasped that with the development of shaped-charge ammunition the era in which the tank totally dominated the land battle was coming to an end, to be replaced by scientific co-operation between arms.

Rather more to the point, therefore, was the issue of the first of the second-generation tank destroyers, the Jagdpanzer IV, to the tank-destroyer battalions of the panzer divisions towards the end of 1943, where it gradually replaced the Marders. Also known as 'Guderian's Duck', it followed the layout of the conventional assault gun, with the fighting compartment forward. The superstructure consisted of well-angled armour plate, extended to the stern plate, overall height being only six feet one inch (1.85 m). Initially armed with the 75mm PaK 39, the vehicle was later up-gunned with the more powerful 75mm L/70 KwK 42, the main armament entering the vehicle through a 'Pig's Head' mantlet, to the right of which a conical hatch concealed a machine-gun.

Shaken by the Stalingrad débâcle and the turn events were taking in Africa, Hitler recalled Guderian to duty on 1 March 1943, appointing him Inspector-General of Armoured Trops with wide-ranging responsibilities including the equipment, organization and training of the Panzerwaffe in the broadest possible sense. This brought not only the Army's panzer and panzer-grenadier divisions within his orbit but also the armoured troops of the Waffen SS, the Luftwaffe and even the armoured trains. The only exception was the Assault Artillery which retained its autonomy, much to Guderian's annoyance, and in this even Hitler opposed him. The reason was not, as General Schmundt, the Führer's adjutant, suggested, that this was the only branch of their arm in which artillerymen could aspire to the award of the coveted Knights' Cross; rather it was an acceptance that at the tactical level the Assault Artillery performed their task so efficiently as not to justify outside interference. Indeed, while Guderian was never one to accept a rebuff with good grace, he clearly appreciated the scale of the Assault Artillery's contribution.

> Anti-tank defence will devolve more and more on the assault guns, since all our other anti-tank weapons are becoming increasingly ineffective against the new enemy equipment … All divisions on the main battlefronts, therefore, need to be supplied with a certain complement of these weapons; the secondary fronts will have to make do with a higher command reserve of assault guns, while the divisions are for the time being equipped with self-propelled anti-tank guns. In order to economise on personnel and material, a gradual amalgamation of the assault gun battalions and tank destroyer battalions is necessary.*

In the event only a few favoured divisions ever possessed their own organic assault gun battalion, including *Grossdeutschland*, the Luftwaffe's *Hermann Goering* Division and the senior Waffen SS panzer divisions. The irony was that from this time onwards there would be long periods when the tank element of most panzer divisions fell to such a dangerously low level that out of sheer necessity the shortfall would have to be made up with assault guns, which could obviously provide heavy fire support

* *Panzer Leader*

but could hardly be expected to carry out the same functions as the tanks themselves.

Guderian's status was officially the equivalent of an army commander, yet in reality he was almost his own master, being merely required to 'consult' with Zeitzler, the Army's Chief of General Staff, and answerable only to the Führer. Shortly before his appointment it was suggested at a General Staff conference that Germany's entire tank-manufacturing capacity should be devoted to building Tigers and Panthers. Closer examination of the question revealed that, with the exception of chassis required for use in assault-gun construction, the manufacture of the PzKw III had ceased the previous autumn; that the Panther had yet to enter its mass-production run; and that, if no more PzKw IVs were to be built, Germany's total monthly output for the time being would consist of twenty-five Tigers, a situation which would result in her rapid defeat in the very near future. Needless to say, the idea was hastily dropped.

After the traumatic experiences of the past year, Guderian began the considerable task of setting the Panzerwaffe as a whole back on its feet. He immediately advised Hitler that the Panther would not be ready for active service before July or even August 1943; as it transpired, even this proved over-optimistic. In the meantime the up-gunned PzKw IV would remain the mainstay of the tank battalions, and its production would be accelerated. He also emphasized the type of equipment that was required, including the second generation of tank-destroyers, approved a simplified version of the SdKfz 251 half-track series for the panzergrenadiers and also the re-equipment of the armoured reconnaissance battalions with an increasing proportion of the smaller SdKfz 250 half-track series, although it was stressed that the need still existed for a fast, well-armed armoured car, this being standardized as the eight-wheeled SdKfz 234 series.

The demand for new types of fighting vehicles, the constant current and retrospective up-gunning and up-armouring process, the endless stream of internal and external modifications, the need to produce a bewildering variety of spares, the universal shortage of raw materials and the sheer scale of the problem had so overburdened the German armaments industry that it was in danger of grinding to a standstill. Luckily for Hitler, he had recently appointed a man of rare administrative genius, Albert Speer, as Minister of Armaments. Guderian and Speer got on very well and the latter was able to cut through the tangle that had arisen and increase the number of AFVs, leaving the factories for the Front. The fundamental point of Speer's rationalization was that industrial production was the proper province of industrialists and not that of military bureaucrats, and by setting up specialist committees of the former he was able to resolve many of the difficulties which had arisen.

Another area in which the Panzerwaffe benefited from Guderian's appointment as Inspector-General was that of training methods. As a senior commander who had seen his share of the sharp end of war, he knew exactly how his tank crews thought, what they talked ·about and what amused them. Therefore, rather than produce the usual stodgy manuals for issue with the Tigers and Panthers, he designed *humorous* booklets entitled *Tigerfibel* and *Pantherfibel* (*Tiger Primer* and *Panther Primer*). Written in everyday soldier's slang, these covered every aspect of maintenance and life aboard a tank, a multitude of 'do's and don'ts' for each crew member, easily remembered rhyming mottoes and numerous cartoons, prominent among which was a shapely blonde lady who urged the reader to ever greater efforts in the frankest and most personal manner possible. Such of these booklets as have survived are now treasured possessions.

Guderian felt that nothing would be gained by committing the Panzerwaffe to a fresh offensive after the *rasputitsa* and indeed that it would require the remainder of 1943 to complete its re-equipment programme. He was told, however, that a major offensive was a political necessity, and the only question outstanding was the form it would take.

It was now generally accepted that the destruction of the USSR lay beyond Germany's power. On the other hand it was felt that, if the Soviet Army could be sufficiently weakened by another major defeat, it might be possible to negotiate some sort of peace with the Kremlin, based on the *status quo ante bellum*.

A conference was held at Munich on 3 May to discuss the details, attended by Hitler and his OKW Staff, General Zeitzler, Chief of Army General Staff, Field Marshals von Manstein and von Kluge, commanding respectively Army Groups South and Centre, General Model, commander of the Ninth Army, Guderian and Speer. The plan which Hitler introduced had been prepared by Zeitzler and was clearly based on the principles of *Vernichtungsgedanke*. Its target was the huge salient centre on Kursk, one hundred miles (160 km) across the seventy (112 km) deep, that had remained in the German line when the great thaw brought Manstein's counter-offensive to a halt. The method involved converging attacks directed through the salient's flanks by Army Groups South and Centre, trapping so many divisions

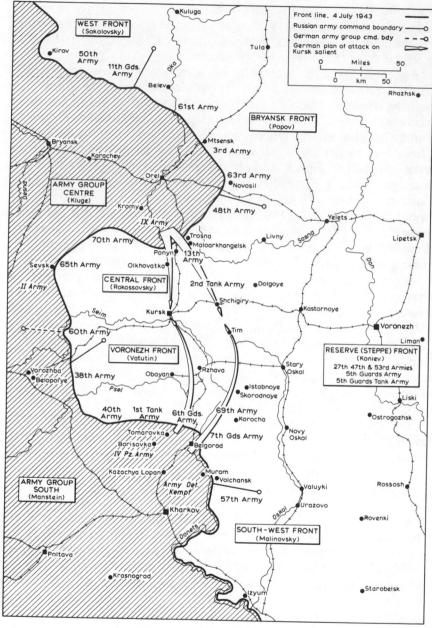

Front line, 4 July 1943 ————
Russian army command boundary ——o
German army group cmd. bdy — – –o
German plan of attack on
Kursk salient

Miles
0   50
0   km   50

WEST FRONT
(Sokolovsky)

Kuluga

Tula

Kirov   50th
          Army
              11th Gds.
              Army

Belev

61st Army

BRYANSK FRONT
(Popov)

Bryansk
     Karachev

Mtsensk

3rd Army

Orel

63rd Army

Novosil

Rhazhsk

ARMY GROUP
CENTRE
(Kluge)

Kromy

48th Army

Yelets

Lipetsk

IX Army

70th Army

Trosna
Maloarkhangelsk

Livny

Sosna

Ponyri   13th
         Army

Sevsk   65th Army

II Army

Olkhovatka

2nd Tank Army

Dolgoye

Kastornoye

CENTRAL FRONT
(Rokossovsky)

Kursk

Seim

Shchigiry

Voronezh

60th Army

Tim

VORONEZH FRONT
(Vatutin)

RESERVE (STEPPE) FRONT
(Koniev)
27th 47th & 53rd Armies
5th Guards Army
5th Guards Tank Army

Vorozhba
Belopol'ye

38th Army

Oboyan

Psel

Rzhava

Stary
Oskol

Liski

Ostrogozhsk

40th
Army

1st Tank
Army

6th Gds.
Army

69th Army

Istobnoye

Skorodnoye

Korocha

Novy
Oskol

Tomarovka

Borisovka

IV Pz. Army

7th Gds Army

Belgorod

Kazachya Lopan

Murom
Volchansk

Valuyki

Rossosh

ARMY GROUP
SOUTH
(Manstein)

Army Det.
Kempf

57th Army

Urazovo

Oskol

Rovenki

Kharkov

Donets

SOUTH-WEST FRONT
(Malinovsky)

Poltava

Krasnograd

Izyum

Starobelsk

Operation Zitadelle, July 1943

within this double envelopment that the Soviet Army would be decisively weakened just as it had been the previous year when the Izyum salient was neutralized.

Opinions were sharply divided among those present. Kluge supported the idea, but Manstein felt that, while it might have worked in April, he now had serious reservations. Zeitzler's view was that the Tigers and Panthers would guarantee success. Guderian responded that the Panther's teething troubles were far from over and that whatever the outcome tank losses were bound to be heavy at a time when reserves should be conserved to meet the anticipated Allied landing in France; in this he received Speer's support. For his part, Model spoke only the truth when he pointed out that the objective was so obvious that the Russians were not only fortifying the walls of the salient in depth but had also concentrated their armour in suitable counter-attack zones. He could hardly have suspected that the enemy were being kept fully informed of German intentions by the Lucy spy-ring, which had penetrated OKW some time earlier, and that eventually the defences of the salient would consist of three fortified zones, totalling twenty-five miles (40 km) in depth, covered by 20,000 guns of various types, of which over one third were anti-tank weapons, and corseted by minefields laid to a density of 2,500 anti-personnel and 2,200 anti-tank mines per mile of front.

Despite the very cogent objections which had been expressed, Zeitzler's plan was ultimately accepted by the conference, thereby committing all that remained of Germany's offensive capacity to what was, in effect, nothing more than a gamble. The implications of failure were so horrendous that a week later Hitler told Guderian that his stomach churned whenever he considered them. What aggravated the situation even further was that the operation, code-named Zitadelle, could not proceed until an adequate number of Panthers had reached the panzer divisions; the greater the delay, the stronger the Russian defences would become and the more completely they would recover from the mauling Manstein had given them earlier in the year. At length, it was decided that the offensive would begin on 5 July; at the earliest possible moment a Hungarian deserter advised Zhukov of the fact.

On Army Group South's sector the principal attack force would be Hoth's Fourth Panzer Army, deployed with the three panzer-grenadier divisions of the SS Panzer Corps (*1st Leibstandarte SS Adolf Hitler (LSSAH), 2nd Das Reich* and *3rd Totenkopf*) on the right and the XLVIII Panzer Corps (3rd and 11th Panzer Divisions and Panzergrenadier Division *Grossdeutschland*) on the left, the southern flank of the operation being covered Operational Group

Kempf, which included the III Panzer Corps (6th, 7th and 19th Panzer Divisions). Also at Hoth's disposal was sPzAbt 503 with three fully equipped companies mustering forty-five Tigers; additionally, each of the favoured divisions' panzer regiments contained a Tiger-equipped heavy company, *Grossdeutschland* possessing fourteen, *LSSAH* thirteen, *Das Reich* fourteen and *Totenkopf* fifteen, so producing an unprecedented concentration of 101 Tiger Model Es.

To the north, Army Group Centre's attacks would be made with Model's Ninth Army, which included the XLVII Panzer Corps (2nd, 9th and 20th Panzer Divisions plus sPzAbt 505 with two Tiger companies) and the LI Panzer Corps (18th Panzer Division plus 653 and 654 Heavy Tank-Destroyer Battalions, both equipped with Elefants).

For this, the largest tank battle in history, the Germans deployed 2,700 tanks and assault guns, 10,000 artillery weapons, 2,500 aircraft and 900,000 men. The Soviets enjoyed a two-to-one advantage in artillery but in other respects their strength was not markedly superior to that of their opponents, consisting of 3,300 tanks and assault guns, 2,650 aircraft and 1,337,000 men. These forces were deployed in three Fronts, the northern half of the salient being held by Rokossovsky's Central Front and the southern half by Voronezh Front, now commanded by Vatutin following Golikov's removal after the disasters of February, while in the immediate rear lay Koniev's Reserve or Steppe Front.

Things began to go very badly wrong for Germany even before Zitadelle opened on 5 July. Fears that the Panther was being committed to action prematurely were amply justified by the long lines of breakdowns, mainly transmission failures and engine fires, that marked the route between railheads and operational assembly areas. Further breakdowns and battle casualties incurred during the first day's fighting reduced the number of Panthers available to the Fourth Panzer Army from a theoretical 200 to a mere forty, a situation which showed little sign of improvement.

The epithet most frequently applied to Operation Zitadelle is that it was the 'Death Ride of the Panzers', and however theatrical this might sound there are nevertheless comparisons to be made with the Light Brigade's attack at Balaclava and the charge of von Bredow's 12th Cavalry Brigade at Mars-la-Tour sixteen years later. It might also be said that it represented a mechanical version of trench warfare, for the battle rapidly evolved into a brutal contest of attrition in which scientific generalship had no part to play. Model's wing of the attack advanced a mere ten miles (16 km) against opposition that would rather die than abandon a foot of ground, and was then brought to a complete standstill. Lacking machine-guns for local defence, the huge Elefants fell victim one after another to Soviet tank-hunting teams once their own escorting infantry had been pinned down; those that survived the battle were later sent to Italy, where a different type of war was about to commence. In the south, resistance was no less bitter but Hoth somehow managed to advance almost twenty-five miles (40 km). The climax of the battle was reached on 12 July when the 700 tanks of the Fourth Panzer Army met the 850 of General P.A. Rotmistrov's Fifth Guards Tank Army in a gigantic mêlée which raged around the village of Prokhorovka. The Russians chose to fight at murderously close range in order to discount the marked gunnery advantage possessed by the Tiger, but even so when they drew back to re-group they left behind half their number. Fourth Panzer Army had lost about 300 tanks in the encounter, including seventy Tigers, most of which had to be left on the battlefield.

At this point Manstein at least felt reasonably close to success, although whether Army Group South still possessed the capacity to exploit a breakthrough after incurring such frightful losses is a matter open to doubt. As it was, events elsewhere compelled Zitadelle's abandonment. On 10 July the Allies landed in Sicily, and three days later Hitler told his senior commanders that the Eastern Front would have to be stripped of troops to form fresh armies which were to be sent to Italy, which he correctly assessed as being on the verge of collapse. Simultaneously, the Russians had also commenced their own counter-offensive with an attack against the Orel salient – a mirror image of the Kursk salient and lying immediately to its north – using Sokolovsky's West Front and Popov's Bryansk Front. The Second Panzer Army was badly mauled and Manstein reluctantly transferred several panzer divisions to Kluge so that Model's rear could be adequately protected against the Soviet advance. On 17 July Hitler declared officially that Zitadelle had run its course.

Each side had lost somewhat in excess of 1,500 tanks, but for the Russians this was less serious since they could recover many of their casualties from the battlefield and in any event the output of their factories was far greater than that of Germany's. For Guderian and Speer it was heartbreaking to see the weapon they had painstakingly re-forged so blunted that never again could it be used to achieve a decision.

There was, too, another aspect of Zitadelle to consider. The German armour had always fought in close partnership with the

Luftwaffe, which had so often pulverized the opposition in its path. Thus, the huge land battles which had just taken place in the Kursk salient had been accompanied by air battles which reached new heights of intensity as the two contending tactical air forces strove desperately but in vain to impose a decision. This lack of success was one of a number of deeply depressing factors which led to the suicide of Colonel-General Hans Jeschonnek, the Chief of Air Staff. Jeschonnek had always been a fervent apostle of close tactical air support but in the opinion of his successor, General Günther Korten, the Luftwaffe's first priority had now become the defence of the homeland against the growing air offensive being mounted by the RAF's Bomber Command and the US Eighth Air Force. This led to a steady withdrawal of Luftwaffe units from the Russian Front and meant that from now on the Panzerwaffe would be forced to operate with ever-decreasing air support.

The immediate consequence was the accelerated development of vehicles for anti-aircraft defence, using both tank and half-tracked chassis. One of the earliest consisted of various combinations of 20mm and 30mm cannon mounted on obsolete PzKw 38(t) chassis and was issued in small numbers to the anti-aircraft platoons of tank battalions in 1943. Always regarded as a stop-gap, this vehicle was replaced the following year by several designs employing the chassis of the PzKw IV in combination with a number of single 37mm Flak 43 or quadruple 20mm cannon mountings. The half-track based anti-aircraft vehicles included the SdKfz 251/17 with a single 20mm cannon or the SdKfz 251/21 with a triple 15mm or 20mm cannon mounting, supplemented by unarmoured versions of the 251 series and the semi-armoured SWS (Schwerer Wehrmachts-schlepper, heavy army tractor), one version of which was armed with the 37mm Flak 43 and served with the panzergrenadier divisions. On their own, these measures could not hope to provide a defence against heavy and sustained air attack, so that, as the Luftwaffe's influence continued to decline, much of the German movement of necessity took place at night while during the day strict attention had to be paid to vehicle camouflage and concealment. Another effect of the Allied bomber offensive was to deprive the Eastern Front of thousands of priceless 88mm dual-purpose guns, held back to defend Germany's cities and industrial plants when they could have been taking their toll of Russian tanks and aircraft.

In the meantime Zhukov's counter-offensive gained momentum. On the southern flank of the Kursk salient, Steppe

Front came into the line on the left of Voronezh Front, and both went over to the attack so that by 23 July Hoth and Kempf had been forced to abandon all the ground bought at such terrible cost and were back where they had started when the battle began. South-West Front (Malinovsky) and South Front (Tolbukhin) simultaneously brought pressure to bear on the southern end of the German line, causing Manstein to divert yet more of his armour to pinch out a bulge which threatened to erupt into a breakthrough on the Mius sector. Immediately *Stavka* switched the emphasis back to Voronezh and Steppe Fronts, so that Belgorod fell on 5 August and Kharkov had to be abandoned on the 22nd.

Guderian sensed that with the failure of Zitadelle the strategic initiative had passed irrevocably to the Soviets, and so did every German general who knew his business. Army Group Centre remained under continuous pressure but was saved from disaster by Hitler's decision to abandon the dangerous Orel salient, not because of the threat posed to the troops therein but because he wished to send them to Italy. Nonetheless, it was pressed steadily back beyond Smolensk, and by November its positions lay west of the Berezina. Lacking reinforcements, the strength of von Kluge's formations dwindled steadily; for example, the Third Panzer Army, still commanded by Reinhardt, lost one third of its strength between May and October and was so stretched that ultimately each of its divisions covered 25,000 yards of front instead of the more usual 15,000. The Third Panzer Army actually possessed comparatively few armoured formations and, as Guderian had predicted, much of the burden had fallen on the Assault Artillery and tank-destroyer battalions; it was largely due to them and to a flexible artillery response that the line held at all. On 27 October Kluge was injured in a traffic accident and sent home on sick leave, his place being taken by Field Marshal Ernst Busch.

It was, however, against Army Group South that the weight of the Soviet effort was directed, for it was in this area that Stalin believed Germany could be decisively beaten. Together, Voronezh and Steppe Fronts possessed a local superiority of 3:1 in men, 4:1 in guns and 3:2 in aircraft. The disparity in tanks and assault guns was even greater at 6:1, the reasons being that the Russians had been able to recover their casualties from Zitadelle while the Germans had not, and that Russian tank production was now outstripping German by a wide margin. Matthew Cooper makes the point that prior to Zitadelle the average tank strength of Manstein's eleven panzer divisions was ninety-five, of which seventy-eight were fit for action, but that after the six months of more or less continuous fighting that followed the respective figures were eighty and twenty while in one case a division could field only six tanks.* Looking back on this period, Manstein himself wrote in his book *Lost Victories*, 'Henceforth Army Group South found itself waging a defensive struggle which could not be anything more than a system of improvisations and stop-gaps. To maintain ourself in the field, and in so doing wear down the enemy's offensive capacity to the utmost, became the whole essence of this struggle.'

This put the matter at its simplest, for Manstein was also hobbled by Hitler's obstinate refusal to abandon the Donbass, whose economic assets were, he claimed, 'vital' to Germany's cause. While Army Group South's line buckled and threatened to cave in under intense pressure, Manstein urged the Führer time and again to sanction a withdrawal to the Dniepr before the front disintegrated in ruin. That he eventually succeeded by mid-September can be regarded as one of the major achievements of his career.

The Dniepr, with a width varying between 400 yards and two miles, is Europe's third largest river. Having taken the decision to retire behind it, Hitler promptly declared that it was Germany's Eastern Rampart; unfortunately, it took rather more than his imagination to make it secure. With the panzer divisions covering their rear, the army group's columns converged on selected crossing-points at Kiev, Kanev, Cherkassy, Kremenchug and Dniepropetrovsk, leaving behind them a 'scorched earth' zone in which it was hoped – vainly as it turned out – that the Russians would be unable to operate for a while. In fact, the Soviet armies were actually very close seconds in the race to the Dniepr and, since the Germans could not be strong everywhere along its length, were soon able to seize and rapidly expand bridgeheads of their own.

The only crumb of comfort which Manstein was able to provide for OKW was news of the complete rout of a major Soviet airborne drop by three parachute brigades near Kanev on 24 September. Of the 7,000 paratroopers involved, only 2,300 survived to join local partisan groups; the remainder were killed or captured, the 5th Guards Parachute Brigade being virtually wiped out when it landed on top of the 10th Panzergrenadier Division.

On 20 October the Central Front was re-named by *Stavka* the

* *The German Army 1933-1945* p.465

Belorussian Front, while Voronezh Front, Steppe Front, South-West and South Fronts became respectively the 1st, 2nd, 3rd and 4th Ukrainian Fronts. This merely underlined the continuing nature of the Russian offensive as fighting returned to the western areas of the Soviet Union. On 6 November Kiev fell, followed by Zhitomir on the 12th, an event which led to the removal of Hermann Hoth from command of the hard-pressed Fourth Panzer Army. By the end of the year the Eastern Rampart had been overrun and the German army in the Crimea had been cut off, yet still the re-vitalized Soviet Army continued to attack throughout the winter. When the spring thaw finally brought a lull, Manstein's front rested approximately along the line of the Carpathians and the pre-war Russo-Polish frontier.

The Russians had now become more used to handling their tank armies, which generally consisted of two tank and one mechanized corps, a Soviet corps being approximately the equivalent of a Western or German division. However, they still had control and communications problems once a battle was in progress, and no matter how able their higher direction of the war might have been, they were still forced to rely heavily on rehearsals and repetition in their tactics. In theory the normal attack would consist of intense artillery preparation and be led by heavy tanks; a second wave, this time of T-34s and infantry, would eliminate what remained of the defenders, while a follow-through wave of T-34s, light T-60s, T-70s and more infantry would pass through the breach so created and press on to the objective, which would be consolidated during the final phase. If the attack failed, it would be repeated again and again until it succeeded, passing over the same ground and being launched at the same times of day, and would be abandoned only if all the available troops had been used up. As a method of waging war against experienced troops, this was horrifyingly expensive in men and material and it was only the Soviet Army's vast resources, *coupled with the fierce motivation of the ordinary Russian soldier*, that enabled *Stavka* to do so.

The fact was that 'Ivan', as the Germans knew him, was a frightening enemy not just because he was tough, hardy and well disciplined, but because he hated so deeply. Like every soldier, Ivan wanted to live, but the more of his country that was liberated, the more evidence there was to see of the barbaric lunacies perpetrated by the Nazi infrastructure, the Gestapo and the Allgemeine SS, so that he was quite prepared to die exacting his revenge.

The majority of Russian tank crews were still regarded as being deficient in tactical skills, although this would slowly improve, and the primary aim of the German defence remained the separation of the enemy's tanks from his infantry so that neither could give the other the support they required. This was usually achieved without difficulty since the latter, being completely unprotected, were easily pinned down by defensive fire. Ironically, the Soviet Army *could* have solved this problem by using turretless T-34 hulls as Kangaroo armoured personnel carriers in the same way the British and Canadian armies used Sherman and Ram hulls to carry an infantry section, a solution which would probably have been cheaper in the long term anyway, as production of T-34 chassis was already rising to a rate well in excess of 20,000 per annum. In the immediate post-war period the Russians' analysis of these battles led directly to their adoption of the APC with all the zeal of the newly converted.

The Panzerwaffe, an arm of service conceived with the strategic offensive in mind, was perforce required by this continued reversal of German fortunes to adopt its techniques to a swiftly changing environment. The sword-and-shield method of active defence, for example, also evolved into a hammer-and-anvil means of destroying an attacker who could be held against the anvil of the PAK-front and then struck with the hammer of an armoured counter-attack against his flank and rear. Likewise, the deep strike into the Russian rear, as demonstrated by Manstein in February 1943, remained a valid concept. These and other techniques including delaying and blocking tactics, defensive pincers, flank attacks and envelopments all followed each other in rapid succession throughout this traumatic period, which provides ample food for thought for anyone interested in the possible course of the land battle should the Warsaw Pact ever decide to invade Western Europe, and with this in mind its study is arguably even more rewarding than that of better-known periods in the Panzerwaffe's history.

In November 1943 von Mellenthin was still serving as chief of staff of the XLVIII Panzer Corps, and he was delighted to learn that General Hermann Balck, who had so distinguished himself while leading the 11th Panzer Division the previous winter, had been appointed corps commander. Mellenthin had a sincere regard for Balck, whose abilities at the tactical-operative level he believed equalled those of von Manstein in the operative-strategic area. Balck's first task as defined by Colonel-General Erich Rauss, the new commander of Fourth Panzer Army, was the recapture of Zhitomir and the stabilization of the front west of Kiev, and for this

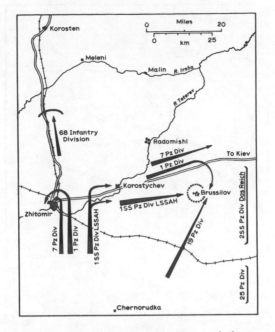

*XLVIII Panzer Corps' capture of Zhitomir and elimination of the
Brussilov pocket, 15-24 November 1943*

he was given the largest concentration of armour available,
including the 1st, 7th, 19th and 25th Panzer Divisions, 1st SS
Panzer Division *LSSAH* and a battlegroup from 2nd SS Panzer
Division *Das Reich*, plus the 68th Infantry Division.

Following the German tradition, Balck and Mellenthin sat down
separately to prepare plans and then accepted the best features of
both. The XLVIII Panzer Corps was to advance northwards from
Chernorudka to Zhitomir, its right flank protected by the 25th
Panzer Division and the *Das Reich* battlegroup, its left by the 7th
Panzer Division and 68th Infantry Division, with the 1st Panzer
Division and *LSSAH* in the centre. All went exactly as planned.
The armoured fist smashed through the Soviet line on 15
November, and while *LSSAH* swung right to form a protective
shoulder, 1st and 7th Panzer Divisions captured Zhitomir without
difficulty during the night of the 17th/18th. The Russian Third
Guards Tank Army (5th and 6th Guards Tank Corps and 1st
Guards Cavalry Corps) mounted counter-attacks at Korostyshev
that afternoon and did so again west of Brussilov next day but these
were successfully held. Balck promptly took the decision to entrap
the enemy army within a pocket. Throughout the 20th *LSSAH*

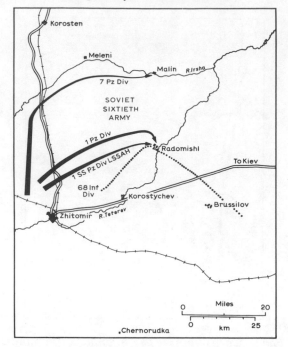

XLVIII Panzer Corps' attack on Radomyshl, 6-15 December 1943

hammered away at the Russians from the west, serving to focus their attention in that direction. Simultaneously, the 1st Panzer Division was driving east along the Zhitomir-Kiev highway with the 7th Panzer Division still covering its left flank, while the 19th Panzer Division approached the eastern edge of the battle area from the south-west, knocking out sixteen tanks and thirty-six anti-tank guns as it broke cleanly through the Soviets' defensive screen. With the coming of darkness, both the 1st and the 19th went into leaguer, little realizing that in Balck's world people seldom halted, rested or slept. The enraged corps commander had expected them to effect their junction that very night and ordered them to complete the encirclement after dusk the following evening; this was achieved by 2100 hours.

By 24 November the pocket had been eliminated, the booty including 153 tanks, 70 guns and 250 anti-tank guns. Three thousand Russians had been killed and many more were captured but a large number had managed to work their way out of the trap, including all the senior commanders and their staffs.

At the end of November Balck received orders from Army Group South to eliminate those Soviet formations now positioned north of the Zhitomir-Radomyshl road, as these were well placed to attack the left wing of any German thrust from Brussilov towards Kiev. He decided to strike a concentrated blow at the enemy's right flank north of Zhitomir, following which the 1st Panzer Division and *LSSAH* would roll up the Russian line from west to east. Simultaneously the 7th Panzer Division, now commanded by Major-General Baron Hasso von Manteuffel and for once operating at full strength, would cross the Zhitomir-Korosten highway much further north and execute a deep strike into the Soviet rear in the direction of Malin; this was to be the critical phase of the operation, and the day before the division moved off combat engineer units were escorted along the route of its approach march by armoured cars repairing the bridges it would require. Elaborate precautions were taken to screen the German intentions; for example, no formal orders group involving the divisional commanders and their staffs was held, and the divisions themselves moved into their assembly areas only at the last possible moment, under cover of darkness.

All three panzer divisions crossed the Zhitomir-Korosten highway at 0600 on 6 December, with the closest possible co-operation from the Luftwaffe. Thanks to excellent planning and preparation, the operation succeeded brilliantly, and during the next few days the area between the Teterev and the Irsha rivers was completely cleared of Russian troops. In one pocket near Radomyshl 3½ divisions were encircled and destroyed, together with thirty-six tanks and 204 anti-tank guns. It was also clear from the huge stockpiles of ammunition and other supplies that the Soviets had been preparing to return to the offensive in the area. The sudden appearance of German armour coming out of the blue seriously unsettled the Russians, eliciting tetchy responses from those whose contact reports were greeted with startled incredulity: 'Ask the Devil's grandmother, then!' These frantic exchanges were also heeded in amused silence by the German wireless intercept operators; as von Mellenthin so drily put it, 'Whenever the Devil and his near relations are mentioned in Russian signals, one can assume that a crack-up is at hand!'

As the XIII Corps moved up to take over the newly captured ground, the XLVIII Panzer Corps was directed north-westward against more Russian formations which were believed to be on the point of effecting a penetration of the front to the south of Korosten, held for the present by the German LVII Corps. On 15 December, therefore, 7th Panzer crossed the Irsha and established a bridgehead around Malin while 1st Panzer and *LSSAH* drove west and then swung north to cross the river. Balck now had the enemy hemmed in on three sides, but he did not know their

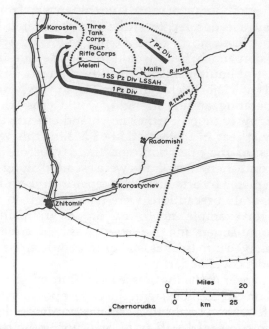

XLVIII Panzer Corps' attack on a superior Soviet concentration at Meleni, 16-23 December 1943

strength. For the next few days the three panzer divisions strove unsuccessfully to turn the salient into a pocket but it was soon clear that the Russians were not intimidated, and their counter-attacks grew in strength and ferocity to a level at which they could barely be contained. Then, on 21 December, a map was found on the body of a Soviet officer, revealing that the XLVIII Panzer Corps was tackling no fewer than three tank and four rifle corps which had been assembled for the recapture of Zhitomir. In this respect Balck, albeit unwittingly, had foiled the enemy's designs, but he wisely abandoned his attempt at encirclement and went onto the defensive. Almost at once, the Russians broke through again on the previous month's battlefield at Brussilov, so emphasizing the continuous nature of the offensive/defensive cycle, yet during this period the Fourth Panzer Army, of which the XLVIII Panzer Corps was the spearhead, had destroyed two Russian armies, mauled a third and captured or destroyed 700 tanks and 668 guns. Even so, such was the enemy's inherent strength that, when Vatutin's 1st Ukrainian Front developed its fresh offensive, it recovered all the ground that Balck's efforts had regained, and a great deal more besides.

Further south, fighting continued to rage along the great Dniepr

Bend. On 5 January 1944, a grey winter day of poor visibility, General Ivan Koniev's 2nd Ukrainian Front initiated attacks that ultimately succeeded in isolating Kirovgrad within a double-envelopment. The town lay in the sector of the German Eighth Army, and its immediate area was under the control of the XLVII Panzer Corps with the 3rd, 11th and 14th Panzer, 10th Panzergrenadier, 2nd Parachute and 376th Infantry Divisions under command. This apparent concentration of strength was deceptive as the Germans could field a total of only fifty-six tanks and 109 assault guns against an estimated Soviet tank strength of 620, while the infantry divisions were stretched painfully thin; the 10th Panzergrenadier Division, for example, had only 3,700 men with which to cover a front of eleven miles (17 km).

Outnumbered by eight to one, the Germans were forced back through the town, and substantial numbers were cut off in the northern suburb of Lelekovka. This group continued to put up a stiff fight and proved to be a major stumbling-block in the path of Russian units trying to establish an assembly area for a full-scale break-out to the west; with the assistance of a relief force, it managed to fight its way out during the night of 9 January. Some Russian armour did manage to penetrate as far as Malii Viski, the village in which the XLVII Panzer Corps had established its command post, but were driven off with serious loss by the 3rd Panzer Division.

German reinforcements began entering the southern fringe of the battle during the evening of the 9th, when the vanguard of *Grossdeutschland* turned back a number of Soviet probes. However, two Russian infantry divisions and their supporting armour had already moved past *Grossdeutschland*'s left flank, and throughout the next two days these were first isolated and then eliminated. Despite these set-backs and numerous spoiling attacks, the Soviet intention clearly remained to break out to the west. On 15 January a seven-mile (10 km) gap had been blasted in the new German line between Gruznoye and Vladimirovka, and the Russians concentrated all their resources to exploit this the following day. Unfortunately for them, the fresh 3rd SS Panzer Division *Totenkopf* had just entered the battle zone and promptly counter-attacked, riding roughshod over their preparations to such effect that the gap was closed off the following day.

This ended twelve days of heavy fighting in the Kirovgrad area. The Germans had been handicapped from the outset by their lack of reserves; nor were they able to create any by withdrawing to shorter lines on other sectors, such measures being specifically forbidden by Hitler himself. The Russians had employed no fewer than thirty-one infantry divisions in this series of operations, and these had been so weakened that many regiments were reduced to a mere 300-400 men, while the number of tanks available for action had dropped to approximately 120 by 17 January.

Kirovgrad may have only been a limited success for the Russians but it contributed directly to a serious German reverse. The fighting had left a German-held salient lying north of Kirovgrad and south of the recent Soviet gains on the Zhitomir sector. This contained two major formations, the XI Corps, under Lieutenant-General Stemmermann, and XLII Corps, under Lieutenant-General Lieb, a total of ten divisions, plus the 5th SS Panzer Division *Wiking*, recruited partly in Scandinavia, and the *Wallonien* brigade, composed of Belgian Nazi volunteers whom Lieb described as 'likeable fellows, but too soft for this business'.

Stavka decided that this salient should be isolated by converging thrusts across its rear by 1st and 2nd Ukrainian Fronts. This was accomplished without undue difficulty by 6 February, the pocket thus formed sometimes taking its name from Cherkassy, some miles away to the east, and sometimes from Korsun, a village and airfield in its centre. Continuous attacks were kept up against its perimeter, which contracted steadily, and on 9 February a *parlementaire* was sent through the German lines with a surrender demand, which was ignored.

Nevertheless, the position of Group Stemmermann, as the 50,000 men inside the pocket were now called, was extremely serious. An appreciation of the overall situation confirmed that the only direction in which a break-out attempt seemed likely to succeed was south-westerly, towards Lisyanka, towards which the First Panzer Army's III Panzer Corps, commanded by General Hermann Breith, an old friend of Guderian and already a holder of the Knights' Cross with Oakleaves, would also attack until an escape corridor had been opened. The Eighth Army's XLVII Panzer Corps was to have assisted by driving into the enemy's flank from the south but had already been worn down by the fighting at Kirovgrad, and its strength was further eroded by deliberate Soviet holding attacks; by 3 February, in fact, it could muster only twenty-seven fit tanks and thirty-four assault guns, so the scale of its contribution was very limited.

During its final days the pocket was compressed into an area measuring eight miles by five (13 km by 8), in the centre of which lay the village of Shanderovka.

The break-out was scheduled to take place during the night of 16/17 February. Casualties had been heavy, and it was with extreme reluctance that Stemmermann and Lieb agreed that the wounded would have to be left behind, attended by a number of doctors and orderlies. The troops began assembling after dusk and started moving off at 2300 hours, with Lieb leading the advance guard and *Wiking* covering the left flank. Throughout the night the columns of men, horse-drawn guns and wagons, trucks and tanks moved slowly across the rolling, wooded landscape, still covered with snow below which the ground was turning to mud. Hope rose steadily but at 0700 the Germans were detected as they entered a steep-sided hollow south of Dzhurzhentsy. The Russians immediately directed artillery fire onto the massed target, increasing in volume and accuracy as the light grew stronger. Because of the icy mud, very few tanks managed to climb the slippery hillsides, and most of the remaining vehicles, guns and heavy equipment had to be abandoned. Lieb and his staff, who were mounted, rallied as many men as possible and then rode alongside the tanks in a desperate attack which broke through the Russian cordon between Hill 239 and Pochapintsy. By 1300 only one obstacle remained – the Gniloy Tikich stream, varying between thirty and fifty feet (7.62 and 12.7 metres) in width, and ten feet (2.54 metres) deep. Here the last of the tanks were driven into the icy water and the remainder of the fugitives floundered across as best they could, under fire the while, reaching the III Panzer Corps' lines at Lisyanka at about 1600.

The Russians claimed that during the reduction of the Cherkassy/Korsun pocket they inflicted 55,000 casualties on the Wehrmacht and took over 18,000 prisoners – substantially more, in fact, than were originally present. German accounts say that 35,000 men took part in the breakout and that 30,000 got through. On one issue, at least, there was no dispute, and that was that, despite the number of men who had escaped, both German corps and the 5th SS Panzer Division *Wiking* required complete re-equipment and were unfit for action for several months. Wherever the columns had left the shelter of the trees or crossed open, level ground, they had been savaged by tanks which had driven over them, and where units had broken in panic the fugitives had been cut down in an orgy of slaughter by the vengeful Cossack cavalry; in this manner *Wallonien* had been all but obliterated, while General Stemmermann had died fighting among his rearguard. Koniev's reward was to be made a Marshal of the Soviet Union.

That so many reached freedom was due entirely to the III Panzer Corps, which at this period consisted of the 16th and 17th Panzer Divisions, joined by the 1st Panzer Division and *LSSAH*, thereby illustrating the way in which the crack divisions were transferred from corps to corps along the front as the need arose. Undoubtedly the most unusual unit in the corps – and indeed the Panzerwaffe – was the Heavy Panzer Regiment Bäke, named after its commander, Lieutenant-Colonel Dr Franz Bäke, a veteran of the tank battle south of Cambrai in October 1918 and a much-decorated panzer leader who at Kursk alone had been awarded the Tank Destruction Badge on three occasions for the single-handed destruction of an enemy armoured vehicle with a hand-held weapon. Bäke's command consisted of two tank battalions, one of them sPzAbt 503 with thirty-four Tigers and the other II/Panzer Regiment 23 with forty-seven Panthers, plus a self-propelled artillery battalion and an engineer battalion with specialist bridging skills.

The regiment was formed in January and its first task was to counter a thrust at Vinnitsa by five tanks corps. It went into action during the evening of the 26th and during the next five days and nights of fighting it destroyed no fewer than 267 enemy tanks and 156 guns of various types in the area Oratow/Balabanowka, a fine tribute to the gunnery characteristics of the German vehicles.* The scale of the German loss startled many senior officers and led them to ask for clarification; it amounted to one Tiger and four Panthers! The regiment had then provided the cutting edge of the III Panzer Corps as it drove to the relief of Group Stemmermann, having to fight its way through extremely tough opposition engendered by Stalin's *diktat* that no one should be allowed to escape from the trap. sPzAbt 503 was withdrawn from Russia in the spring for conversion to Tiger Model Bs, its place in Heavy Panzer Regiment Bäke being taken by sPzAbt 509, which had been active under Army Group South since the previous November.

Army Group South was now being pressed steadily westwards, unable to concentrate sufficient reserves with which to strike a decisive counter-blow because of Hitler's insane orders to stand fast on unsuitable positions. On 24 March the 1st Ukrainian Front had reached the Dniester, and five days later its advance guards were penetrating the foothills of the Carpathians, the effect being to cut off the First Panzer Army, which was already engaged with the 2nd Ukrainian Front to the east and south. Because of the number of occasions on which German troops were trapped by a combination of the Soviets' advance and

* The disastrous faults exhibited by the Panther at Kursk had been urgently remedied by design modifications. Despite being slightly heavy at forty-five tons (45,720 kg), the vehicle evolved into one of the finest medium tanks of the war, with some reservations regarding its automotive aspects.

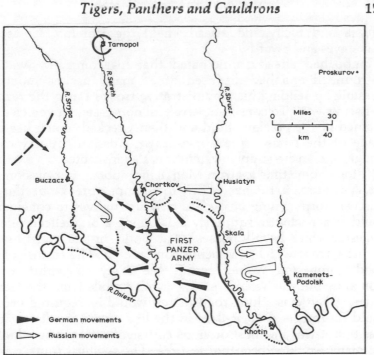

First Panzer Army's break-out from the pocket at Kamenets-Podolsk

Hitler's refused permission to withdraw, this period of the war is often referred to as that of the *Kesselschlachten* – Cauldron Battles.

Having been brought up in the traditions of *Vernichtungsgedanke* and having employed it so effectively themselves during the early years of the war, it was clear to many German commanders that, in the opening stages at least, just who is surrounding whom is a matter of mental attitude, and that the sooner a break-out was attempted, the greater was its chance of success. So grew the concept of the 'wandering pocket' in which trapped formations fought their way back to their own lines through the enemy mass; it goes almost without saying that such a concept relied almost exclusively for its success on the accumulated expertise of the Panzerwaffe.

The First Panzer Army was isolated in the area Kamenets-Podolsk on 25 March, on which date it consisted of nine under-strength panzer divisions, one panzergrenadier division, ten infantry divisions and several smaller formations, including Panzer Regiment Bäke. Since 5 November 1943 it had been commanded by General Hans Valentin Hube, a World War I infantryman who in recent years had served with distinction in

Russia and Sicily and already held the Knights' Cross with Oakleaves and Swords.

Hube had already anticipated that his command would be surrounded and had disposed of as many useless mouths as possible by sending his administrative troops far to the rear, out of harm's way. To conserve petrol, all non-essential vehicles were drained of the precious fluid and then wrecked, much use being made of the *panje* – the horse-drawn Russian country cart or sledge, and an air-supply system was also instituted.

It took some time for von Manstein to obtain permission from OKW for the First Panzer Army to attempt a break-out, but once this was forthcoming Hube had two alternatives to consider. He could either adopt a southerly axis, using a bridgehead over the Dniester which he still possessed at Hotin, or head west towards the new front which was being constructed. The former offered good going and would permit the army to withdraw into Romania, but this would remove it for a while from the German order of battle as a long road-march would be required before it could resume its proper place in the line; a further disadvantage was that it was the most obvious course of action, one which the Russians would expect him to take. The western route was less attractive, as it meant traversing broken country and involved crossing three rivers which ran from north to south into the Dniester – the Sbrucz, the Sereth and the Strypa; to be weighed against this, however, it offered the possibility of a junction with a relief force, was the shortest route to the restored German line and was not a direction that would seem attractive to the Russians themselves.

Manstein made no bones about the fact that, while the southern alternative was superficially more attractive, its adoption would merely postpone the evil hour and probably lead to a second and fatal encirclement of the army. He therefore ordered Hube to direct all his effort to the west and immediately flew to the Führer's headquarters on the Obersalzberg to explain the situation and demand fresh troops with which the Fourth Panzer Army could mount a relief operation. The discussion was acrimonious but eventually Hitler gave way and released the newly formed II SS Panzer Corps, consisting of the 9th SS Panzer Division *Hohenstaufen* and the 10th SS Panzer Division *Frundsberg*, which had been panzergrenadier divisions until October 1943; these, together with the 100th Light and 367th Infantry Divisions, would form the Fourth Panzer Army's relief force.

Once the decision to strike west had been taken, Hube planned and fought a brilliant operational battle. An elaborate deception plan, based on vehicle movements and false radio traffic, was set in motion to convince the enemy that the break-out would be made across the Dniester. The armour was split into three groups designated Northern Attack Force, Southern Attack Force and Rearguard, and the staff prepared route and movement tables for the rest of the army. Morale within the pocket was good, partly because the troops already knew what to expect from previous experience, partly because they were given a detailed briefing. As II SS Panzer Corps, 125 miles (201 km) away at Tarnopol, moved into its assembly areas for the drive east, the Luftwaffe prepared to land further supplies of fuel and ammunition inside the pocket as it moved west.

The break-out took place during the night of 27/28 March under cover of a blizzard which shrouded the scale of the movement. The two Attack Forces, led by Panther battalions, broke through the Russian screens without difficulty, secured crossings of the Sbrucz the following day and advanced on the Sereth. It took the Russians a little while to work out what was going on, and some of their units were sent chasing phantoms to the south in the belief that the Germans had escaped in that direction. However, once the Northern Attack Force reached the Sereth on 29 March, the cat was out of the bag. Koniev ordered his Fourth Tank Army to cross the Dniester and advance into the German flank between the Sbrucz and the Sereth. This move was met by the Southern Attack Force and roughly handled, while the crossing of the Sereth continued without interruption.

The Russians next began moving armour from north and south into the path of the First Panzer Army, simultaneously attacking its rearguard, which contained most of the Tigers. On 1 April the weather, hitherto favourable to Hube and his men, began to turn against them. A three-day blizzard made movement difficult, and then a sudden thaw produced the sort of quagmire in which the Russian armour performed to better advantage than the German. The progress of the embattled pocket slowed to a few miles a day. On the other hand, the Luftwaffe continued to bring in supplies and take out the wounded, a most important morale consideration since no German wished to become a prisoner of the Soviet Army. Even better, Hube managed to establish radio contact with the II SS Panzer Corps, approaching slowly from the west.

Gradually the gap between the two armoured formations narrowed until on 15 April both Attack Forces reached the Strypa and effected a crossing. Next day, near Buczacz, Hube's advance guard met that of the II SS Panzer Corps. It only remained for the rearguard to come in and the First Panzer Army was back in its place in the line, having destroyed no fewer than 357 Soviet tanks and forty-two self-propelled guns during its remarkable feat. Hube had shown himself a panzer leader of Balck's calibre at the operational level and was immediately promoted to the rank of Colonel-General. On 20 April he was awarded the Diamonds to his Knights' Cross, one of only twenty-seven such awards made during World War II, but he was killed in an air crash the following day on his way to receive the decoration.

The loss of Hube's potential was a grave blow to the First Panzer Army and to the Panzerwaffe as a whole, but three weeks earlier Germany had also lost the services of two of her ablest commanders. On 30 March the Führer's personal Condor aircraft collected von Manstein and von Kleist (the latter still commanding the rump of Army Group A, part of which was trapped in the Crimea) from their respective headquarters and flew them to the Obersalzberg. That evening Hitler awarded them both the Swords to their Knights' Crosses, thanked them courteously for their services, and then dismissed them from their commands, mentioning that Manstein would probably be found another appointment before long, presumably in the west; this, of course, proved to be an empty promise. Manstein had few doubts that the immediate cause of his dismissal was his public victory in the argument over the employment of the II SS Panzer Corps, but he knew full well that Goering, Himmler and Keitel resented his past success as much as they did his attitude of professional independence, and had intrigued against him for reasons of their own.

Many of Germany's best panzer leaders were now dead or prisoners in enemy hands or had been dismissed their posts. In their place Hitler appointed his own favourites, men who in some cases possessed ability and in others merely the capacity to solve problems in the short term. To emphasize that the old order had passed, Army Group South became Army Group North Ukraine under Colonel-General Walther Model, while Army Group A became Army Group South Ukraine under the command of the intensely ambitious Colonel-General Friederich Schörner, a former mountain troops officer whose dedication to the Nazi cause had not gone unrewarded.

The April mud finally brought an end to ten months of continuous fighting in the south. The Soviet Army had paid a terrible price to liberate its homeland, yet it grew visibly stronger with every month that passed. Once the *rasputitsa* had passed, it would attack again, on a scale never before experienced. In the meantime the stormclouds gathered in the west as well, black with the menace of a renewed war on two major fronts.

9. The Hydra Strikes

During the second half of 1944 the Eastern Front came dangerously close to complete collapse on several occasions, yet tempting as it might be to regard these circumstances as a simple compound of Hitler's intransigence and the Russian application of sheer mass, there were numerous factors involved which interacted on each other to produce results that were to prove fatal to the German cause.

At the highest level, the conspirators' failure to kill the Führer with their bomb on 20 July was to have dire consequences for the Army as an institution. Hitler would never again trust his generals, and as a mark of his contempt even the traditional military salute became illegal on 23 July, while henceforth even a whiff of suspicion or perhaps an anonymous denunciation from within the ranks was enough to ruin an officer or place him in fear of his life. Among those most heavily implicated were General Ludwig Beck, the former Chief of Army General Staff who had played so important a part in the formation of the Panzerwaffe, and General Erich Höpner, one of its most distinguished commanders; Beck, who would have become Head of State if the plot had succeeded, was permitted to commit suicide, but Höpner faced a firing squad. In the reign of terror which was to last until the war ended, many more senior officers would be put to death savagely, forced to commit suicide or sent to concentration camps. That many more generals were fully aware of the plot is beyond question, and these men found themselves on the horns of an insoluble dilemma; on the one hand they viewed the concept of assassination with all the horror of those raised to believe that the Army was above politics, especially in time of war; on the other, they could not find it in themselves to betray the conspirators despite adequate knowledge of their intentions.

The average German soldier and civilian, mercifully unaware of the true manner in which the war was being directed, still had faith in the Führer's ability to snatch victory from defeat, and there was very little support for the plot, despite a decline in the Nazi Party's popularity.

One of those punished directly after the explosion was Zeitzler, Chief of Army General Staff since 1942. Although Zeitzler was his own man – and had actually rebuked Hitler for speaking derogatively of the German officer corps – initially he had got on surprisingly well with the Führer. Recently, however, their relationship had deteriorated sharply and Zeitzler had angrily and repeatedly requested that he be relieved of his responsibilities, which consisted in the main of trying to reconcile Hitler's decisions with reality. Hitler dismissed him the day after the *coup*, denying him the prestige of wearing uniform, to emphasize the fact of his disgrace.

In Zeitzler's place Hitler appointed Guderian, complimenting himself on his own wisdom in placing the Panzerwaffe apart from the Army's command structure under its own Inspector-General, since not one armoured unit had thrown in its lot with the conspirators. This begged the question that in three widely separated theatres of war the German armour was too firmly embedded in combat and too far removed from the seat of power to have the potential for palace revolutions, and that in any event the conspiracy did not extend to the level of the troops. Nonetheless, it was apparent that Hitler now regarded Guderian as being one of very few long-serving senior commanders who could still be trusted, although it was made absolutely clear to the new Chief of Army General Staff that he was effectively a cypher forbidden to issue orders on his own authority and that all decisions would be made by the Führer himself. In this way, even such checks and balances as had formerly existed within the German higher command echelon had now been removed, the absolute control of the Third Reich's armies being exercised by a brain already damaged by the onset of Parkinson's disease and the tertiary or cerebral effects of syphilis contracted by Hitler in Vienna in his seedy Bohemian youth.

Thus fell the stars of many former panzer leaders who had served their country well. Few rose to replace them, but outstanding among them was that of Field Marshal Walther Model, formerly commander of the 3rd Panzer Division and XLI Panzer Corps, now one of Hitler's favourites. Wherever trouble threatened, there Model was sent to restore the situation; in 1944, for example, he successively commanded Army Group North from January until the end of March, then Army Group North Ukraine from April until 28 June, following which Army Group Centre was added to his responsibilities until he was appointed to command the Western Front on 17 August. Mellenthin tells us that he was 'an alert, dapper, fiery little man, never separated from his monocle, and although a soldier of great driving power and energy, yet he could hardly be regarded as an adequate substitute for Manstein. In particular, Model was too prone to interfere in matters of detail and to tell his corps and army commanders exactly where they should dispose their troops'.

Comings and goings at the highest levels apart, the morale of the German soldier on the Eastern Front remained unshaken. After the Casablanca conference the Allies had unwisely declared that their primary war aim was to secure the unconditional surrender of Germany, the implication being that it was the German people who were the enemy rather than Hitler, his henchmen and the evil apparatus of Nazism. Consequently, the Army fought with renewed determination to keep the Russians out of its homeland, coming to regard itself as the rampart of European culture against the onset of the Bolshevik horde. This attitude is reflected, *inter alia*, on the dedication plate of the history of Panzer Regiment 35, which shows a soldier's grave in a bleak Russian landscape, together with the legend '*Ihre Gräber sind eine Verpflichtung für die Welt: Freide!*' ('Their graves represent a debt owed by the World – Freedom!'). Startling as this might seem to the British or American reader, it was nonetheless a genuine source of motivation, and one which was more fiercely potent than the simple spirit of adventure which had marked the invasion of the Soviet Union three years earlier.

In addition to retaining its morale and tactical expertise, the Panzerwaffe was better supplied with equipment during 1944 than at any other time in its history, thanks to the efforts of Speer. Despite the rising intensity of the Allied bombing offensive against the centres of armaments production, a grand total of over 19,000 fighting vehicles left the factories for the front, including 8,328 medium and heavy tanks, 5,751 assault guns, 3,617 tank-destroyers and 1,246 self-propelled artillery carriages of various types.

Of the second generation of tank-destroyers, the Jagdpanzer IV had already entered service, and there followed in rapid succession the Hetzer (Trouble-maker), Jagdpanther and Jagd-tiger. The Hetzer was based on the chassis of the obsolete PzKw 38(t) tank and was issued to the tank-destroyer battalions of infantry divisions. It possessed an angled superstructure, was protected by 60mm armour plate and was armed with the 75mm L/48 PaK 39 gun offset to the right of the fighting compartment, plus a roof-mounted machine-gun that could be operated by remote control from inside the vehicle. The Hetzer was much admired for its fine lines, but not by its crews who were forced to endure the cramped and inconvenient conditions imposed by the layout. The driver, located at the left front, suffered least but was badly placed if forced to leave the vehicle in a hurry. Behind him sat the gunner, with the loader bringing up the rear, on the left of a gun designed to be loaded from the right and out of easy reach of the ammunition bins. The commander sat in isolation at the right rear of the fighting compartment, his only optical aid being periscopic binoculars which had to be used through the open hatch. Another effect of offsetting the gun to the right was unequal arcs of traverse, so that while eleven degrees were obtainable to the right, the juxtaposition of breech and side armour permitted only five degrees to the left. In mitigation, it must be admitted that offsetting was the only method by which the gun, four men and forty-one rounds of large ammunition could be fitted into the space available. In spite of the grumbles it provoked, the Hetzer produced good results and was adopted by the Swiss Army after the war.

By way of contrast, many regard the forty-five-ton (45,720 kg) Jagdpanther, armed with the 88mm L/71 PaK 43/3 gun capable of penetrating every British, American or Russian tank in service, as being the best tank-destroyer design of the war. As its name implies, the vehicle was based on the Panther chassis, the five-man crew being housed in a well-angled armoured superstructure whose 80mm front plate was laid back to provide the equivalent protection of 160mm thickness in the vertical. The Jagdpanther had a useful speed of 28 mph (45 kph), could stow eighty rounds of ammunition and possessed a secondary armament of a machine-gun in the glacis; its principal faults lay in the inevitable limitations imposed on main armament traverse by the adoption of a fixed fighting compartment, and its height of eight feet eleven inches (2.72 metres) which made concealment difficult. The Jagdpanther was issued to heavy tank-destroyer battalions, where it replaced the Nashorn.

A needless outgrowth of the same idea was the Jagdtiger, based on the Tiger B chassis, although the vehicle is of some interest in that it was the most powerfully armed AFV to see active service during the war, mounting a 128mm L/55 PaK 80 gun, the heavy rounds for which were split for ease of handling by the loader, the disadvantage of this being that it made for a slower rate of fire than tank-destroyers which employed fixed ammunition. Protected by 250mm frontal, 80mm side and 40mm roof armour, the Jagdtiger stood at nine feet three inches (2.82 metres) and, despite weighing over seventy tons (71,120 kg), could still achieve 23 mph (37 kph). On the other hand, the complex electro-mechanical transmission was subject to failure, and the weight factor made recovery very difficult. Only forty-eight of these monsters were completed during 1944 – as opposed to 228 Jagdpanthers, some being issued to heavy tank-destroyer battalions and others to SS Panzer corps.

The very fact that tank-destroyers and assault guns now outnumbered tanks was a tacit acknowledgement that the Panzerwaffe was irrevocably committed to performing a defensive role. Again, so many panzer divisions, including the favoured SS divisions which received a more regular allocation of equipment, were sent to France to counter the Allied invasion in June that the influence of the remainder, stretched painfully thin along the Eastern Front, was reduced to that of tactical intervention, rarely reaching the operative level, and only once achieving a short-lived result of strategic significance. At times panzer divisions, still the most potent weapons at the disposal of army group commanders, remained split among hastily assembled battlegroups drawn from several formations, in spite of the fact that they were themselves already operating well below strength. Of necessity, the philosophy concerning their employment became that of the fire brigade, containing one crisis after another, while the Tiger battalions provided a similarly stabilizing influence at corps level. This constant employment, coupled with the renewed nightmare of fighting a war on two major fronts, in itself created a degree of equipment wastage that coutner-balanced the improvements Speer had managed to effect in manufacture and supply.

It is, however, also necessary to examine the events of the latter half of 1944 from the Russian perspective, as only then does the full extent of the demands made upon the Panzerwaffe become apparent. This is a period which the Soviets understandably regard as being critical in the development of their own theories of armoured warfare and to which they devote much study, their conclusions being that, despite being worsted time and again in tactical encounters by German skill and battlecraft, they generally achieved their objective at the operative level, albeit at a terrible price, while at the strategic level they dictated events from start to finish.

The fact was that the Soviets had digested the lessons of previous years and there had been a dramatic improvement in their ability to handle large mechanized forces. It was true that they still relied on rigid centralized pre-planning and that their version of deep penetration operations was slower and more methodical than the German Blitzkrieg technique, but they had overcome many of their command problems by establishing forward headquarters which controlled each phase of their breakthrough and exploitation operations. They had also improved their communications and logistics apparatus, without which it would have been impossible for them to have embarked on the sort of operations they contemplated, and for this Allied aid was in a large measure responsible. This included tens of thousands of vehicle radio sets and over one million miles of telephone cable, 1,500 locomotives, 9,800 freight cars and 540,000 tons of rails, 356,000 motor trucks and 50,000 jeeps. True as it might be that the Russian infantryman could support himself in the field for long periods without the logistic backing found in German and Western armies, as far as the armoured formations were concerned they consumed huge quantities of fuel, ammunition and spares, and if these were not forthcoming everything quickly ground to a halt; the 'army without baggage' of popular myth is, therefore, something of a half-truth.

The offensives mounted by Soviet Fronts now involved simultaneous operations mounted directly against the German Front *and* one or both flanks with the object of achieving a major encirclement. Whereas in 1943 such operations had been conducted to a depth of fifteen to twenty miles (25-30 km) with a view to entrapping between six and twelve divisions, in 1944 the degree of confidence gained encouraged the execution of operations to a depth of 93-200 miles (150-200 km) in which up to eighteen German divisions might be trapped. In this new climate of optimism the task of individual armies which made up the fronts was to conduct operations to a depth of 62-93 miles (100-150 km) with the object of destroying between three and six divisions. During such major offensives a front might expect to advance a total distance of 250-312 miles (400-500 km) in two to three weeks, while for an army the corresponding figures would be 93-112 miles (150-180 km) in one or two weeks.

In 1943 the Soviet Army had been capable of an offensive deployment to a density of 150-180 guns and mortars and thirty to forty tanks, tank-destroyers and self-propelled artillery weapons per kilometre of front; by mid-1944 this had risen to, respectively, 200-250 guns and 70-85 AFVs per kilometre. In overall terms, the Wehrmacht on the Eastern Front found itself having to contend against local superiorities of 3-5:1 in manpower, 6-8:1 in tanks and artillery, and 3-5:1 in combat aircraft.

The Russian offensives opened with successive assault echelons which suppressed the German defences and created gaps through which mobile groups would pass deep into the enemy hinterland. These mobile groups varied in size according to the function they were intended to perform. The front mobile group, for example, might consist of one or two tank armies or one or two tank corps plus one or two cavalry mechanized groups, while the army mobile group consisted of one or two tank or mechanized corps reinforced by the army commander with additional artillery and anti-aircraft units.* Once through the forward defences, tank armies tended to move along parallel axes in pre-formed columns which were ready to deploy, their order of march determined by the need or otherwise to hold off the sort of fast-moving counter-stroke the Panzerwaffe had become so adept at delivering. Much movement took place at night, and within any twenty-four-hour period of an offensive a tank army would expect to cover a minimum of six to nine miles (10-15 km). Groups of varying size and composition were also employed at both front and army level to operate well ahead of the main body and seize ground of critical importance, bridges, road and rail junctions before a coherent defence could be established to protect them; known at the time simply as forward detachments, these groups can be regarded in many respects as the ancestors of the present-day Soviet Army's operational manoeuvre groups.

A further example of expanding Russian confidence was evident in a change of attitude to encircled enemy forces. While once they had followed the traditional method of establishing two cordons around a pocket – one to contain the defenders and the other to hold off relief attempts – it was now felt that only an inner cordon was necessary, and the troops which would have been detailed to form the outer now continued their advance without interruption.

Simultaneously, Soviet armaments production continued to soar, 29,000 tanks, assault guns and tank-destroyers being built in 1944, including 11,000 up-gunned T-34s equipped with an 85mm main armament mounted in an enlarged turet, and 2,000 IS-2 (IS = Iosef Stalin) heavy tanks, both of which entered service in the spring and were encountered in increasing numbers as the year progressed. In comparative gunnery terms, there was now not a great deal separating the contending tank fleets. The German 75mm L/48 gun which armed the PzKw IV had a muzzle velocity of 2,461 feet per second, to which the Panther's 75mm L/70 offered a considerable improvement at 3,068 ft/sec, while the T-34's 85mm L/51.5 produced 2,599 ft/sec. In the heavy category the Germans still possessed a slight advantage, the

---

* The composition of these formations can be found in the Appendix D, containing comparative orders of battle.

relevant figures for the 88mm L/56 of the Tiger E and the 88mm L/71 of the Tiger B being respectively 2,657 ft/sec and 3,340 ft/sec, compared with the IS-2's 122mm L/45 which produced only 2,562 ft/sec, although this was partly discounted by the fact that the Russian weapon fired a much heavier round (25 kg as opposed to 10 kg).

Although the IS-2 was coarsely finished and lacked the sophisticated gun-control equipment of the Tigers, it was actually better protected than the Tiger B with a maximum armour thickness of 160mm compared with the German vehicle's 150mm; indeed, within the limitations imposed by its intended use, it was a formidable fighting machine whose arrival was far from welcome to the already hard-pressed Panzerwaffe. Von Manteuffel recalled that, when his *Grossdeutschland* Division's Tigers first met the new Russian heavies at Targul Frumos, Romania, in May, they opened fire at 3,000 metres and were horrified to see their rounds flying off the thick frontal castings. Not until the range had closed to within 1,800 metres did the new Soviet tanks begin to lurch to a standstill, belching smoke and flames. This, however, lay well within the range in which the Tigers were themselves vulnerable to the Stalin's 122mm gun, and it was at once apparent that they could no longer expect to inflict the carnage they had in the past without also suffering grievously in return.

In the nature of its operations between June and December, the Soviet Army resembled a huge, enraged and vengeful hydra which shot out one head after another to fasten its fangs into its opponent's body, while simultaneously other heads engorged allies before spitting them out as fresh enemies. Hitler and his OKW staff believed that after the *rasputitsa* the Russians would renew their offensive in the Ukraine and concentrated most of the German armour to counter this. However, Stalin and *Stavka* had correctly evaluated the real weakness of Germany's strategic situation and calculated that a successful offensive directed against the over-extended Army Group Centre would also isolate Army Group North once the Russian spearheads had reached the Baltic, thereby causing irreparable damage to, if not the actual destruction of, both army groups.

The truth was that Army Group North was an anachronism and a luxury Germany could no longer afford, notwithstanding Hitler's belief that its presence encouraged Finland to remain in the war. There was no longer any pretence that Leningrad could be captured; the city had been relieved with a local offensive the previous winter and the Wehrmacht pushed away to the west. Moreover, now that Germany had been forced onto the defensive everywhere, the logical process would have been to abandon the Baltic states and disband the army group, since this would not only have shortened the front by several hundred miles but also enabled the formations so released to be re-constituted as a much-needed strategic reserve; such, however, was not the manner in which affairs were conducted.

Busch, the commander of Army Group Centre, had correctly deduced that his sector was to be the target of the next major offensive. He requested permission to withdraw most of his command behind the Berezina so that the Russian blow, when it came, would strike empty space. The effect of this, coupled with a scorched earth policy and the practice of holding only a forward outpost line while the majority of the troops remained out of artillery range in their main position some twelve miles (19 km) to the rear, would be to dislocate the carefully phased Soviet timetable and create such disorder and confusion among the attacking echelons that a prompt counter-stroke would pay handsome dividends. This was exactly what Zhukov and Vasilevsky had anticipated while they were planning the offensive, and they were both astonished and delighted when nothing of the sort happened; they could hardly have anticipated that Hitler would reject Busch's appreciation out of hand, telling him to stand and fight where he was.

Deployed against Army Group Centre were Bagramyan's 1st Baltic Front, Chernyakovsky's 3rd Belorussian Front and Rokossovsky's 1st Belorussian Front. In terms of manpower the two sides were evenly matched, but the Russians possessed a superiority of 4,000 tanks to 900 German, 28,600 guns against 10,000, and 5,300 aircraft against 1,300.

The offensive itself, codenamed Bagration, opened symbolical-ly on 22 June, the third anniversary of Barbarossa, with a pre-emptive strike by the Red Air Force which all but removed the Luftwaffe from the battle. Consequently, those German formations which were not immediately swamped under a flood of armour found themselves harried or pinned down by swarms of tactical attack aircraft. The Soviet armoured commanders had had it hammered home to them that what counted was speed and, despite considerable losses, they went to their work with a will, isolating one objective after another with double envelopments during a more or less continuous advance. In this way, large numbers of German troops were cut off at Vitebsk on 27 June, at

Mogilev on the 28th, at Bobryusk on the 29th and east of Minsk on 3 July. For those trapped within these pockets there was no hope of relief, for now no fewer than forty tank brigades and numerous cavalry mechanized groups were in full cry across what had once been eastern Poland with none to deny them, reaching Wilno on 13 July, Lublin on the 23rd and Brest-Litovsk on the 28th.

When the offensive at last ran down as it approached the Vistula, it had torn a 250-mile (400 km) gap in the German line, advanced 450 miles (720 km) in four weeks and, by Guderian's estimation, eliminated the equivalent of twenty-five German divisions. Whether the Soviets still possessed the means or, more significantly, the will to assist the abortive rising of the Polish Home Army inside Warsaw, or whether German defensive measures actually prevented the Russians intervening, as Guderian suggested, is a matter for debate elsewhere. According to Soviet sources the advance was finally halted by a prepared defence in depth east of the city and by a concentration of armour which included the 4th and 19th Panzer Divisions, 3rd SS Panzer Division *Totenkopf* and 5th SS Panzer Division *Wiking*, joined by the Luftwaffe's Panzer Division *Hermann Goering*. Whatever the truth, the virtual destruction of Army Group Centre during Operation Bagration remains one of the Soviet Army's most significant achievements and is regarded by many as one of the decisive events of World War II.

Only on the outer flanks of the offensive was the Panzerwaffe able to impose its own will on the enemy to any degree, and then the respite gained was brief. Balck's XLVIII Panzer Corps launched a two-fisted counter-attack between the Strypa and the Sereth on 14 July, with mixed results. The 1st Panzer Division followed its instructions implicitly and halted the Soviet advance on the Oleyev sector after some hard fighting, but the commander of the 8th Panzer Division chose to ignore the approach-route he had been allocated along forest tracks east of Zlochuv and decided instead to use a major road along which Balck had specifically forbidden movement; the consequence was that the division became a prime target for Soviet ground-attack squadrons and was strafed again and again in column. Mellenthin was sent to take temporary command of the division three days later, when it had recovered sufficiently to be detailed for the relief of the trapped XIII Corps, encircled to the north. This time the officer commanding its panzer regiment decided needlessly to regroup his assault force only thirty minutes before the attack was due to commence, and in full view of the enemy. Mellenthin had no

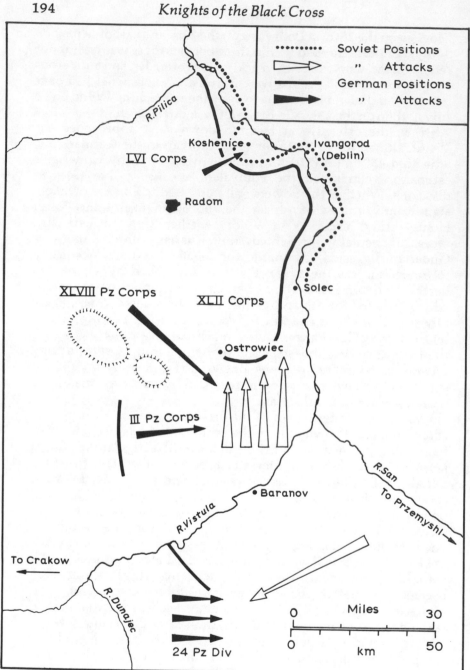

Fourth Panzer Army contains the Soviet breakthrough at the Baranov bridgehead, August 1944

option but to dismiss him and cancel the operation. The XIII Corps managed to fight its way out on the 20th at the cost of all its artillery and heavy weapons.

Army Group North Ukraine's line was now leaking like a sieve, and through the many gaps the armoured columns of Koniev's 1st Ukrainian Front were pouring in a mounting flood that was to drive it back across the Vistula.

As July turned to August, Model was frantically trying to close the gap which had opened between the First and Fourth Panzer Armies with the re-constituted Seventeenth Army, presently de-training in the area of Cracow. Only the 24th Panzer Division was available to screen this operation from Soviet forces advancing westwards from Przemyshl, the commander of which formed several battlegroups which engaged in a series of fast-moving 'hit-and-run' actions which thoroughly unsettled the Russians and enabled the Seventeenth Army to establish itself.

Balck was appointed commander of the Fourth Panzer Army on 28 July and took von Mellenthin with him as his chief of staff. He was immediately confronted with a difficult situation on the Baranov-Sandomierz sector where four Soviet armies (First and Third Guards Tank Armies, Fourth Tank Army and Fifth Guards Army) had established a major bridgehead across the Vistula west of its junction with the San and were launching heavy and continuous attacks on the right flank of the XLII Corps between Ostrowice and Solce. The German formation put up a spirited defence and, when Balck directed the III Panzer Corps to attack the enemy's left rear, the Russians were forced to halt their attack. However, before they could re-deploy to meet the threat the XLVIII Panzer Corps also crashed into their left flank, forcing them onto the defensive within a much reduced area. Next, Balck decided to eliminate a smaller bridgehead around Kosenice, lying some forty miles (64 km) downstream on the sector of LVI Corps. For this operation the concentrated corps artillery of the XLII and LVI Corps was supplemented by the divisional artillery of three panzer divisions, and although only six infantry battalions were employed in the attack, they received the direct fire support of no fewer than 120 assault guns. Needless to say, the Russian troops holding the bridgehead, amounting to two or three divisions, simply vanished amidst a tempest of direct and indirect gunfire.

Meanwhile, on the northern flank of Army Group Centre, Bagramyan's 1st Baltic Front had broken through to the Gulf of Riga, isolating Army Group North. Immediate steps were taken to re-open communications between the two army groups by converging attacks intended to slice through the neck of the Soviet salient. The major effort would be made from the west and be spearheaded by the XL Panzer Corps operating under the control Third Panzer Army, now commanded by Colonel-General Raus; the corps consisted of the 4th, 5th 14th and *Grossdeutschland* Panzer Divisions and was able to field approximately 400 tanks and assault guns. The German counter-attack commenced on 14 August and was directed at Shauliya and Yelgava but was able to make only slow progress in the face of the most determined opposition put up by the Soviet 51st, 2nd Guards and 5th Guards Tank Armies. However, to the north a strong battlegroup under the tank ace Colonel Count Strachwitz captured Tukums and re-opened a narrow corridor to Army Group North on 21 August.

For all the success of Bagration and its related operations, the Russians were still not the tactical equals of the Panzerwaffe, as demonstrated by the following incident, only one of many which took place along the front.

The Panthers of I/Panzer Regiment 35 had taken part in the battles to re-establish contact with Army Group North, but after the capture of the commanding Hill 920 that commanded by Sergeant Christ began to give trouble. The driver reported a major oil leak and increasingly defective steering; consequently, when the rest of the unit moved off, there was nothing for the Panther to do but remain where it was and await a tow back to workshops.

After a while Christ heard the squeal of tracks and the rumble of tank engines to his right and, knowing that no German armour remained in the area, dismounted to investigate. Some panzergrenadiers told him that they had spotted a T-34 in a wood opposite their position. The sergeant crawled forward through the underbrush until he could observe with his binoculars. Visible at the edge of the trees were not one but two T-34s, and his professional examination revealed that they were Model 43s, 76.2mm-gun versions up-armoured to 110mm and fitted with a cupola, sometimes referred to in German accounts as T-43s. Painfully the ailing Panther was nursed into a firing position. The gunner set the range, laid his aiming mark on the first target and pressed the firing button. The round struck and was immediately followed by another; for some reason the enemy tank did not burn, but its crew scrambled out. Christ promptly engaged the second tank, which burst into flames at once. Simultaneously, the muzzle flashes of two more tanks were spotted to the right of the burning vehicle, although the Russians were not engaging the Panther and seemed oblivious of its presence. These were also set ablaze with one round apiece.

Christ decided not to push his luck too far and reversed until the Panther was turret-down behind the crest. His instinct proved to be correct for another pair of T-34s appeared close to the original targets, this time with their guns traversed towards him. Using the cupola's counter-rotation device to give his gunner the correct line, he edged the Panther forward until it was hull-down and then let fly. An immense internal explosion blasted one of the newcomers apart. Suddenly, the first T-34 to be hit attempted to make good its escape, its driver having evidently clambered back aboard while Christ's attention had been distracted. A third 75mm round was punched through its plating and this time it burned like a torch. At this point the Panther's ammunition supply failed, and when yet two more T-34s appeared on the right Christ's driver and operator leaped out and ran to a nearby lorry to bring up fresh rounds. These were fired as quickly as they were handed aboard, and soon the Germans' sixth victim was blazing. The seventh followed in rapid succession when it unwisely broke cover. This finally broke up the Russian counter-attack, and during the evening Christ and his men received their reward in the shape of a tow to workshops and some rest after what had clearly been a busier day than usual.

From the Baltic to the northern slopes of the Carpathians the line had once again achieved a state of temporary stability, but in the meantime the hydra had lashed out again, this time to strike down Germany's Balkan allies. On 20 August Malinovsky's 2nd and Tolbukhin's 3rd Ukrainian launched a major offensive against Army Group South Ukraine. Led by the Sixth Guards Tank Army, this burst into Romania in an advance which covered 250 miles (400 km) in twelve days. This was materially assisted by the fact that Romania herself changed sides on the 25th, her troops promptly turning their weapons on their recent allies or seizing the Danube bridges to prevent their withdrawal. During the ensuing débâcle no fewer than sixteen German divisions were lost.

Next the Soviets swarmed across the Bulgarian frontier. Bulgaria was in the curious position of being at war with Great Britain and the United States but not with the Soviet Union; now she, too, defected, Guderian reflecting bitterly on the loss of the eighty-eight PzKw IVs and fifty assault guns which had been supplied to the Bulgarian Army. These developments threatened to isolate the German Army Groups E and F, stationed respectively in Yugoslavia and Greece, so that they had to be withdrawn rapidly north into Hungary. Simultaneously, the Wehrmacht was compelled to put down a serious rising in Slovakia.

In the far north, Finland concluded a separate peace with the Soviet Union on 2 September. On 10 October the Baltic sector erupted again, 1st Baltic Front reaching the coast near Memel while 2nd and 3rd Baltic Fronts closed in on Riga and Leningrad Front swept through Estonia. The remnants of Army Group North, amounting to some thirty-three divisions, was bundled back into the Courland peninsula and the Memel perimeter and blockaded there. Guderian was extremely bitter that Schörner, the army group commander, had allowed his panzer divisions to be trapped in a situation where they could make little further contribution to the war. Eventually several were evacuated by sea but two, the 12th and 14th, remained under siege until the end.

On 20 October the 2nd, 3rd and 4th Ukrainian Fronts turned their attention to Hungary, Germany's last remaining friend in Europe, Italy having surrendered the previous year and been turned round by the Allies. Even the Hungarian government would gladly have settled its differences with the Kremlin but it was prevented from doing so by some timely cloak-and-dagger work in Budapest on the part of Otto 'Scarface' Skorzeny and his associates. Yet on the Hungarian plains near Debrecen, in ideal tank country, Colonel-General Freissner's Army Group South – as Army Group South Ukraine had been renamed – won the Panzerwaffe's last important success in the east. Here a series of cut-and-thrust tank battles lasting several days culminated in the isolation of three Soviet corps by the 1st, 23rd and 24th Panzer Divisions, the pocket formed being rapidly eliminated by the Sixth Army. This action undoubtedly put a brake on Soviet intentions in Hungary, but the delay imposed was short-lived and by the end of the year Budapest was under siege.

Both sides now gathered their strength for the last round. Few entertained any doubts that Hitler's Reich had long to live, for the disasters in the east had been matched by similar events in France and the erosion of the last major defence line in Italy, although it was tantamount to suicide to voice such thoughts in public. In June, July and August Germany had sustained one million casualties on the Eastern Front alone and to make good these losses those who had previously been exempt from military service, including the very young, the old and the sick, were conscripted and formed into so-called Volksgrenadier divisions. Their armoured counterparts were thirteen panzer brigades numbered 101 to 113. These bore no relation to the brigades consisting of two two-battalion armoured regiments with which the panzer divisions had begun the war; instead, their establishment amounted to a single mixed tank/assault-gun battalion, a battalion or two of panzer grenadiers and such artillery and supporting troops as could be scrounged together.

They represented a hasty marriage between vehicles newly delivered from the factories and crews which had just emerged from the instructional schools. Mellenthin comments that in some cases their training had not even reached company level, and because of this and the lack of opportunity to gain any tactical expertise, their losses tended to be disproportionately high.

At the beginning of December the private fears of most Germans were centred on whether it would be the Western Allies or the Soviets who overran their country first. There were no illusions as to what a Russian invasion would mean after the terrible events that had taken place in the east. A majority of senior officers favoured the creation of a strong central armoured reserve which could be used to stabilize the Eastern Front while the war in the west took its course. Such a reserve had been assembled in secret and consisted of two fully equipped panzer armies, yet perversely it was not at the Russians that Hitler intended launching this concentration of force, but at the Americans.

10. Italy and the Campaign in the West

The Allies were not slow in following up their victory in North Africa and on 9 July 1943 launched their successful invasion of Sicily. It was at once apparent to those German troops on the island that their Italian comrades no longer had any wish to continue fighting, so that they were compelled to make a fighting withdrawal which concluded with an expertly conducted evacuation across the Straits of Messina the following month. Much of the burden of the fighting fell on that part of the Panzer Division *Hermann Goering* which had not been sent to Africa, the 15th Panzergrenadier Division (formed around a nucleus of survivors from the lost 15th Panzer Division) and the seventeen Tigers of 2/sPzAbt 504, whose 1st Company had also been lost in Tunisia.

Italy was itself invaded on 3 September. Hitler was well aware that in the wake of Mussolini's downfall in July the situation of German units there was precarious, and he began pouring in reinforcements not simply to contain the Anglo-American landings but also to disarm the Italian Army, should the need arise. This period witnessed the Panzerwaffe's greatest level of involvement in the Italian campaign, including those units which had just been evacuated from Sicily, the XIV Panzer Corps (29th Panzergrenadier Division and 1st Parachute Division) and LXXVI Panzer Corps (16th and 26th Panzer Divisions); the 1st SS Panzer Division *LSSAH* also entered the arena briefly between August and October before returning to Russia.

When a second landing took place on the Gulf of Salerno on 9 September, the 16th, 26th and part of the *Hermann Goering* Panzer Divisions, the 15th and 29th Panzergrenadier Divisions all converged of the Allied beachheads and put in such vigorous counter-attacks that for a while the success of the operation hung in the balance. Serious losses were inflicted on the invasion forces but in the end the fearful weight of naval gunfire support tipped the scales and forced the Germans to withdraw northward. Simultaneously, there was sporadic fighting between German and Italian troops in various parts of the country when some of the latter resisted attempts to disarm them following the public announcement of Italy's surrender. The fiercest of these short-lived clashes took place in Rome and Corsica, the former potentially the most serious since it involved the re-constituted Ariete Armoured Division and threatened the communications of those German formations already heavily engaged to the south. Elsewhere, thousands of Italian soldiers simply disbanded themselves and joined partisan units in the hills, particularly in the north.

The Wehrmacht's commander-in-chief in Italy for most of the succeeding campaign was Field Marshal Kesselring, whose objectives were first to tie down as many enemy divisions as possible so that they could not be used in the invasion of western Europe when the time came, and subsequently to prevent the Allies breaking through into the Balkans behind the army groups contesting the Soviet advance. Nonetheless, in German eyes Italy remained a secondary theatre of operations, despite the bitterness of some of the fighting, and one in which the rules of mountain warfare were paramount. The story of the campaign, therefore, became one of the Allies having to fight their way painstakingly through one elaborately constructed defence line after another, with expert demolitions delaying their progress as the Germans withdrew cleanly from one ridgeline to the next; only one major attempt was made to outflank the defences by means of an amphibious landing at Anzio, but this failed to fulfil its promise and was quickly contained by prompt German reaction.

In such a style of warfare the role of the Panzerwaffe was entirely tactical and supportive, with tank-destroyer and assault artillery units becoming closely involved in the fighting around fixed positions while the major mechanized formations were grouped behind the front to counter the unlikely prospect of an Allied breakthrough. They were, therefore, under-employed to the extent that the number of armoured divisions present in Italy was progressively reduced as the campaign continued, the 16th Panzer Division being posted to Russia late in 1943, followed by Panzer Division *Hermann Goering* in July 1944, while the 15th Panzergrenadier Division was sent to France in September 1944. After its losses in Tunisia and Sicily and the early battles in Italy, sPzAbt 504 went to Holland to rest and refit but returned to Italy in June 1944 after a short spell on the Eastern Front and remained there for the rest of the war.

During 504's absence a newly raised Tiger battalion, sPzAbt 508, arrived in Italy. The personnel of this unit had been closely involved in the field trials of an armoured, self-propelled demolition charge known as the Goliath. These little vehicles resembled miniature versions of the lozenge-shaped British tanks of World War I, the intention being that they should be pointed towards their objective and then allowed to motor slowly across No Man's Land, the charges being detonated by remote control once they had reached their target. The device was first used at Kursk and is also known to have been employed against the Polish Home Army during the Warsaw Rising, but it made its début against the Anglo-American armies at Anzio. This proved to be interesting but abortive as the tracks were vulnerable to any sort of fire; persistent legend has it that at least one example was caught, turned round and sent back from whence it had come! 3/sPzAbt 508 was present at Anzio from February to May 1944 and may have been involved, although the impression given is that it fought as a conventional tank company. sPzAbt 508 remained in Italy until January 1945, when it handed over its remaining Tigers to spzAbt 504 and returned to Germany.

The Italian landscape was particularly suitable for the type of long-range defensive shooting in which the German armour possessed a distinct advantage over its Allied counterparts because it possessed not simply better weapons but also first-rate optical gunsights. For example, on 22 June 1944, shortly after sPzAbt 504's return to the line near Massa Marittima, a single Tiger platoon stopped a Fifth Army attack dead in its tracks near Parolla, destroying eleven of the twenty-three Shermans which were leading the American assault. 'Like shooting ducks on a pond,' was the German verdict on the engagement; the Sherman crews could but agree and abandoned the twelve survivors, which were captured during a counter-attack. The Allies remained out-gunned throughout the campaign and elsewhere in Europe, although the gap narrowed with the introduction of several new weapons, including the 90mm gun of the M-36 tank destroyer, the 76mm gun fitted to later models of the Sherman and to the M-18 tank-destroyer, and the British 17-pdr which armed the Sherman Firefly and later the Comet cruiser tank, as well as the Achilles and Archer tank-destroyers. The 17-pdr gave approximate parity with the Panther, but the only real answer to emplaced Tigers firing at long range remained a medium artillery concentration.

Veterans of the Eastern Front who later fought in Italy or the West were shocked by the volume, accuracy, flexibility and rapid response of the British and American artillery which was able to switch its fire around the battlefield in a manner hitherto unknown, often joined by tank and tank-destroyer units employed in the supplementary artillery role when the front was static for any length of time. Another unpleasant surprise was the efficient control of ground-attack squadrons which were always waiting to pounce with cannon fire, bombs and rockets; though individually inaccurate, each rocket possessed the impact of a medium artillery shell, so that the arrival of a salvo in close succession and proximity was a terrifying experience. All in all, it was a foolish tank commander who failed to change his position once he was aware that his vehicle had been spotted.

The Italian campaign also contained a most unpleasant surprise for Allied armoured units in the shape of a ground-mounted Panther turret. This was emplaced on top of a rectangular steel box which had been dug in to a depth of approximately ten feet (two metres). The box consisted of two portions, the top plate of the upper incorporating the turret ball-race while a manhole in the floor was located over an iron ladder leading down into the lower portion. This was six feet seven inches high and was divided into three compartments, the first of which was lined with board and contained three bunks for the crew and an escape manhole, the second the main access hatch and the ladder, while the third served as a storeroom for food and ammunition and also contained electric batteries and a switchbox. Electric light was provided and fumes were dispersed by fans in the roof. The entrance was located some forty feet away and consisted of a slit trench sloping steeply downward and covered at its deeper end with beams and earth. The turret protruded only inches above the ground, being generally so well camouflaged as to be completely invisible to approaching tank crews until it opened fire. It was first encountered in May 1944 in the carefully fortified switch line lying behind the western end of the Gustav Line, referred to in Allied accounts as the Hitler Line but more correctly in German histories as the Senger Line, and again later the same year in the deep defensive belt known as the Gothic Line.

Such points of interest apart, there were few lessons to be learned from the Panzerwaffe's operations in Italy, although its contribution to a tenacious defence ensured that this continued until the war's end.

On 1 June 1944 there were 156 German divisions engaged on the Eastern Front, twenty-seven in Italy and fifty-four in the West awaiting the Allied invasion of France. In theory the last, with 850,000 men, represented some twenty per cent of the available strength, but in practice many of the infantry divisions were below their establishment and some contained soldiers of dubious loyalty, including former Polish and Russian prisoners of

war, a high proportion of whom spoke no German; after the
Normandy landings those Poles that could wasted no time in
joining their countrymen fighting among the British. Included in
the German total in the West were ten panzer divisions and one
panzergrenadier division with an overall tank strength of 1,552.
Superficially, this equalled approximately thirty per cent of the
Panzerwaffe's strength, but some of these divisions were
recovering and refitting after their experiences on the Eastern
Front, while others still had units serving in the East and three
had no combat experience at all; the *average* divisional tank
strength amounted to seventy-five vehicles.

The position of Commander-in-Chief West was held by von
Rundstedt, who exercised theoretical command over Rommel's
Army Group B (Seventh and Fifteenth Armies) in the invasion
sector and von Blaskowitz's Army Group G (First and Nineteenth
Armies) in southern France. There was universal agreement
among senior commanders that the panzer divisions would play a
decisive role when the invasion came, but deep-seated
disagreement as to the form this should take. Rommel, chastened
by his defeat in Africa and his experience of Allied air power, was
in favour of defeating the invaders before they could establish
themselves ashore. 'If the enemy once gets his foot in, he'll put
every anti-tank gun and tank he can into the bridgehead and let
us beat our heads against it, as he did at Medenine. To break
through such a front you have to attack slowly and methodically
under cover of massed artillery, but we, of course, thanks to the
Allied air forces, will have nothing here on time. The day of the
dashing cut-and-thrust tank attack of the early war years is past
and gone.'* Guderian, with von Rundstedt's complete agreement,
expressed the contrary view: 'Our opinion was that it all
depended on our making ready adequate reserves of panzer and
panzergrenadier divisions; these must be stationed far enough
inland from the so-called Atlantic Wall, so that they could be
switched easily to the main invasion front once it had been
recognised.'†

Herein lay the nub of the problem. Hitler had always thought
that the Allies would make their major landing north of the Seine
in the Pas de Calais area, and although he later also considered
Normandy as a possible invasion site, he continued to regard this
as the main danger area and was encouraged to do so by an
elaborate Allied deception plan. After considering the conflicting

* *The Rommel Papers*, ed. B.H. Liddell Hart
† *Panzer Leader*

views of the officers most concerned, he decided in May to establish an OKW Reserve consisting of I SS Panzer Corps under the command of SS General Sepp Dietrich which, *subject to his own approval*, could be committed as Rommel suggested. This reserve lay outside Rundstedt's authority and, to compound the inevitable confusion that would arise from such a compromise, the rest of the armour was placed under General Freiherr Geyr von Schweppenburg's Panzer Group West, which was constructed more as a training organization than as an operational headquarters. Many of the signals relating to this matter and to the deployment of German armoured formations after the Allied landings on 6 June were picked up and interpreted by the *Ultra* interception unit in Britain and promptly passed forward.

Much, therefore, hinged on the manner of the I SS Panzer Corps' employment during the first hours of the invasion. Dietrich, its commander, was one of Hitler's oldest friends, a well-built street-brawler who had found his vocation during the Nazi Party's violent rise to power, been prominent in the elimination of the SA leadership during the Night of the Long Knives, and was a former commander of 1st SS Panzer Division *LSSAH*. Coarse of manner, he retained his sergeant-major's instinct for a smart turn-out and although a competent panzer leader could hardly be described as brilliant. The three armoured divisions which constituted his corps, 21st Panzer Division, the Panzer Lehr Division and 12th SS Panzer Division *Hitlerjugend*, were the best equipped in France. 21st Panzer Division contained a few old Afrika Korps hands and was a reincarnation of the division which had been lost in Tunisia, lacked a Panther battalion but had 127 PzKw IVs and was positioned closest to the invasion sector; Panzer Lehr, located at Le Mans, was commanded by Lieutenant-General Fritz Bayerlein, a former chief of staff of Rommel's in North Africa, and had been raised from the panzer schools' demonstration units in Germany, being equipped with no fewer than 190 tanks, forty assault guns and 612 half-tracks, an establishment which rivalled that of *Grossdeutschland*; *Hitlerjugend*, composed of teenage soldiers, was situated between 21st Panzer and Panzer Lehr and was also well up to strength, with 177 tanks and twelve assault guns, becoming notorious for the dedicated and self-destructive savagery with which it fought throughout its career.

The careful preparation which the Allies had put into every aspect of their invasion plans paid ample dividends on all save Omaha Beach, no difficulty being experienced in getting ashore and consolidating beach-head defences. In contrast, the response

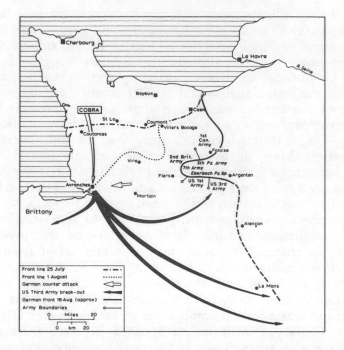

Normandy – the American break-out and the Falaise pocket, July 1944

of the I SS Panzer Corps was turgid and piecemeal, thanks to the sanctions imposed on its use. Only Feuchtinger's 21st Panzer Division possessed limited standing orders which permitted it to counter-attack, but even then the divisional commander remained uncertain for several hours which local higher formation he was subordinate to. At length he was told to advance north and restore the German Front between Caen and Bayeux. The division advanced in two columns which were quickly detected, coming under sustained air attack and naval gunfire. Losses had begun to mount even before the spearheads had worked their way through Caen, and at 1600 hours the attack was brought to a standstill by the British 3rd Division's anti-tank gun screen, a second attempt being foiled by artillery fire and hull-down tanks. By the time his division had withdrawn and gone into leaguer, Feuchtinger had only seventy battleworthy tanks left. Nonetheless, 21st Panzer had effectively prevented the capture of Caen that day, and had its attack been launched during the morning, its effect would have been even greater.

Notwithstanding repeated requests from von Rundstedt, Hitler refused to release the Panzer Lehr and *Hitlerjugend* Divisions until late that afternoon, and although this enabled them to make at least part of their approach march into the battle zone under the protective cloak of darkness, they could hardly avoid the effects of non-stop strafing the following morning. This was so serious that Panzer Lehr was unable to get into action for a further forty-eight hours while *Hitlerjugend*, having been so harassed and delayed on route that it averaged only 4 mph (6.40 kph), arrived with dry petrol tanks in its pre-action replenishment area only to find that its dump had already been turned into an inferno.

Rommel's option, that of halting the invasion at the water's edge, therefore no longer existed, while its alternative, that of inflicting a decisive defeat on the invaders inland, beyond the reach of naval gunfire, was never put to the test, as Hitler continued to believe that the Normandy landings were a feint and that sooner or later the Allies would make their main invasion effort in the Pas de Calais. His policy, therefore, remained one of strict containment, disregarding the constant exposure of his troops to the crushing effect of the warships' fire and the swarms of ground-attack aircraft flying from airfields in southern England. Indeed, the Allies were able to build up their strength faster than Army Group B, for the RAF and USAAF had also thoroughly disrupted communications in the German rear, dominating road and rail routes by day, while at night the French Resistance groups emerged to ambush convoys and blow up vital bridges.

Five days after the landings Rommel advised OKW that daylight movement in the battle zone had become an impossibility, while for 60 miles (100 km) beyond the front was effectively cut off until nightfall. The result was not only to reduce vital supplies of ammunition and fuel to a trickle but also to delay the arrival of fresh panzer divisions ordered to converge on Normandy. The 2nd Panzer Division, for example, although originally positioned just north of the Seine, was forced because of blown bridges to make a detour of 160 miles (256 km), and its leading elements did not start entering the forward area until 13 June; even then, a further week elapsed before it could report itself as being complete. The 17th SS Panzergrenadier Division, stationed 200 miles (320 km) away at Bayonne, was unable to complete its journey until the 17th. The 9th and 10th SS Panzer Divisions, transferred from the Eastern Front, took longer to cross France than they had the rest of Europe and did not reach the front until 25 June. The 2nd SS Panzer Division *Das Reich* had over 450 miles (720 km) to travel from Toulouse and arrived slowly between 26 and 30 June, its panzer regiment having been delayed by fuel shortages; further delays had been caused by Resistance units which repeatedly ambushed the division's columns along the way. *LSSAH* reached the front from Belgium on 29 June. The 116th Panzer Division, formed recently in France from the remnants of the 16th Panzergrenadier Division on the latter's return from Russia, remained near Dieppe watching the Pas de Calais until it too was committed to the fighting in Normandy late in July, being joined by the 19th Panzer Division from the south in early August.

The strategy proposed by Hitler was the separation of the two Allied armies by a concentrated thrust to the coast, following which all efforts would be directed at the elimination of the British Second Army; once this had been achieved, he believed that the neighbouring US First Army would ask for terms. The late arrival of the panzer divisions destroyed any slight chance of success this plan might have had, although the plan itself ensured that the bulk of the German armour was concentrated opposite the British and Canadian sectors. This was exactly what the Allies themselves hoped to achieve in order to distract German attention away from American preparations for a major break-out from the southern flank of the beachhead, and to this end Montgomery mounted a series of crumbling offensives which sucked the German armour into a tactical vortex as soon as it arrived and held it there.

First came Epsom, which lasted from 26 June until 1 July, pushing across the Odon south-west of Caen and securing a foothold on the feature known to the British as Hill 112. This gently rolling feature was quite unremarkable in itself save that its summit provided panoramic views in every direction, ensuring that it witnessed some of the bitterest fighting of the campaign. To the Germans the hill became known as Kalvarienberg (Mount Calvary), while their opponents referred to the whole locality as Death Valley. On 10 July Operation Jupiter enabled the British to tighten their grip on the hill, but for the next three weeks savage fighting raged across its slopes and among the adjacent villages in the Odon valley. Prominent in the defence of the feature were the Tigers of sSS-PzAbt 102, whose crews were often unable to dismount for hours at a time because of the British massed artillery fire.

On 8 July most of Caen was captured by means of an attack from the north which followed in the wake of a pulverizing bomb carpet. Another bomb carpet heralded the opening of Operation Goodwood south-east of the city on 18 July, in which no fewer than three British armoured divisions (the Guards, 7th and 11th) attempted to capture Bourguebus Ridge and, if the opportunity arose, break out into open country. Opposing this thrust were the 21st Panzer Division, *LSSAH* and *Hitlerjugend*, reinforced with thirty Tigers from the heavy battalions and seventy-eight of the redoubtable 88mm dual-purpose guns, dug in, camouflaged and waiting. The British under-estimated not only the strength of the defence but also its depth, so that after three days of fighting they had obtained a very limited success at the high cost of over 200 tanks destroyed or out of action. On the other hand, Goodwood seemed to reinforce the impression that the real danger from the Allies lay at the northern end of their line, so that by the last week of July the British and Canadians were faced with the 2nd, 21st, 116th, 1st SS, 9th SS, 10th SS and 12th SS Panzer Divisions and four Tiger battalions, while opposite the Americans there were only the Panzer Lehr and 2nd SS Panzer Divisions and the 17th SS Panzergrenadier Division available to buttress the line held by increasingly weary infantry divisions.

The writing on the wall was now plain enough for all to see – the German Army in France was bleeding to death. Ten days after Goodwood its losses in personnel amounted to over 127,000 men, yet it had received fewer than 15,000 reinforcements. On 15 July Rommel estimated that he had lost 225 tanks for which only seventeen replacement vehicles had arrived. The truth was that the Panzerwaffe, designed by its architects as a weapon of mobile strategic offence, was being steadily battered to pieces while performing a static tactical defence. Such counter-attacks as it was able to make, including the thrust through Bayeux to the coast favoured by Hitler, which took place on 29 June, were quickly halted and smashed up.

There was the occasional flash of brilliance which momentarily lightened the gloom, but they were few and far between. On 13 June the British 7th Armoured Division attempted a wide right hook, which, had it succeeded, would have levered the defenders of Caen out of their position and cut off the Panzer Lehr Division. Shortly after dawn the vanguard passed through Villers-Bocage and halted on the road leading to the summit of Hill 213, tanks, carriers and half-tracks closing up nose-to-tail to allow sufficient room for the relief point units to pass by. Unknown to those in the column, they were being observed from the high ground by SS Lieutenant Michael Wittmann, a tank ace credited with 119 kills on the Eastern Front who had been awarded both the Knights' Cross and Oakleaves in January 1944 while serving with the 13/SS Panzer Regiment *LSSAH*. Now, Wittmann was commanding 2/sSS-PzAbt 101, which on this morning mustered six Tigers, only four of which were battleworthy, the battalion having just completed a difficult approach march from Beauvais. Nearby was No. 1 Company, also reduced to a handful of tanks.

Recognition of a quick kill was instinctive. Wittmann broke cover, his first round striking a half-track with such force that it was hurled, blazing, across the highway. The Tiger then lumbered the length of the column, destroying one vehicle after another, impervious to everything that was fired at it in return, breaking into the village to inflict yet more carnage before Wittmann ordered his driver to turn off the main street and return across country to Hill 213. The solo action had lasted a mere five minutes but had brought the advance of the 7th Armoured Division to a standstill.

That afternoon sSS-PzAbt 101 and elements of 2nd Panzer Division launched a counter-attack on Villers-Bocage which eventually recovered the village after heavy fighting in which three Tigers were destroyed, a further three, including Wittmann's, immobilized, and several of 2nd Panzer's tanks knocked out; 7th Armoured's losses during the day amounted to twenty-five tanks, fourteen carriers and fourteen half-tracks, the majority incurred during the morning. On the recommendation of General Bayerlein of Panzer Lehr, Wittmann was awarded the Swords to his Knights' Cross and was promoted on the spot. He was offered an appointment at an officers' tactical school but declined and was killed on 8 August during an engagement with a troop of British Shermans, at least one of which was a 17-pdr Firefly.

There were, too, occasions during the normal course of the fighting when, for every German tank destroyed, the Allies lost four. This was something they were quite prepared to tolerate in the short term, for in 1943 American tank production had reached a figure of 29,500 and was actually cut back to 17,500 the following year, to which must be added the 5,000 British tanks constructed in 1944. Thus, for the Allies, tank losses were made good almost at once, while for the Panzerwaffe in Normandy they were irrevocable.

Small wonder, then, that when Keitel at OKW telephoned von Rundstedt to ask what was to be done in an impasse in which the armies in Normandy could neither remain where they were nor embark on a war of manoeuvre without being destroyed, the Commander-in-Chief West made his famous retort: 'Make peace, you fools! What else can you do?' He was promptly relieved of his command and replaced by von Kluge on 3 July, although the latter had no fresh solutions to the problem and was no more

master in his own house than Rundstedt had been. On 17 July
Kluge was also required to assume direct command of Army Group
B when Rommel's staff car was attacked from the air and overturned; seriously injured, Rommel was evacuated to Germany, his
eventual fate being enforced suicide in the aftermath of the attempt
on Hitler's life.

At the southern end of the Allied line Lieutenant-General Omar
N. Bradley's Twelfth Army Group was ready to initiate its break-
out operation, code-named Cobra, on 19 July, but poor flying
weather led to its being postponed until the 25th, on which date
there were 645 tanks deployed opposite the British and Canadians
but only 190 opposite the Americans. Once again, the Allies
employed a bomb carpet to batter their way through, hitting
Panzer Lehr particularly hard, as Bayerlein later recalled. 'After an
hour I had no communication with anyone, even by radio. My
front lines looked like the face of the moon and at least 70 per cent
of my troops were out of action – dead, wounded, crazed or
numbed. All my forward tanks were knocked out and the roads
were practically impossible.'

During the next few days the US First Army continued its steady
advance on Avranches through visibly disintegrating opposition.
Von Kluge did not react until the 28th, when he ordered the 2nd
and 116th Panzer Divisions to move into the danger zone from
their positions opposite the British sector. Montgomery immediately instituted a series of holding offensives designed to prevent
the transfer of any more German armour, commencing with
Bluecoat on 30 July. This pushed the British Second Army's line
southwards towards Mont Pinçon and Vire and in places achieved
deep and unexpected penetrations. These new gaps in his front
were plugged by von Kluge with the 21st Panzer Division and at
least one Tiger battalion, their twenty-mile (32 km) journey taking
five hours, during which they were harried incessantly by Allied
fighter-bombers. Sir Miles Dempsey, the Second Army's commander, maintained the pressure to such good effect that Kluge was
further obliged to commit the II SS Panzer Corps (9th and 10th SS
Panzer Divisions). The holding strategy was then prolonged along
the Allied left, with two Canadian offensives, Totalize and Trac-
table, aimed at Falaise; these succeeded in further pinning down
the German armour and were barely contained by *Hitlerjugend* at
the cost of its own virtual destruction.

The effect of these operations was to create a hard shoulder
against which the major German field army in France was to be
crushed, a process begun with the activation of Lieutenant-General
George S. Patton's US Third Army on 1 August. Patton's four

streamed through the gap at Avranches in succession, the VIII Corps into Brittany, the XV Corps reaching Le Mans on 8 August having covered seventy-five miles (120 km) in three days, the XX Corps heading south to the Loire before swinging east, followed by the XII Corps. The bulk of Third Army was, in fact, executing a giant wheel towards the Seine, pivoting on the First Army's VII Corps at Mortain.

The *Vernichtungsgedanke* tradition was as deeply ingrained in von Kluge as in any German officer of equivalent rank for him not to recognize at once that, with his right held and with his left irretrievably turned, any northward pressure by Patton was bound to entrap his entire command. His professional advice to the Führer, therefore, was that the panzer divisions should provide a screen behind which the rest of the army should withdraw beyond the Seine. Hitler rejected this sound advice out of hand, proposing instead a large-scale counter-attack through Mortain to the coast at Arromanches, the effect of which would be to close off the gap and isolate Patton's army, which would cease to pose any threat once it had exhausted its supplies and probably disintegrate. The choice of location was made entirely from the map and without any understanding of what conditions were like at the front, particularly as regards Allied air superiority. Kluge was ordered to concentrate eight panzer divisions for the task, an impossibility in itself, but eventually managed to assemble four, all well below strength, equipped with a total of 185 tanks and assault guns.

Thanks to *Ultra*, the Allies received several days warning of the attack, the preparations for which were confirmed by air reconnaissance and normal intelligence activity. Known as Operation Liège, it began early on the morning of 7 August, aided by poor flying-conditions. The 2nd Panzer Division managed to advance some seven miles (12 km) before being fought to a standstill by Combat Command B 3rd Armored Division. *Das Reich* also enjoyed some initial success, recapturing Mortain but not the nearby Hill 317, whose determined American garrison directed artillery concentrations onto the stalled columns. Elsewhere, on the extreme right of the counter-offensive, the 116th Panzer Division was itself placed on the defensive by an American spoiling attack while in the centre *LSSAH* made little or no headway. Worse still, by noon the sky had cleared, the remnants of ground mist had been burned off by the sun, and the deadly fighter-bombers arrived in swarms, bombing and strafing at will. For the rest of that day and all the next it was the Americans who attacked, so that by 9 August the Germans were back where they had started.

Nonetheless, von Kluge fully intended to renew his efforts on 10

August and had regrouped with the object of doing so when his intelligence staff advised him that Patton's corps had now started to wheel north. His request to Hitler that the panzer divisions employed at Mortain be re-deployed to meet the threat was ignored, and from that point onwards events moved at a pace they could no longer be controlled. Under pressure from the British and Canadians in the north and from the Americans in the west and south, by 16 August three major German formations, the Seventh Army, Fifth Panzer Army (as Panzer Group West was now known) and Panzer Group Eberbach, which consisted mainly of the divisions employed at Mortain, were pinned inside a pocket some twenty-five miles (40 km) long and fifteen (24 km) wide. This continued to shrink by the hour so that on the evening of the 17th the only exit from the trap was a six-mile (9 km) wide gap through which fugitives, motor vehicles of every type, horse-drawn transport and artillery sought safety to the east, harried by the Allied air forces and artillery.

When the gap was finally closed on the 21st, only 40,000 of the estimated 100,000 men in the pocket had managed to escape from the trap, partly because Kluge had, upon his own initiative, withdrawn the II SS Panzer Corps and used it to keep open the neck of the sack for as long as possible by counter-attacking from the outside, and partly because almost every piece of equipment except personal weapons had been abandoned.

Von Kluge did not survive his army, but the reasons for his death were different. Hitler believed that his attitude towards the Mortain counter-stroke had been half-hearted, although this was less than just. Then, on 15 August, the Field Marshal had been forced to spend several hours sheltering in a ditch from air attack, out of contact with his own headquarters and therefore with OKW, his absence being interpreted by the Führer as a clandestine attempt to negotiate surrender terms with the Allies. He was promptly dismissed and, after considering his position, took his own life. Although innocent of any charges of professional neglect, he was, ironically, an unwilling conspirator in the 20 July bomb plot and knew that by now the Gestapo would be fully aware of his involvement.

His replacement was Field Marshal Walther Model, the Führer's favourite trouble-shooter on the Eastern Front. There was, in fact, little that Model could do beyond save what he could from the wreck. Those divisions which relied on the horse as a prime mover stood no chance at all, while the panzer divisions were reduced to an average of ten tanks and a few hundred men. Even the line of the Seine proved indefensible so that the Allied armies found no difficulty in securing bridgeheads and fanning out across France. Understandably, there were bitter reflections that in Normandy the Panzerwaffe had simply been squandered and that this in turn had prevented the establishment of a viable armoured reserve with which to counter the sweeping Allied advances, as opportunities did arise during which telling blows could have been struck at an enemy grow supremely confident in victory; what might have been the response of a von Manstein as Patton's US Third Army outran its fuel supplies, or of a Balck when presented with the long exposed flank of the British Second Army as it roared northwards across the Belgian frontier to Brussels and Antwerp, must remain a matter for speculation.

A further factor which complicated Model's position was the landing of General Alexander Patch's US Seventh Army on the southern coast of France on 15 August. Blaskowitz, the commander of Army Group G, received permission to withdraw and did so expertly, with the 11th Panzer Division covering the Nineteenth Army during its retreat up the Rhône valley, fighting its way through an ambush at Montélimar and subsequently counter-attacking at Bourg. Army Group G's withdrawal ended at the German frontier but Blaskowitz, an old enemy of Himmler's, was made a scapegoat for the loss of southern France and replaced by Balck as army group commander. Elsewhere, von Rundstedt was reinstated as Commander-in-Chief West on 5 September, leaving Model free to command Army Group B.

One of the most remarkable aspects of the German Army at this period was its resilience. Very quickly the remnants of units from the shattered front, soldiers on leave, Luftwaffe troops, men of below average physical fitness and the personnel of training depots and instructional schools were assembled into divisions which, while in themselves seldom impressive, were quite adequate for the task of manning the interlocked line of bunkers which formed Germany's West Wall. Nonetheless, the fact remained that on 7 September Army Group B possessed only a hundred tanks, which were outnumbered in the ratio of twenty to one. Nor was there any immediate prospect of adequately refitting the skeletal panzer divisions in the West, Hitler having directed that, in view of the even greater catastrophies that had befallen in the East, most of the Panther and PzKw IV production should be allocated there, although von Rundstedt's command did receive the much smaller number of Tiger Bs and Jagdpanthers being completed. This decision was doubtless influenced by the belief that once within the West Wall a static defence could be maintained for the moment, while in the East mobile warfare continued to predominate. In addition, Rundstedt was allocated ten of the newly constituted but partially trained panzer brigades; his own opinion was that the resources of these formations would have been better employed if they had been absorbed into the existing panzer divisions, where their inexperience presented less of a threat to themselves, and he was proved right.

Simultaneously the Allies, unprepared either mentally or logistically for the scale of the German collapse in France, temporarily outran their supplies and were brought to a standstill until these caught up with them. The time so gained permitted the Germans to consolidate their defences so that, when they started to probe forward again, they began to meet increasingly tough resistance. The prospect of the war ending in 1944 began to dwindle but General Eisenhower, the Allied Supreme Commander in Europe, permitted Montgomery's Twenty-First Army Group to attempt a crossing of the Rhine, which, if successful, could result in a thrust deep into the German industrial heartland of the Ruhr. This operation, known as Market Garden, involved the First Allied Airborne Army being dropped to seize bridges over the Maas north of Eindhoven, the Waal at Nijmegen and the Rhine at Arnhem. The divisions which were to carry out these tasks, respectively the US 101st Airborne, the US 82nd Airborne and British 1st Airborne, were then to be relieved in quick succession by the rapid advance of the British XXX Corps.

Market Garden began on 17 September with everything going according to plan at Eindhoven and Nijmegen. At Arnhem, however, the British parachute and glider troops dropped within sight of Model's new headquarters, located in the western suburb of Oosterbeek. Model was quite used to this sort of hurly-burly after his months on the Eastern Front and, moreover, he was for once able to act without the paralysing influence of OKW restraining him. As luck would have it, SS General Wilhelm Bittrich's II SS Panzer Corps was refitting nearby after its ordeal in Normandy and, although still well below their establishment, both its divisions were quite adequately equipped to deal with lightly armed paratroops whose isolated endurance was clearly limited. Once it became obvious that the Arnhem road bridge was the British objective, Model established a cordon intended to isolate the town from the dropping zones to the west. This was only partially successful, for the 2nd Battalion The Parachute Regiment, commanded by the future Major-General Sir John Frost, managed to slip through and seize the northern end of the bridge, holding it against impossible odds for several days, thereby complicating the German response to the British XXX Corps' northward drive.

Next, the 9th SS Panzer Division *Hohenstaufen* was detailed to contain the remainder of the 1st Airborne Division within Oosterbeek, while the 10th SS Panzer Division *Frundsberg* attempted to recapture the northern end of the bridge and establish blocking positions on the Nijmegen-Arnhem road. The former was achieved with comparatively little difficulty, but the determined opposition put up by Frost's men at the bridge meant that *Frundsberg*'s tanks could be got across the Rhine only by means of the ferry at Pannerden, eight miles (13 km) upstream from Arnhem. All of this consumed priceless time during which the British XXX Corps and the US 82nd Airborne Division came ever closer to securing a crossing of the Waal at Nijmegen. In the event it was the Germans who won the race, establishing a defensive front south of Elst under Major Hans-Peter Knaust, the commander of an armoured battlegroup which had been rushed from Germany to join *Frundsberg* as soon as the airborne drops took place. Knaust had lost a leg at Moscow in 1941, and although its wooden substitute caused him constant pain, his energy was in no way impaired. Thus his Tigers and Panthers were quickly able to halt the XXX Corps' drive on Arnhem once the Nijmegen bridge had fallen. The problem for the British armour was that it was unable to deploy off the road, this being carried on high embankments bounded by deep ditches, while for various reasons the weight of artillery and air support that had been available in Normandy was now absent. The attempt to drive through to Arnhem had to be abandoned, and for Lieutenant-General Brian Horrocks, commanding the XXX Corps, the question had now become one of evacuating as much of the 1st Airborne Division from Oosterbeek as possible. An imaginative but complicated series of operations ensued in which Knaust's position was bypassed to the west and the 1st Polish Parachute Brigade dropped on the southern bank of the Rhine opposite the embattled division, but only 2,000 of the original 10,000 men who had landed at Arnhem could be ferried to safety. Knaust was awarded the Knights' Cross for his considerable part in this, one of the Panzerwaffe's last successes in the West.

Meanwhile, in Lorraine Hitler had ordered the Fifth Panzer Army, commanded by General Hasso von Manteuffel, to mount an offensive intended to eliminate the American bridgeheads over the Moselle. Manteuffel's armoured formations included the 11th and 21st Panzer Divisions and the 15th Panzergrenadier Division, all of which were worn out and at only a fraction of their proper strength, plus the newly raised 106th, 111th, 112th and 113th Panzer Brigades. The latter first displayed their inexperience during two preliminary operations. On 8 September the 106th launched an attack on the northern flank of the US Third Army but was repulsed with the loss of all save nine of its forty-four tanks and assault guns. This was followed on the 12th by a major action between the much stronger 112th Panzer Brigade, which went into battle with ninety-eight tanks, and the French 2nd Armoured Division, at Dompaire south of Luneville. The 112th had much the worst of the encounter, leaving sixty of its tanks on the field, and ten days later had been reduced to a single Panther and six PzKw IVs. However, when the offensive itself began on 18 September, the 111th and 113th Panzer Brigades, each with a strength comparable to that of the 112th, managed to establish a local superiority over Combat Command A of the 4th Armored Division in the area of Arracourt, north of Luneville. In normal circumstances this should have been sufficient to guarantee a German victory, as CCA contained only a single tank battalion, but under the leadership of Major-General John S. Wood 4th Armored had become one of the best formations in the United States Army.

When the dust cleared after four days of fighting, CCA had lost fourteen Shermans and seven Stuarts; in sharp contrast, the 111th had been reduced to a mere seven tanks and eighty grenadiers, while the 113th was in little better state. By the time the offensive had run down at the end of September, at least half the 350 Panthers and PzKw IVs which had been employed lay wrecked on the autumn battlefield, while many of the survivors had to be returned to workshops for heavy repair.

Despite these set-backs, at the beginning of October von Rundstedt could dispose of some 500 tanks and assault guns along the Western Front, 239 of which were on Army Group B's sector. In general terms this represented an improvement, although the majority of Allied commanders were entitled to doubt whether the Panzerwaffe's capacity for action exceeded the sort of spoiling attack launched by the 9th Panzer and 15th Panzergrenadier Divisions, in company with the Parachute Division *Erdmann*, against the eastern flank of the Nijmegen Corridor at Meijel on the 26th. This caused the over-extended US 7th Armored Division to give ground, threatened the headquarters of the British Second Army and was potentially so dangerous that the 15th (Scottish) Division and the 6th Guards Tank Brigade had to be rushed into the area to stabilize the situation.

And yet plans for a major German offensive were already well in hand. Hitler accepted that the Wehrmacht no longer possessed the capacity seriously to damage the Soviet Army, but he believed that if he could inflict a major defeat on the Western Allies they might accept a stalemate which in turn would give him the additional strength to hold off the Russians in the East. This was to be done using the method that had proved so dramatically successful in 1940, namely a concentrated armoured thrust directed through the Ardennes, although this time the objective was to be the port of Antwerp. The effect of this would be to entrap the American, British and Canadian armies operating in the Low Countries, placing them in a situation identical to that in which the BEF, French and Belgians had found themselves in $4\frac{1}{2}$ years previously and similarly compelling their eventual evacuation or surrender. There was, however, a very important difference between the projected operation, confidently code-named Wacht am Rhein (Watch on the Rhine), and von Manstein's Sichelschnitt concept. In the latter case the limited road system in the Ardennes had coincided with the south-westerly direction of the German advance, whereas the new proposal envisaged a thrust-line to the north-west, a shift of ninety degrees to the right which took it across the grain of the country and offered very few roads going in the desired direction; such was the penalty of working from the map table without the ability to visualize and interpret the terrain involved.

Notwithstanding, Hitler was delighted with his brainchild and sent copies of the detailed draft plan to von Rundstedt and Model, having scrawled 'NOT TO BE ALTERED' on the cover. Both at once saw the impossibility of what was being demanded and submitted alternative plans which would have placed the defence of the Western Front on a sounder footing. These were immediately rejected out of hand by Hitler, who was determined to emulate the darkest hours of his hero Frederick the Great by winning a startling series of victories just when his enemies believed he was finished. With the bomb plot such a recent memory and the Gestapo actively engaged in collecting evidence against the senior command echelon, it was a very courageous individual indeed who was prepared to argue at length with the Führer. Those who still felt bound to do so out of a sense of duty now took the precaution of obtaining the active support of colleagues who were either fervent Nazis or members of the Waffen SS. In this dangerous game the street-wise SS General Sepp Dietrich, whose opinion Hitler might just have heeded, declined to participate, commenting with a guffaw, 'If ever I want to get shot, that's how I'll go about it!'

In return for his loyalty Dietrich was promoted and given command of the newly constituted Sixth Panzer Army, which was intended to take the lead during Wacht am Rhein and so teach the Army its business. Manteuffel's Fifth Panzer Army was to operate on Dietrich's left, with Brandenberger's Seventh Army protecting its own left flank. The offensive would be launched along a front of eighty-five miles (136 km) running from Monschau in the north to Echternach in the south, most of which was known to General Hodges' US First Army as the Ghost Front because nothing ever happened there.

The immense preparations and large-scale movements required for the German offensive were largely misinterpreted by the Allies. *Ultra* certainly picked up a regular series of signals dealing with the withdrawal of SS Panzer divisions for refitting, the formation of the Sixth Panzer Army, the concentration of fighter aircraft in the West and requests for air cover above the railheads closest to the Eifel, but these were believed to relate to the establishment of an OKW reserve and a re-deployment of assets to meet renewed Allied offensives north and south of the Ardennes. When von Manteuffel's Fifth Panzer Army vanished from the Lorraine sector but re-appeared near Aachen, this fitted the same pattern. There was, too, doubt that Germany still possessed sufficient fuel for a major assault and that, even if she had, it would not be delivered through the Ardennes.

The greatest Allied delusion, however, lay in the belief that it was von Rundstedt who controlled events in the West and that he was re-grouping his forces with the sound military common sense with which he had always been credited, when the reality was that Hitler was in absolute command and determined to commit an act of folly which lay beyond the bounds of Allied imagination. Even so, there were a few officers who guessed the truth but were ignored, while a great many more were uneasy that something unpredictable and certainly unpleasant was about to happen; among the latter was Eisenhower himself who, recalling the fate of the over-confident US II Corps during its first serious engagement with the Panzerwaffe in North Africa, commented to a member of his staff on 7th December that the Allies might be on the verge of 'a nasty little Kasserine'.

Meanwhile, on the German side of the lines troops continued to pour secretly into their assembly areas, tanks, guns and half-tracks moving into position amid the snow-laden woodlands which they shared with carefully camouflaged fuel- and ammunition-dumps. The armoured formations had been re-fitted to a degree thought impossible only weeks since and once more there was an air of confident expectation abroad among the troops. Only among the most senior commanders was morale at a

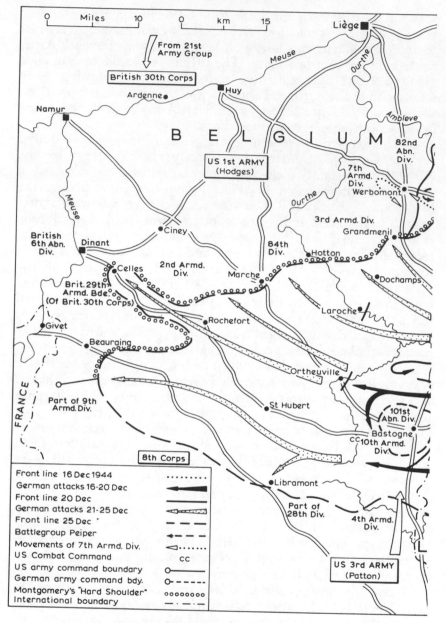

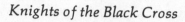

The Battle of the Ardennes Bulge, December 1944

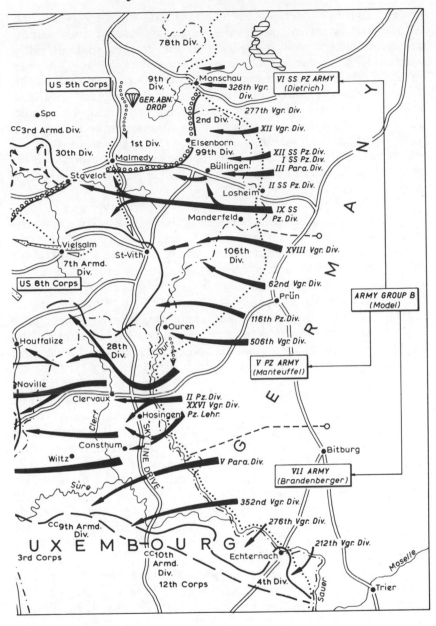

78th Div.

US 5th Corps

9th Div.
Monschau
326th Vgr. Div.

VI SS PZ ARMY
(Dietrich)

GER. ABN. DROP

2nd Div.
277th Vgr. Div.

Spa
CC 3rd Armd. Div.

1st Div.

Elsenborn
99th Div.

XII Vgr. Div.

30th Div.
Malmedy

Büllingen.

XII SS Pz. Div.
I SS Pz. Div.
III Para. Div.

Stavelot

II SS Pz. Div.
Losheim

Manderfeld

IX SS Pz. Div.

Vielsalm

St-Vith

106th Div.

XVIII Vgr. Div.

7th Armd. Div.

US 8th Corps

62nd Vgr. Div.

Prün

ARMY GROUP B
(Model)

116th Pz. Div.

Ouren

506th Vgr. Div.

Houffalize

28th Div.

V PZ ARMY
(Manteuffel)

Noville

Clervaux

II Pz. Div.
XXVI Vgr. Div.
Pz. Lehr.

Hosingen

Consthum

Bitburg

Wiltz

V Para. Div.

Süre

VII ARMY
(Brandenberger)

352nd Vgr. Div.

CC 9th Armd. Div.

276th Vgr. Div.

L U X E M B O U R G

3rd Corps

CC 10th Armd. Div.

Echternach

212th Vgr. Div.

12th Corps

4th Div.

Trier

Moselle

Sauer

"SKY LINE DRIVE"

Clerf

Our

low ebb as they contemplated the uncertain future. Even Dietrich, whom Rundstedt curiously described as 'decent but stupid', protested bitterly but in private to his cronies that all Hitler wanted him to do was to cross a river (the Meuse), capture Brussels and then go on and take the port of Antwerp; and all this during the worst period of the winter when the Ardennes were waist-deep in snow and there was no room to deploy four tanks abreast, let alone six armoured divisions; when it did not get light until eight in the morning and was dark again at four in the afternoon; with divisions recently re-formed and composed in the main of raw, untrained recruits and, to cap it all, at Christmas, too!

Wacht am Rhein was to have commenced in November but was postponed until 16 December and actually mounted under the amended code-name Herbstnebel (Autumn Fog). At 0530 2,000 German guns blasted out along the Ghost Front, and some 240,000 men moved to attack the weakest sector of the Allied line, accompanied by 1,200 tanks and assault guns; in immediate opposition there were for the moment only 80,000 men, many of them green or resting after the earlier fighting elsewhere along the West Wall, and a light screen of armoured cavalry units. Bad flying weather kept the Allied air forces grounded and according to the meteorologists' forecast would continue to do so for several days, causing optimism to soar. Few suspected even at this stage that the entire fuel stock amounted to only twenty-five per cent of what was regarded as the absolute minimum for this huge undertaking and that the capture of American bulk supplies was critical. Only a handful of senior officers reflected that, even if all went well, when the time came to swing north-west towards Antwerp the bulk of the German strength should be disposed on the outer edge of the wheel, i.e. with Manteuffel's Fifth Panzer Army, and not on the inner edge as at present with Dietrich's Sixth Panzer Army; this was a principle that both Schlieffen and Manstein had grasped instinctively, and with which Moltke the Younger had meddled fatally in 1914.

Even so, it could hardly be gainsaid that Herbstnebel had achieved complete surprise both as to its time and place and at every command level. As Eisenhower had feared, there was 'a nasty little Kasserine' when the inexperienced commanders of two regiments belonging to the raw US 106th Division surrendered shortly after they had been cut off on the Schnee Eifel. Elsewhere, shaken units were overrun or forced to give way before the assault while behind the shattered front English-speaking Trojan Horse parties organized by Otto Skorzeny, dressed in American uniforms and riding in captured American vehicles, did their best to foment panic, chaos and confusion for several days.

On the all-important northern sector, however, events turned out very badly. A paratroop drop at Baraque Michel ended in complete disaster, while at Elsenborn the attack of the Volksgrenadiers who were to punch a hole in the American line through which *Hitlerjugend* was to pass met such determined resistance from the US 2nd and 99th Divisions that little or no progress was made. Some way to the south, however, the vanguard of *LSSAH*, a battlegroup commanded by SS Lieutenant-Colonel Joachim Peiper, broke through the armoured cavalry screen in the Losheim Gap and embarked on its tortuous, massacre-strewn route westwards, hoping to secure an American fuel-dump intact. Initial success was achieved, too, by the Fifth Panzer Army, the 116th Panzer Division breaking away towards Houffalize while the XLVII Panzer Corps (2nd Panzer, Panzer Lehr and 26th Volksgrenadier Divisions) captured Clervaux and advanced on Bastogne, an important road and rail junction which was the hub of communications within the Ardennes.

Very soon, however, it was apparent that the stubborn if disconnected resistance being offered by the Americans was costing priceless time. Further, the Allies were by now fully conversant with the mechanics of Blitzkrieg and quickly identified Antwerp as the strategic objective. Reinforcements were rushed into the area, including Eisenhower's strategic reserve, the 82nd and 101st Airborne Divisions. Patton's Third Army was ordered to wheel north and drive into the shoulder of the German penetration while Montgomery was made responsible for containing the enemy advance within the northern edge of what had already become known as 'the Bulge', using Hodges' US First Army for the purpose as he rapidly re-deployed the British XXX Corps into a blocking position along the Meuse. Thus, instead of meeting progressively less resistance as they advanced, the task of the German spearheads became harder with every mile they covered.

Manteuffel's troops continued to make good progress for a while. Bayerlein drove Panzer Lehr hard, side-stepping obstacles in his path, and would probably have captured Bastogne during the night of 18/19 December had not his division been brought to a standstill by atrocious going. By the time it had dug itself out of the mud, the opportunity had passed, the garrison of the town having been reinforced to the point at which it was capable of withstanding a determined siege. Leaving the infantry to conduct this, 2nd Panzer and Panzer Lehr had no alternative but to bypass

Bastogne and continue westwards with dwindling fuel supplies.

Meanwhile, *Hitlerjugend* was still stalled at Elsenborn, and although Battlegroup Peiper had made considerable progress along the twisting Ambleve valley, it had failed to capture the vital fuel-dumps, one of which was set ablaze by its defenders under the very muzzles of its guns. Blown bridges barred its further progress and newly arrived American formations closed in from the north, severing its communications with the rear. Peiper was now trapped and, after holding out for several days in the vain hope of relief, was forced to abandon all his equipment and escape on foot under cover of darkness. Only a fraction of his command got through, leaving behind in the littered snow the equivalent of a medium tank battalion, ten Tigers, seventy half-tracks, assault guns and anti-aircraft vehicles. In fairness, it must be said that Peiper's thrust probably caused more concern at the headquarters of US First Army than any other single event during the battle.

For their part the Allies continued to believe that the driving force behind the offensive was von Rundstedt, although beyond suggesting that Herbstnebel be cancelled altogether or confined to re-establishing a portion of the front along the Meuse, the Commander-in-Chief West declined to contribute to the tragedy, maintaining a sphinx-like detachment worthy of von Seeckt. As the commander of Army Group B, however, Model was more closely involved and as the battle developed put forward the entirely logical suggestion that the as-yet uncommitted II SS Panzer Corps, now consisting of the 2nd *Das Reich* and 9th *Hohenstaufen* SS Panzer Divisions, should be used to reinforce Manteuffel's success. Hitler would not hear of it, for although Dietrich had produced disappointing results it was quite unacceptable to him that the SS should be seen to be playing a subsidiary role to the Army; the II SS Panzer Corps would, therefore, be committed on the Sixth Panzer Army's left flank, along with his own Führer Escort Brigade, a small armoured unit formed from his immediate personal bodyguard. The effect of this was to cause the abandonment of the stoutly held positions which the Americans had established around St-Vith, which was captured on 21 December.

By now Herbstnebel was well behind schedule, but on the 23rd the beginnings of the German wheel to the north-west could be detected in attacks by *Das Reich* on Grandmesnil and the 116th Panzer Division on Hotton, less than ten miles (16 km) to the west. Both attacks were held with difficulty and would probably have achieved more if they had been co-ordinated; at one time the two divisions would automatically have been placed under the command of a single corps headquarters for the delivery of a concentrated blow, but in the prevailing circumstances they belonged to different – and apparently competing – armies whose operations were scrutinized minutely by OKW, and that was that. OKW did, however, allocate its last armoured reserves to the Fifth Panzer Army the same day; these consisted of the 9th Panzer and 15th Panzergrenadier Divisions, the latter being promptly sucked into the siege of Bastogne. But perhaps the most significant event of 23 December was the improved weather which allowed the Allied air forces to intervene in the battle for the first time, establishing a domination over the front and the German rear areas as far back as the Eifel railheads.

West of Bastogne, the 2nd Panzer and Panzer Lehr Divisions, hamstrung by dwindling fuel supplies, maintained a slow progress towards the Meuse with the leading battlegroup of 9th Panzer following in their tracks. On 24 December, 2nd Panzer passed through Celles and crossed the last ridge separating it from the river but was brought to a standstill by the fire of tanks and artillery belonging to the British 11th Armoured Division, already deployed to cover the crossing-sites at Dinant.

Next day the concentrated US 2nd Armored Division attacked 2nd Panzer from the north, inflicting the loss of eighty-two tanks, eighty-three guns and 500 vehicles of various types in exchange for twenty-eight of its own, simultaneously holding off a Panzer Lehr battlegroup; many of the German vehicles were found to have been abandoned with not a drop of fuel in their tanks. Christmas Day also witnessed the repulse of a major attack on Bastogne, and on the 26th Patton's armoured spearhead broke through from the south and established contact with the garrison.

There was no alternative for Manteuffel other than to order what remained of his armour to withdraw. Herbstnebel had failed and although fierce fighting would continue to rage around Bastogne for a while, by the end of January 1945 the front was back in roughly the same position it had been in when the battle began. The cost to Germany amounted to 100,000 personnel casualties, 800 irreplaceable tanks and the pointless consumption of much of her tiny fuel stock. The Americans sustained 81,000 casualties and the British 1,400, the Allied tank loss also being in the region of 800, although this was made good within weeks.

Yet despite the obvious failure of his plans by 26 December, two days later Hitler was still babbling to Rundstedt about 'the tremendous easing of the situation which has come about – a transformation such as nobody would have believed possible a fortnight ago!' The problem was that, while Herbstnebel *had* delayed the Western Allies' final advance by approximately six weeks, the Soviet Army was able to mount its next offensive exactly on time and gain enormous territorial advantages in consequence. That was the as-yet unseen price which had to be paid for squandering Germany's last viable armoured reserve.

11. A Present for the Führer

The Panzerwaffe began 1945 with twelve panzer and panzer-grenadier divisions deployed along the Western Front and the equivalent of some 32½ in the East, all differing widely as to their strength and combat potential. Of those facing the Soviets, Guderian had been able to husband 12½ armoured divisions which were to be committed on the most dangerous sectors when the Russians resumed their offensive, an achievement for which Hitler personally thanked him, commenting that, 'The Eastern Front has never before possessed such a strong reserve as now.' To this the Chief of General Staff tartly retorted that, 'The Eastern Front is like a house of cards – if the front is broken at one point, the rest will collapse!' He and his staff knew only too well the vast scale of the Soviet preparations and were disgusted that the Führer and OKW refused to accept the carefully prepared evidence presented to them, preferring to ignore the truth because it conflicted with their own wistful belief that such an appalling situation could possibly exist.

It was certainly true that the Soviet Army had been badly hurt during the battles of the previous year – to the point, in fact, that ten per cent of its effectives were now women, who could even be found manning tanks on occasion. But the ranks were once more full again and there was no shortage of equipment: north of the Carpathians alone there were 2,204,000 Russians poised to attack 400,000 Germans; over 6,000 tanks opposed by only 1,100; 32,000 artillery weapons of various kinds preparing to pulverize a front which could dispose of a mere 4,000; and 4,700 aircraft against which the Luftwaffe could put up only 270. Moreover, the Soviets sensed that final victory now lay within their grasp and were determined to finish the task in the shortest time possible.

The Eastern Front erupted again on 12 January, the Russian advance swamping the defences and rolling across Poland to Germany's eastern borderlands until by 2 February its leading elements had established themselves on the Oder, only fifty miles (80 km) east of Berlin itself. *Stavka* then initiated slower-paced offensives which, by the end of March, had overrun Silesia and cleared the coast of Pomerania. A short pause ensued while Zhukov's First Belorussian Front and Konev's First Ukrainian Front prepared for their double-envelopment of Berlin, which was completed by 25 April. Meanwhile, the Western Allies had reached the left bank of the Rhine, and by the end of March they had established firm bridgeheads across the great river barrier. Their subsequent break-out trapped most of Model's Army Group B within the industrial basin of the Ruhr, where it ultimately surrendered. Two years earlier Model had been sharply critical of von Paulus for allowing himself, a German field marshal, to be taken alive by the enemy; now, in the same situation himself, he remained true to his ideals and committed suicide. There remained little the remaining German forces in the West could do save impose delay on the armoured spearheads which probed across Germany into Czechoslovakia and Austria, reached the Baltic and made their initial contact with the Soviet advance guards near the Elbe on 25 April.

Given the higher direction of the war, the wonder is that the German Army held out for so long. Hysteria led to the creation of new army groups whose commanders were changed with bewildering frequency as week followed disastrous week; the appointment of Himmler as commander of Army Group Vistula was only one symptom of the total unreality pervading the atmosphere at OKW. Everywhere Hitler thought he saw treason, treachery and cowardice among the officers he now hated but was forced to rely on. An early casualty was Colonel von Bonin, Guderian's own Chief of Operations Staff, who was made a scapegoat for the unauthorized withdrawal of the tiny Warsaw garrison and sent to a concentration camp. Taking their cue from their masters, prominent Party officials, members of the Allgemeine SS and Gestapo *apparatchiks*, knowing they would receive short shrift from the Soviets and the Western Allies alike, began arriving at headquarters close to the front, not to take part in the defence of their homeland but to arrest, try, demote, imprison or execute on the spot any officer they believed guilty of doing less than his duty. The criterion set was simply a matter of success or failure, and since the odds always favoured the latter, what amounted to a reign of terror persisted until the very last days of the Third Reich. On 28 March, after a series of public disagreements with Hitler, Guderian was himself ordered to take six weeks' sick leave, which was tantamount to dismissal. Keitel revealed the depths of OKW's ignorance by suggesting that he spend it at Bad Liebenstein, only to be told that the resort was now in American hands. Undeterred, the field marshal then proposed Bad Sachsa in the Harz Mountains, but to this Guderian drily responded that he preferred to choose a location which would not be overrun by the enemy during the next forty-eight hours.

The story of the Panzerwaffe during these four months is largely the story of its individual divisions. No coherent strategy was ever evolved and while local counter-offensives were mounted these were all quickly halted; the enemy possessed too many tanks, too many anti-tank guns and too many aircraft for it to be otherwise, while the constant fuel shortage inhibited formations attaining even the limited objectives they had been set. Tank, assault-gun and tank-destroyer units remained capable of inflicting serious loss and causing delay but were themselves subject to attrition and became progressively weaker. Little in the way of reinforcements reached them, most of the dwindling resources being formed into *ad hoc* panzer divisions constructed around a handful of tanks and panzergrenadiers, seldom exceeding the size of a regimental battlegroup. These short-lived formations received names rather than numbers, including *Clausewitz, Feldherrnhalle 2, Holstein, Munchberg, Jütebog* and *Kurmark*.

However, the final days of the Panzerwaffe were not marked by a series of fatal conflicts on a stricken field; rather, the demise of the arm came about as a result of the severing of the arteries of mechanized war. When supplies of fuel, lubricants, spares and ammunition ceased to flow, armoured formations were forced to destroy their equipment as they withdrew, so that when the fighting finally ended the once-proud divisions had been reduced to mere skeletons of their former selves, with survivors trying to surrender to the Western Allies before the Russians caught up with them.

Only in Hungary was the Panzerwaffe able to influence the fighting to any degree and then but briefly. On 18 January, having completed a difficult approach march along snow-covered mountain roads to the northern edge of Lake Balaton, the IV SS Panzer Corps attempted to break through to the besieged garrison of Budapest. Its spearheads set such a cracking pace that by the evening of the next day they had covered forty miles (64 km) and reached Dunapentele on the Danube. The thrust then swung north between the Danube and the eastern shore of Lake Velencei as far as the River Vali, which was reached on the 22nd. The IV SS Panzer Corps was now only fifteen miles (24 km) short of the

Budapest perimeter but the Soviets had wasted no time in moving
reinforcements into a blocking position, and further progress was
impossible. By 27 January the corps' flank and rear were being
subjected to such intense pressure that it had to be withdrawn and
Budapest left to its fate.

Even so, Hitler was sufficiently impressed to believe that he
still possessed the power to repeat the imagined triumph of
Herbstnebel in the east and on 22 January ordered Dietrich's
Sixth SS Panzer Army to leave the Ardennes and move to
Hungary, contrary to the advice of Guderian, who felt that it
would be better employed in Poland.* As a further justification
for the move, Hitler was able to point out that as the Allied
bombing offensive against Germany had all but eliminated her
capacity to produce synthetic oil, it had become a matter of vital
necessity that the Hungarian oilfield at Nagykanizsa should be
protected at all costs, although the truth was that this was so small
as to be incapable of producing more than a fraction of the
Wehrmacht's requirements.

Details of the army's movement orders were picked up by *Ultra*
and promptly passed to the Russians by the British Military
Mission. The Allied air forces also did everything they could to
make the passage as difficult as possible, fighter-bomber attacks
on the tank trains limiting their movement to the hours of
darkness, while rail junctions lying along the route were bombed
in advance, making time-consuming diversions inevitable.

Meanwhile Hitler had also expressed concern that a bridgehead
which the Soviets had seized over the River Hron, which flowed
into the Danube from the north, could be used as a launching
platform for a drive on Vienna. Wöhler, commanding Army
Group South, was able to inform him that the bridgehead was
held by infantry and that the nearest Soviet armoured formation,
the Sixth Guards Tank Army, was known to be refitting out of
the line. It was, therefore, decided that the first of Sixth SS Panzer
Army's formations to arrive, I SS Panzer Corps (*LSSAH* and
Hitlerjugend Panzer Divisions) would be committed immediately.
The attack went in on 17 February led by 150 tanks and assault
guns, achieved complete surprise and rolled over one after
another of the Seventh Guards Army's formations; by the 24th,
having sustained 8,800 casualties and been forced to abandon
most of its heavy equipment, the army was compelled to evacuate
the bridgehead. Shumilov, its commander, was sharply criticized
for failing to take elementary precautions, an attitude obviously

* The honorific 'SS' was granted as a reward for its services in the Ardennes.

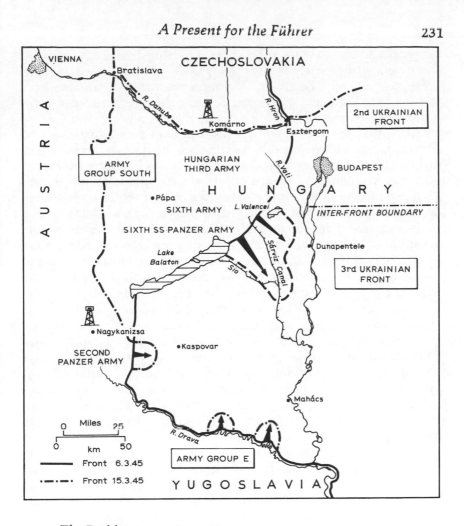

The Frühlingserwachen offensive in Hungary, March 1945

engendered by over-confidence resulting from months of continuous military success. As Hitler had intended, Malinovsky's Second Ukrainian Front temporarily abandoned its designs on Vienna, its commander also being censured for his failure to recognize the significance of the Hron bridgehead.

After this, the Panzerwaffe's last operational victory, the I SS Panzer Corps moved south to participate in what was to be its last major offensive, the code-name for which was Frühlingserwachen (Spring Awakening). The intention was to rip apart Tolbukhin's 3rd Ukrainian Front in two phases, the first of which consisted of a concentrated thrust delivered between Lakes Balaton and Valencei, aimed at Dunapentele; following this, the effort would be split into drives north and south along the Danube, eliminating what remained of Tolbukhin's presence west of the river. The blow would be delivered by the Sixth SS Panzer Army (five panzer divisions, two heavy tank battalions equipped with Tiger Bs, two infantry and two cavalry divisions) and Balck's Sixth Army (five panzer and three infantry divisions).* Flank protection in the north was to be provided by the Third Hungarian Army (one armoured, one cavalry and two infantry divisions) and in the south by de Angelis' Second Panzer Army, now an armoured formation in name only, with one panzergrenadier division, four infantry divisions with assault-gun support, and several small battlegroups; further south still, preliminary attacks were to be launched from the Yugoslav frontier in the direction of Mohacs by Weichs' Army Group E, the object being to draw off Tolbukhin's reserves before the main offensive took place. In total, the joint German/Hungarian commitment to Frühlingserwachen amounted to 431,000 men, 5,630 artillery weapons, 877 tanks and assault guns equipping eleven panzer divisions and four Sturmartillerie brigades, of which 150,000 men, 3,000 artillery weapons and 807 tanks and assault guns would form the main assault groups. In addition, the Luftwaffe made available 850 aircraft to support the operation.

Tolbukhin's command included five armies plus two tank, one mechanized and one cavalry corps, and although its ranks had been thinned by fighting earlier in the year, it still amounted to 407,000 men, 7,000 guns and mortars, and 407 tanks, assault guns and tank-destroyers, while the Seventeenth Air Army could put up 965 aircraft from its forward airfields. Moreover,

* Amid the general climate of paranoia, Balck had lost command of Army Group G and been reduced in status to army commander; von Mellenthin, his long-term chief of staff, was briefly suspended but later appointed to the staff of the Fifth Panzer Army in the West.

Tolbukhin had received ample warning of German intentions from deserters and other sources so that he was able to prepare a Kursk-style defence in depth consisting of three defensive belts each several miles deep and covered by mines, anti-tank guns and a carefully prepared artillery fire control plan.

Army Group E began its diversionary attacks shortly after midnight on 5 March, seizing bridgeheads across the Drava, and at dawn the Second Panzer Army joined in with a thrust aimed at Kaspovar. Following an intense thirty-minute bombardment and air attacks, the Sixth SS Panzer and Sixth Armies delivered their blow later the same morning, this being seriously diluted as the II SS Panzer Corps had been delayed and was unable to get into action until the afternoon of the next day. The contested ground was low-lying and waterlogged because of the spring melt and was so cut up by canals and deep drainage ditches, full to overflowing, that German tank commanders were heard to ask sarcastically if their job could not have been better performed by the Navy! For several days fierce attritional fighting raged, sucking the Soviet reserves into a killing match. Dietrich, too, committed his last reserves, and by the evening of the 9th his most advanced units were almost twenty miles (32 km) ahead of their start-lines, although still without the prospect of a clean breakthrough.

In fact Frühlingserwachen, sometimes referred to as the Ardennes of the East, had all but run its course. Tolbukhin was indeed desperate and repeatedly requested *Stavka* to commit the Ninth Guards Army to the fray. *Stavka*, however, sensed that the German offensive was running down and refused, its intention being to use the army offensively at the correct psychological moment. Early warning of this was provided on the 14th, when thousands of vehicles were reported to be streaming south-west out of Budapest. The blow itself fell two days later, shattering the poorly motivated Third Hungarian Army and exposing the German left flank.

On his own initiative Wöhler courageously declared that Frühlingserwachen had been suspended and then set about the complex task of trying to re-establish the front. Balck's Sixth Army took over the whole of the front between the two lakes while Dietrich extracted his two panzer corps one at a time and moved them north to plug the gap left by the routed Hungarians, forming a new line between Papa and Komarno. *Stavka* now committed the re-fitted Sixth Guards Tank Army, and it was only with the greatest difficulty that Balck was able to prevent the remains of his own army being encircled.

Frühlingserwachen cost Germany over 500 tanks and assault guns, 300 guns and 40,000 men. Worse, the initiative had passed again to Malinovsky and Tolbukhin, this time irrevocably, for on 25 March the Sixth Guards Tank Army, the Fourth and Ninth Guards Armies, burst through the ten-mile gap separating Balck from Dietrich, smashing their way through the Austrian frontier defences and on to Vienna.

The Panzerwaffe had fought its last major battle, and even as Wöhler reached his decision to abandon the offensive, men sensed instinctively that the end could not be postponed for long. Disillusioned, they now fought only to survive and to avoid capture by the Russians. On 23 March Balck advised Berlin of the position, adding that desertion was now rife and that frankly the troops had lost confidence in their leaders. On learning that the Waffen SS formations were as badly affected as any other, Hitler flew into a paroxysm of rage, despatching Himmler to chastise the Party's legions.

The majority of Waffen SS veterans insist that they were soldiers like other soldiers, although history has taken a different view and will probably continue to do so. For most of its existence, the 1st SS Panzer Division *Leibstandarte SS Adolf Hitler* would gladly have sacrificed itself for the Führer, just as the Emperor Napoleon's Guard had sacrificed itself at Waterloo. The difference was that Hitler now groundlessly despised the very men who fought for him, while Napoleon had kept faith with them. *Leibstandarte* had certainly been involved in incidents which brought nothing but shame on its name, but now it did something which was to earn general approval. Having been ordered to remove their prestigious cuff titles as a mark of disgrace for alleged acts of cowardice, its officers and men also stripped off the decorations awarded by a once-grateful Hitler, tossed them into a latrine bucket and sent it to the Führer.

Appendix A: Some Aspects of German Tank Design

General
During the period in which the Panzerwaffe was formed, German medium tank designers were inhibited by a twenty-four-ton (24,380 kg) bridge-loading specification, although this restriction was abandoned as soon as the need for larger tanks became apparent. Nonetheless, the turret rings of the PzKw III and IV were sensibly constructed with sufficient diameter to permit up-gunning without radical re-design. A standard layout was adopted with a rear-mounted engine from which the line of drive ran forward to the clutch and gearbox and thence laterally across the front of the vehicle to the drive sprockets. The PzKw III, IV, Panther and Tiger were all manned by five-man crews consisting, of commander, gunner, loader, driver and hull gunner, the last also performing the task of radio operator.

Gunnery
With the exception of the 37mm gun and the 75mm L/24 howitzer, all main armament weapons were muzzle-heavy in their mountings, the antidote to this being provided by a compression spring in a cylinder which was fitted to the turret wall, so restoring balance. As might be expected in a country with such a highly developed optical industry, telescopic gunsights were excellent, although a little more complicated than those used by other armies. In essence they consisted of two movable plates, the first of which rotated about its own axis with the various armour-piercing, high-explosive and co-axial machine-gun range scales inscribed around the circumference of different quadrants; the second or sighting plate moved in the vertical plane and incorporated the sighting and aim-off markings. The two plates moved simultaneously, the sighting plate rising or falling as the range plate turned. To engage at a selected range, the range wheel was turned until the required marking was opposite the pointer at the top of the sight, and then the sighting mark was laid onto the target using the traverse and elevation controls.

Another useful aid to good gunnery was a clock scale marked around the inside of the commander's cupola. This scale worked on the counter-rotation principle. When the turret was traversed, a pinion which also engaged the teeth of the turret rack drove the scale in the *opposite* direction but at the same speed so that the figure 12 remained in constant alignment with the hull's centreline. This enabled the commander to determine the bearing of his next target and inform the gunner accordingly. The gunner would then traverse onto the bearing ordered, using his own turret position indicator, and would find the gun approximately 'on' for line.

The hull machine-gun presented something of a problem since it was breech-heavy, and although a counter-balance spring corrected this, it also tended to drag the gun into a central position, so making life difficult for the operator, who needed one hand to feed the ammunition belt into the gun. This dilemma was solved by the provision of a moulded rubber cap linked to the butt by a bar; once he had inserted his head into the cap, the operator would lower it to obtain elevation and raise it to obtain depression while still using both hands to serve the weapon.

For a while many German tanks carried a rack of smoke bombs on their stern plate. These could be released by the commander using a pull-wire, enabling the tank to reverse into its own smoke-screen if seriously threatened. In due course these devices were discarded in favour of turret-mounted smoke-grenade dischargers; these should not be confused with the S-mine projectors mounted for a while on the hull of the Tiger E, which were intended for use once the vehicle had broken through into the heart of the enemy position.

Armour
During the years in which the PzKw III and IV were conceived, designers had comparatively little practical experience of obtaining the best protection factor from a given thickness of armour plate, and consequently they employed far more vertical surfaces than would be regarded as acceptable even a few years later, confident that these could resist the fire of the little anti-tank guns of the period but failing to anticipate the speed with which the gun/armour spiral would develop once hostilities commenced. The Tiger E also had its design roots in the same period and was similarly constructed, but in this case the great thickness of armour employed went far to offset the disadvantage. For the PzKw III and IV, however, the problem had to be solved by hasty up-armouring, using bolt-on appliqué plates until the greater

thickness could be incorporated in the manufacturing process. Once the Russian T-34 had revealed its secrets, subsequent AFV designs, including the Panther, the Tiger B, the Jagdpanther and the Hetzer, benefited from the laid-back angle of their frontal armour and other surfaces. In the majority of cases mantlet design was satisfactory, one cast version known as the *Saukopf* or Pig's Head being widely employed in assault-gun and tank-destroyer construction; a notable exception was that of the Panther which, being rounded, could deflect a strike downwards through the roof of the driving compartment.

In general, the protection provided by German armour was comparable with that of its British and American rivals, although the shortage of raw materials meant that a high carbon content was present as a hardening agent, a factor which made satisfactory welding difficult. During the last years of the war many German AFVs were fitted with side-skirts, of either soft metal or wire mesh, as a defence against infantry-launched hollow-charge weapons such as the bazooka.

Automotive
The automotive aspects of German AFV design were soundly engineered and for the most part followed the conventional pattern of the period, although the various final drive and steering systems employed have been described as over-complicated and incorporating too many ball-races. This was particularly true of the Panther and the Tigers, in which a hydraulic regenerative controlled-differential steering unit was employed, similar to the Merritt-Brown system installed in the British Churchill, the most notable product of which was the phenomenon known as the 'neutral turn'. This arose if the driver happened to touch his steering controls when the vehicle was in neutral with the engine running, the result being to set the tank turning on its own axis, with potentially fatal results on a crowded tank park.

German tank engines were designed for use in a temperate climate, and their air filters quickly clogged in the dusty conditions prevailing in North Africa or in southern Russia during the summer months.

Although electric self-starting devices were fitted, there were times when it was not advisable to use these, for example when the battery's life-expectancy was in doubt or when wintry conditions had congealed sump oil to the consistency of treacle. In such circumstances crews could resort to an ingenious geared inertia-starter system, the handle for which was inserted through the stern plate and then swung by two men until the heavy flywheel had reached a speed of 60 rpm, at which point the accumulated power was tripped to turn the main engine.

The PzKw III, Panther and the Tigers all employed a torsion bar suspension. The PzKw IV, however, used leaf springs, an arrangement which proved less than satisfactory as the up-gunning and up-armouring process continued, as the forward springs remained constantly bowed under heavy pressure, causing the vehicle to yaw badly. The interleaved roadwheel system used on the Panther, the Tiger E, the half-track series and other vehicles performed the task of spreading the vehicle's weight evenly but suffered from the serious disadvantage that stones, snow and ice quickly became packed in the spaces between the wheels.

Appendix B: A Short History of the Panzer Divisions

1st Panzer Division. Raised October 1935. Poland 1939. France 1940. Soviet Union 1941-3. Refitted in France. Returned to Eastern Front November 1943. North Ukraine, Carpathians, Hungary and Austria.

2nd Panzer Division. Raised October 1935. Poland 1939. France 1940. Balkans 1941. Soviet Union 1941 – January 1944. Refitted in France. Normandy. Ardennes offensive. Surrendered Plauen.

3rd Panzer Division. Raised October 1935. Poland 1939. France 1940. Eastern Front 1941-5. Hungary and Austria. Surrendered Styria.

4th Panzer Division. Raised 1938. Poland 1939. France 1940. Eastern Front 1941-4. Evacuated from Courland 1945 to Western Front, where it surrendered.

5th Panzer Division. Raised November 1938. Poland 1939. France 1940. Balkans 1941. Eastern Front 1941-4. Courland 1945. Surrendered near Danzig.

6th Panzer Division. Raised October 1939 from 1st Light Division, which had already seen active service in Poland. France 1940. Soviet Union 1941-2. Refitted France. Returned to Eastern Front December 1942. Hungary and Austria. Surrendered Brno, Czechoslovakia.

7th Panzer Division. Raised October 1939 from 2nd Light Division, which had already seen active service in Poland. France 1940. Soviet Union 1941-2. Occupation of Vichy France, November 1942. Return to Eastern Front December 1942. Baltic States. Surrendered Schwerin.

8th Panzer Division. Raised October 1939 from 3rd Light Division, which had already seen active service in Poland. France 1940. Balkans 1941. Eastern Front 1941-5. Hungary. Surrendered Brno, Czechoslovakia.

9th Panzer Division. Raised January 1940 from 4th Light Division, which had already seen active service in Poland. Holland and France 1940. Balkans 1941. Soviet Union 1941-4. Refitted France 1944. Normandy. Ardennes offensive. Trapped in

Ruhr pocket April 1945.

10th Panzer Division. Raised April 1939. One battlegroup fought in Poland later the same year. France 1940. Soviet Union 1941-2. Refitted in France. Assisted in repulsing the Dieppe Raid August 1942. Sent to Tunisia December 1942 and lost in general surrender of May 1943. Not re-formed.

11th Panzer Division. Raised August 1940 from cadre supplied by 5th Panzer Division. Soviet Union 1941-4. Refitted in France. Covered withdrawal of German forces from southern France to Alsace. West Wall. Surrendered Bavaria.

12th Panzer Division. Raised October 1940. Eastern Front 1941-5. Surrendered Courland.

13th Panzer Division. Raised October 1940 from cadre supplied by 2nd Panzer Division. Eastern Front 1941-5. Destroyed January 1945 during the defence of Budapest. Re-formed as Panzer Division *Feldherrnhalle 2*.

14th Panzer Division. Raised August 1940 from cadre supplied by 4th Panzer Division. Balkans 1941. Soviet Union 1941-3. Lost at Stalingrad. Re-formed France, October 1943. Eastern Front, November 1943 – May 1945. Evacuated from Courland in the final days of the war.

15th Panzer Division. Originally raised as 15th Light Division in August 1940 from a cadre supplied by 10th Panzer Division. North Africa 1941-3. Lost in general surrender of May 1943. Re-formed July 1943 as 15th Panzergrenadier Division.

16th Panzer Division. Raised August 1940 from a cadre supplied by 1st Panzer Division. Balkans 1941. Soviet Union 1941-3. Lost at Stalingrad. Re-formed France March 1943. Italy. Returned to Eastern Front November 1943. Surrendered Brno, Czechoslovakia.

17th Panzer Division. Raised October 1940. Eastern Front 1941-5. Ceased to exist April 1945.

18th Panzer Division. Raised October 1940. Eastern Front 1941-3. Following heavy losses in November 1943, the division was reorganized as the 18th Artillery Division.

19th Panzer Division. Raised October 1940. Eastern Front 1941-5. Remnants trapped in pocket near Prague May 1945.

20th Panzer Division. Raised October 1940. Eastern Front 1941-5. Surrendered near Prague May 1945.

21st Panzer Division. Raised originally as the 5th Light Division in February 1941, assumed permanent title July 1941. North Africa 1941-3. Lost in general surrender of May 1943. Re-formed France July 1943. Normandy 1944. West Wall. Transferred to Eastern Front January 1945.

22nd Panzer Division. Raised September 1941. Eastern Front March – December 1942. Disbanded due to heavy losses January 1943.

23rd Panzer Division. Raised October 1940, but incomplete until September 1941. Eastern Front March 1942 – May 1945. Hungary.

24th Panzer Division. Raised February 1942 from units of the 1st Cavalry Division. Eastern Front 1942-3. Lost at Stalingrad. Re-formed France April 1943. Italy August 1943. Returned to Eastern Front October 1943. West Prussia January 1945. Surrendered Schleswig-Holstein.

25th Panzer Division. Raised February 1942. Eastern Front October 1943 – March 1944. Refitted Denmark April 1944. Returned to Eastern Front September 1944. Destroyed Austria 1945.

26th Panzer Division. Raised October 1942. Italy July 1943 – May 1945. Surrendered near Bologna.

27th Panzer Division. Raised September 1942 but sent to the Eastern Front before it was complete. Dispersed in detachments during the Stalingrad operations, the division never re-formed and by January 1943 had ceased to exist.

116th Panzer Division. Raised April 1944 by converting the 16th Panzergrenadier Division. Normandy 1944. Ardennes offensive. Trapped in Ruhr pocket April 1945.

Panzer Lehr Division. Raised November 1943 from the demonstration units of the various panzer schools. Normandy 1944. Ardennes offensive. Trapped in Ruhr pocket April 1945.

Panzer Division Grossdeutschland. Originally raised as a panzergrenadier division from the crack motorized infantry regiment of the same name in May 1942, *Grossdeutschland*'s armoured status was confirmed during the winter of 1943-4, although its tank strength had always exceeded that of Army or Waffen SS panzer divisions. Officially elevated to corps status on 13 December 1944, being grouped with Panzergrenadier Division *Brandenburg*, joined later by the Führer Escort Brigade, the Führer Grenadier Brigade (both of which achieved theoretical divisional status) and the Panzergrenadier Division *Kurmark*, although the arrangement was not homogeneous. As an armoured formation, *Grossdeutschland* served throughout on various sectors of the Eastern Front, ending the war in East Prussia, although some of its units had been evacuated by sea and saw limited service in the West.

Parachute Panzer Division Hermann Goering. A Luftwaffe formation raised in mid-1942 as a panzergrenadier division.

Elements of this were lost in Tunisia as a result of the general surrender of May 1943. Sicily 1943. Italy 1943 – July 1944. Eastern Front July 1944 – May 1945. Elevated to panzer corps status in October 1944 by the addition of a panzergrenadier division. The designation Parachute was honorific.

*1st SS Panzer Division Leibstandarte SS Adolf Hitler.** Raised as a panzergrenadier division in July 1942 from Hitler's bodyguard regiment, which had already seen active service in Poland 1939, France 1940, the Balkans 1941 and the Soviet Union 1941-2. Occupation of Vichy France 1942. Returned to Eastern Front spring 1943. Italy August – September 1943. Returned to Eastern Front October 1943. Designated panzer division 22 October 1943. Refitted in Belgium May 1944. Normandy 1944. Ardennes offensive 1944. Hungary and Austria 1945.

2nd SS Panzer Division Das Reich. Raised as a panzergrenadier division in November 1942 from 2nd SS Motorized Division, which had previously seen active service in the Balkans 1941 and the Soviet Union 1941-2. Occupation of Vichy France 1942. Returned to Eastern Front spring 1943. Designated panzer division 22 October 1943. Refitted France February 1944. Normandy 1944. Ardennes offensive 1944. Hungary and Austria 1945.

3rd SS Panzer Division Totenkopf. Raised as a panzergrenadier division in November 1942 from 3rd SS Motorized Division, which had already fought in France 1940 and the Soviet Union 1941-2. Occupation of Vichy France 1942. Eastern Front February 1943 – May 1945. Designated panzer division 22 October 1943. Hungary and Austria 1945.

5th SS Panzer Division Wiking. Raised as a motorized infantry division in December 1940, constituent elements being the SS Regiment *Germania*, which had served in the 1940 campaign in the West, joined by Scandinavian, Dutch and Belgian volunteer units. Designated a panzergrenadier division 9 November 1942 and a panzer division 22 October 1943. *Wiking* served on the Eastern Front throughout its history, frequently sustaining heavy casualties, and latterly took part in the abortive Budapest relief attempt. It was finally destroyed near Vienna in April 1945.

9th SS Panzer Division Hohenstaufen. Raised as a panzergrenadier division in December 1942 and designated a panzer division on 22 October 1943. Stationed in France until despatched to the Eastern Front in March 1944. Returned to France June

---

* Even during the period in which these Waffen SS formations were classed as panzergrenadiers, their tank strength was actually higher than that of the majority of the Army's panzer divisions.

1944. Normandy. Arnhem, Ardennes offensive. Hungary 1945. Surrendered, Austria.

10th SS Panzer Division Frundsberg. Raised as a panzergrenadier division in December 1942 and designated a panzer division in October 1943. Stationed in France until despatched to the Eastern Front in March 1944. Returned to France June 1944. Normandy. Arnhem. West Wall. Transferred to Eastern Front February 1945. Surrendered, Saxony.

12th SS Panzer Division Hitlerjugend. Raised as a panzer-grenadier division in June 1943 from a cadre supplied by *LSSAH*, the majority of its recruits being teenage members of the Hitler Youth organization. Designated a panzer division in October 1943. Stationed in Belgium and France. Virtually fought to destruction in Normandy 1944. Refitted Bremen. Ardennes offensive. Hungary 1945. Surrendered, Austria.

Appendix C: Specimen German Orders of Battle

Whatever the theoretical order of battle of German formations might or might not have been, in practice organization was by no means standard, being dictated by circumstances and the availability of equipment. Very seldom, for example, did their tank strength ever approach that laid down in the tables.

Panzer Division, 1939-40
Panzer Brigade of two regiments, each of two battalions, each battalion consisting of three light/medium companies and one heavy company; mechanized infantry brigade, consisting of a motor-cycle battalion and one lorried infantry regiment of two battalions; motorized artillery regiment, of two battalions; armoured reconnaissance battalion; anti-tank battalion; anti-aircraft battalion; engineer battalion; divisional services.

Panzer Division, 1941
Panzer regiment of two battalions, each consisting of two PzKw III companies and one PzKw IV company; mechanized infantry brigade, consisting of a motor-cycle battalion and two lorried infantry regiments, each of two battalions; motorized artillery regiment of three battalions; armoured reconnaissance battalion; tank-destroyer battalion; anti-aircraft battalion; engineer battalion; divisional services.

The infantry-to-tank ratio had been increased since 1940. The motor-cycle battalion of the mechanized infantry brigade was sometimes merged with the armoured reconnaissance battalion and in due course disappeared altogether. The mechanized infantry were known as motor rifle regiments until mid-1942 and thereafter as panzergrenadier regiments.

This basic structure was maintained throughout the war, with exceptions. From time to time some panzer divisions were reduced to a single tank battalion while others were temporarily equipped with three, depending on the local situation. By 1944 it was normal for one of the panzer regiment's battalions to be equipped with Panthers and the other with PzKw IVs, although because of the overall tank shortage a varying proportion of assault guns had to be accepted in lieu. Some favoured formations, including *Grossdeutschland* and most of the Waffen SS panzer divisions, also possessed an organic assault-gun battalion. As more half-tracked armoured personnel carriers became available, it was normal for one of the division's panzergrenadier regiments to be classed as 'armoured', as *one* of its battalions was in theory equipped with these; the second regiment was 'motorized' but possessed no APCs at all.

Panzergrenadier Division, 1943
Two panzergrenadier regiments, each of three battalions; tank (or assault gun) battalion; reconnaissance battalion; motorized artillery battalion; tank-destroyer battalion; anti-aircraft battalion; engineer battalion; divisional services.

Panzergrenadier Regiment Forming Part of the Above
Three battalions, each of three rifle companies and a heavy weapons company; infantry gun company; anti-aircraft company; engineer company; regimental supply and service troops.

In March 1945 it was proposed to replace the panzer and panzergrenadier divisions with composite formations of battle-group size. These were to have been organized as follows: 'Mixed' panzer regiment consisting of one sixty-four-strong tank battalion and one panzergrenadier battalion equipped with APCs; self-propelled artillery battalion; tank-destroyer battalion; anti-aircraft battalion; engineer battalion; signal and supply services etc.

Some of the scratch 'named' formations referred to in Chapter 12 were similarly organized, although their commanders had to put up with whatever they were given.

Armoured Reconnaissance Battalion of Panzer Division, 1939
Battalion headquarters, including intelligence section; two armoured reconnaissance squadrons, each consisting of one heavy and two light armoured car troops; one motor-cycle machine-gun squadron, consisting of three rifle troops and one heavy weapons troop; one heavy squadron, consisting of a light gun troop (two towed M.18 light infantry guns); anti-tank troop (three to five 37mm anti-tank guns); assault pioneer troop; supply, workshops etc.

The German Army practised deep reconnaissance to a far greater degree than did the British, American or Soviet Armies.

This is reflected in the organization of the battalion, in which the motor-cycle machine-gun and heavy squadrons existed to assist the passage of the armoured car squadrons through the enemy's forward areas and out into his hinterland.

Armoured Reconnaissance Battalion of Panzer Division, 1944

Battalion headquarters; staff company, consisting of an intelligence section, five three-vehicle armoured car troops, one close support troop with three 75mm L/24 howitzer cars, and one tank-destroyer troop with three Puma or SdKfz 234/4 armoured cars; no. 1 armoured reconnaissance company, consisting of eight troops, each equipped with three SdKfz series half-tracks; nos. 2 and 3 reconnaissance companies, each consisting of three three-vehicle troops and a heavy troop with close support and mortar sections, all equipped with the appropriate versions of the SdKfz 250 series half-tracks; no. 4 heavy company, consisting of an assault pioneer troop (seven SdKfz 251/5 or 250/1 half-tracks, thirteen machine-guns and six man-pack flame-throwers), close support troop (six SdKfz 251/9 or 250/8 self-propelled 75mm L/24 howitzers) and a mortar troop (six SdKfz 251/2 or 250/7 80mm mortar-carriers); supply, workshops etc.

Although there was still a need for armoured cars, there were times when the wet season on the Eastern Front made the going impossible for wheeled vehicles, whereas the little SdKfz half-tracks were less inhibited. In addition, these vehicles were able to perform the function previously carried out by the battalion's motor-cycle machine-gun troops, which had suffered severely and were ultimately disbanded. The new organization gave increased flexibility and firepower, although the titles of the companies were deliberately misleading.

Assault Gun Battalion 1941

Three batteries, each of three two-gun troops. Total, eighteen assault guns. Supply, workshops etc.

This organization was expanded the following year by increasing the number of assault guns per troop to three and by equipping the commanding officer and battery commanders with their own assault guns, thereby producing a total of thirty-one guns. After *Barbarossa* the 75mm L/24 howitzer was progressively replaced by the 75mm L/43 and L/48 guns, joined in 1943 by the 105mm L/28 howitzer. In 1943 the title assault gun battalion was changed to assault gun brigade, largely to suggest the employment of formations larger than was actually the case.

This should not be confused with the larger unit introduced the following year.

Assault Artillery Brigade 1944
Brigade headquarters: three Assault Guns 75mm L/48; three batteries, each consisting of battery headquarters (two assault guns 75mm L/48, two troops of four assault guns 75mm L/48, one troop of four assault howitzers 105mm L/28, assault pioneer troop, supply troop, fitters etc; grenadier escort battery; headquarters battery; transport, supply, fitters etc.

Tank-Destroyer Battalion
Three batteries, each consisting of three three-gun troops; headquarters battery: supply, workshop etc.

Appendix D: Comparative Orders of Battle of Opposing Armoured Formations

Soviet Tank Brigade, December 1941
Two tank battalions, each of one heavy company, one medium company and one light company; motor rifle battalion; reconnaissance battalion; supply, repair etc; ten KV, sixteen T-34, twenty T-60.

Soviet Tank Corps, March 1942
Two tank brigades (three in April); one motor rifle brigade; no supply or support units; twenty KV, forty T-34, forty T-60/T-70.

Soviet Tank Corps, July 1942
Three tank brigades; one motor rifle brigade; guards mortar battalion; mortar battery; motor-cycle battalion; armoured car battalion; engineer company; supply, repair etc; ninety-eight T-34, seventy T-70.

Soviet Tank Army, May – June 1942
Two or three tank corps; one to three rifle/cavalry divisions; one separate tank brigade; light artillery regiment; guards mortar regiment; anti-aircraft battalion; 350-500 tanks.

Soviet Mechanized Corps, 1942
Three mechanized brigades with thirty-nine tanks each; one tank brigade (fifty-three tanks), or two tank brigades, or two tank regiments with thirty-nine tanks each; anti-aircraft regiment; anti-tank regiment; guards mortar battalion; armoured car company; engineer company; signals company; supply, repair etc; 175-204 tanks.

Soviet Tank Army, January 1943
Two tank corps; one mechanized corps, at discretion, motor-cycle regiment; anti-aircraft regiment (expanded to AA division in July

248

1943); tank-destroyer regiment (two tank-destroyer regiments after July); howitzer regiment (two self-propelled artillery regiments after July); guards mortar regiment (two mortar regiments after July); signal regiment; aviation communications regiment; engineer regiment; supply, repair etc; 500-650 tanks.

Soviet Tank Corps, July 1943

Three tank brigades, each of sixty-five tanks; motor rifle brigade; mortar regiment; anti-aircraft regiment; self-propelled artillery regiment (SU-76); tank-destroyer regiment (twenty 45mm); tank-destroyer battalion (twelve 85mm); guards mortar battalion; motor-cycle battalion; engineer battalion; armoured car battalion; 208 tanks, forty-nine self-propelled guns.

In December 1943 the armoured car battalion and the tank-destroyer units were deleted from this order of battle; additions included a second self-propelled artillery regiment equipped with SU-85s, and an aviation company.

Soviet Mechanized Corps, September 1943

Three mechanized brigades; one tank brigade; one self-propelled artillery regiment (SU-76); mortar regiment; guards mortar battalion; anti-aircraft regiment; engineer battalion; signals battalion; motor-cycle battalion; supply, repair etc; 204 tanks and twenty-five self-propelled guns.

In December 1943 this order of battle was expanded by the addition of a second self-propelled artillery regiment equipped with SU-85s and a tank destroyer regiment.

Soviet Tank Army, August 1944

Two tank corps; one mechanized corps, at discretion; one light artillery brigade consisting of two 76mm artillery regiments and one 100mm artillery regiment; one light self-propelled artillery brigade consisting of three light SP artillery battalion (SU-76), one machine-gun battalion and one AA machine-gun company; two mortar regiments; one guards mortar regiment; one anti-aircraft division consisting of four AA regiments; one motorized engineer brigade consisting of two motorized engineer battalions and one pontoon-bridging battalion; one motor-cycle regiment; one signal regiment; one aviation communications regiment; supply, repair etc; a thousand tanks and self-propelled guns.

Soviet Tanks Corps, December 1944

Three tank brigades of sixty-five tanks each; one motor rifle regiment; one anti-aircraft regiment; one light self-propelled artillery regiment (SU-76); one medium self-propelled artillery regiment (SU-85/SU-122); one heavy self-propelled artillery regiment (SU-152) in some corps; one light artillery regiment; one guards mortar battalion; one motor-cycle battalion; one engineer battalion; one signal battalion; one aviation company; supply, repair etc; 207 tanks, sixty-three self-propelled guns.

Soviet Mechanized Corps, December 1944
Three mechanized brigades, each consisting of three motor rifle battalions and one tank regiment (thirty-five tanks); one tank brigade (sixty-five tanks); one light self-propelled artillery regiment (SU-76); one medium self-propelled artillery regiment (SU-85); one heavy self-propelled artillery regiment (SU-152) in some corps; one anti-aircraft regiment; one mortar regiment; one guards mortar battalion; one motor-cycle battalion; one signal battalion; one engineer battalion; supply, repair etc; 183 tanks and sixty-three self-propelled guns.

British, Commonwealth and Polish Armoured Division, 1944
One armoured brigade consisting of three armoured regiments and one mechanized infantry battalion; one mechanized infantry brigade of three battalions; one armoured reconnaissance regiment; two self-propelled field artillery regiments; one tank-destroyer regiment; one light anti-aircraft regiment; signals regiment; two engineer squadrons plus one bridging troop; one engineer field park squadron; machine-gun company; supply, divisional service units etc; tank strength; 246 cruiser or medium tanks and forty-four light tanks.

In this context the term 'regiment' is synonymous with 'battalion' in the British service. During the war in North Africa British armoured divisions frequently fought with two – on one occasion three – armoured brigades under command; this imbalance was not compatible with the infantry and artillery resources available.

US Armored Division 1944
Three combat command headquarters; three tank battalions; three armored infantry battalions; three self-propelled artillery battalions; one armored cavalry reconnaissance squadron consisting of three armored car troops, one assault gun troop and one light tank company; one armored engineer battalion; one armored ordnance battalion; one armored signals company; supply, divisional service units etc; tank strength: 195 medium

tanks and seventy-seven light tanks.

American armoured divisions also entered the war with more tank battalions (six) than could adequately be supported by the divisional infantry and artillery, but following the North African campaign this figure was reduced to three, thereby achieving a balance between arms.

Select Bibliography

Belcham, Major-General David, *Victory in Normandy* (Chatto & Windus, 1981)

Carver, Field Marshal Lord, *El Alamein* (Batsford, 1962)

Carver, Field Marshal Lord, *Tobruk* (Batsford, 1962)

Cooper, Matthew, *The German Army 1933-1945* (Macdonald & Janes, 1978)

Cooper, Matthew, and Lucas, James, *Panzer — The Armoured Force of the Third Reich* (Macdonald & Janes, 1976)

Degrelle, Leon, *Campaign in Russia* (Crècy Books, 1985)

Downing, David, *The Devil's Virtuosos* (New English Library, 1977)

Erickson, John, *The Road to Stalingrad* (Weidenfeld & Nicolson, 1975)

Erickson, John, *The Road to Berlin* (Weidenfeld & Nicolson, 1983)

Fraser, General Sir David, *And We Shall Shock Them* (Hodder & Stoughton, 1983)

German Report Series, published by the US Department of the Army:

Pamphlet No. 20-230 *Russian Combat Methods in World War II* (1950)

Pamphlet No. 20-233 *German Defense Tactics Against Russian Breakthroughs* (1951)

Pamphlet No. 20-234 *Operations of Encircled Forces* (1952)

Guderian, General Heinz, *Panzer Leader* (Michael Joseph, 1952)

Halder, General Franz, *Hitler as a War Lord* (Putnam, 1950)

Horne, Alistair, *To Lose a Battle — France 1940* (Little, Brown, 1969)

Jukes, Geoffrey, *Kursk* (Macdonald, 1968)

Jukes, Geoffrey, *Stalingrad* (Macdonald, 1968)

Keegan, John, *Barbarossa* (Macdonald, 1971)

Kesselring, Field Marshal Albrecht, *Memoirs* (William Kimber, 1974)

Kutz, C.R., *War on Wheels* (Scientific Book Club, 1942)

Laffin, John, *Jackboot – The Story of the German Soldier* (Cassell & Co, 1965)

Larionov, V., *et al*, *World War II – Decisive Battles of the Soviet Army*, (Progress Publishers, Moscow, 1984)

Liddell Hart, B.H., *The Other Side of the Hill* (Cassell & Co, 1951)

Lucas, James, *War on the Eastern Front* (Macdonald & Janes, 1979)

Lucas, James and Cooper, Matthew, *Panzergrenadiers* (Macdonald & Janes, 1977)

MacDonald, Charles B., *The Battle of the Bulge* (Weidenfeld & Nicolson, 1984)

Macksey, Kenneth, *Crucible of Power* (Hutchinson, 1969)

Manstein, Field Marshal Erich von, *Lost Victories* (Arms and Armour Press, 1982)

Mellenthin, Major-General F.W. von, *Panzer Battles* (Cassell & Co, 1955)

Mitcham, Samuel W., *Hitler's Legions* (Leo Cooper, 1985)

Perrett, Bryan, *A History of Blitzkrieg* (Robert Hale, 1983)

Purnell's *History of the Second World War*, Volumes I-VI

Ryan, Cornelius, *A Bridge Too Far* (Hamish Hamilton, 1974)

Seaton, Albert, *The German Army 1933-1945* (Weidenfeld & Nicolson, 1982)

Senger und Etterlin, General Dr. F.M. von, *German Tanks of World War II* (Arms and Armour Press, 1969)

Smith, Peter C. and Walker, Edwin, *Battles of the Malta Striking Forces*, (Ian Allan, 1974)

The Vanguard Series of monographs published by Osprey, including the following titles by various authors: *German Light Panzers, PzKw III, PzKw IV, PzKw V Panther, The Tiger Tanks, Sturmartillerie & Panzerjäger, German Armoured Cars & Reconnaissance Half-Tracks, The SdKfz 251 Half-Track, Mechanised Infantry, 6th Panzer Division 1937-1945, 2nd SS Panzer Division Das Reich*, and *Panzergrenadier Division Grossdeutschland*.

Wilmot, Chester, *The Struggle for Europe* (Collins, 1952)

Wykes, Alan, *The Siege of Leningrad* (Macdonald, 1968)

Zhukov, Marshal G., *Greatest Battles* (Macdonald, 1965)

Index

Index